"A perceptive, wonderfully funny memoir about the
Canadian addiction that is hockey from a very good writer
and an OK (it sounds like) player. What other writer can
boast of having had his nose broken by Denis Potvin and
seeing a teammate spanked by a Nanaimo waitress?
Splendid fun."

—Stephen Cole, author of *The Canadian Hockey Atlas*

"Bill Gaston's book stinks like hockey, as all great hockey
books should."

—Dave Bidini, author of *Best Game You Can Name*
and *Tropic of Hockey*

"An amazingly accurate—and often side-splittingly funny—
autobiography of millions of male Canadians."

—*Winnipeg Free Press*

"A hilarious autobiographical romp. It's page-turning, read-
aloud-to-anyone-within-earshot material."

—*Tyee Books*

"Very funny, true-to life celebration of the euphoria that is
hockey." —*Owen Sound Sun Times*

"A lovely book." —*The Globe and Mail*

MIDNGHT HOCKEY

★ ★ ★

all about **BEER,** *the* **BOYS,**
and the **REAL CANADIAN GAME**

Bill Gaston

Anchor Canada

Anchor Canada and colophon are trademarks.

Library and Archives Canada Cataloguing in Publication

Gaston, Bill, 1953–
Midnight hockey : all about beer, the boys, and the real Canadian game /
Bill
Gaston.—Anchor Canada ed.

ISBN 978-0-385-66191-1

1. Gaston, Bill, 1953–. 2. Hockey players—Biography. 3. Victoria
(B.C.)—Biography. 4. Hockey—Anecdotes. I. Title.

GV848.5.G38A3 2007   796.962092   C2007-903365-2

Cover image: Benjamin Lowy / Corbis
Cover design: Kelly Hill
Printed and bound in Canada

Published in Canada by
Anchor Canada, a division of
Random House of Canada Limited

Visit Random House of Canada Limited's website:
www.randomhouse.ca

TRANS   10   9   8   7   6   5   4   3   2   1

To the boundless spirit of Alex Dick
1950–2006

Prologue

MY OLDER BROTHER IAN is a longtime Oilers fan, so when he moved from Edmonton to Toronto, I called to see how things were going. In the background I could hear horns honking, people yelling, and when I asked him about it, he grumbled, "Fuckin' Toronto fuckin' Leafs."

The Maple Leafs had won something spectacularly unimportant—a game maybe, or perhaps they got a shot on goal, or managed to miss the playoffs by fewer points than last year. Whatever the reason, the entire city had spilled out into the streets, whooping and cheering. Later, as Ian elbowed his way down Yonge Street he stopped. Looked around. There were men and women. Young and old. Kids in turbans. Guys in tailored suits. Paunchy oldtimers and noisy *"whoooooo!"* girls perched atop jock-drunk shoulders. Jamaican kids and Vietnamese, laughing, chanting, fingers pointed heavenward. It was Little Italy and Chinatown, new Canadians and old, all jumbled together as they celebrated . . . The Game. Our Game. That singular common denominator that crosses solitudes, that unites us as a nation. It was a beautiful moment.

"So you've converted?" I asked. "A Leafs fan now?"

"Fuck no," he said.

Hockey is many things. It's cold fire. Steel on ice. It's chess played at 200 miles an hour. It's a game of momentum, with strange ebbs and surging flows. But for all its quicksilver perfection, hockey is still a sport played by mortals. Fallible flesh and bone. This is a book about the game beyond the glitz, after the crowds have thinned, when the cheers have died and the lights have dimmed.

For every player who fought his way into the NHL or onto Canada's Olympic squad, there are a hundred more like Bill Gaston: players who were good, very good, but not quite good *enough*. Bill played in the juniors and went pro for a season in France's *Ligue du Sud*. He even skated a game in Switzerland under the banner of "Gaston Bobo," but he never circled an NHL arena to the throbbing sound of his own name.

Told over the course of a season spent with an oldtimers team, *Midnight Hockey* is a tale of tube skates and taped glasses, of guilt-free beer cooling in Zamboni snow and the eroticism of a well-timed breakaway. You'll learn the real difference between "beer-league" hockey and "oldtimers," and you'll finally discover why goalies are insane. (Bill solves this riddle, and it doesn't have to do with them being human targets in a particularly malicious firing range—well, not exclusively anyway.) You'll learn why hockey players represent the highest level of human evolution, and why public urination is something of an art form. A minor art form, true. But an art form nonetheless.

Still, amid the locker-room farts (punchlines, all on their own) and lumberjack burps (ditto), in the sweat-sheen of second-rate strippers and the malty aroma of the mythic Beer Cooler, amid the apocalyptic hangovers and stick-induced vasectomies, there's something else going on here. *Midnight Hockey* is, ultimately, a meditation on mortality—as heartfelt as possible when discussing frozen pucks and drunken players.

This is a book about outgrowing your body, about chasing your younger self down the ice, pokechecking like mad but always two strides behind, as the gap between you gets larger and larger . . . and maybe you catch an ass-view glimpse of your younger self banking one in, but you never do manage to steal that puck. It's about trying to beat life at its own game—and failing, and knowing you will fail, and trying just the same.

It comes in creaks and sighs, old age does. And the temptation is always present to simply run out the clock, to rag the puck—knowing that when you finally do hang up your skates, the game will continue without you. It's bigger than you.

This is a funny book. Terrifically funny. Made all the funnier by the fact that it is so very sad.

Bill Gaston has played oldtimers hockey with judges and farmers, carpenters and professors and priests. All of them tilting at that same blue line: sagging Quixotes, fuelled by ibuprofen and denial, fighting to stay in the game, trying to stave off a final, sudden-death overtime defeat.

"I think that hockey players are good at the game of life," Bill notes, "because they know how to play hurt."

It makes you wonder about our choice of Mountie as National Icon. A scarlet-jacketed Mountie—pure of heart, strong of jaw—would never take someone down with an elbow to the throat. Mounties don't spit and swear or argue with the ref. Mounties shoot straight. They'd never deke out a goalie, let alone suckerpunch an opponent. (At least, not the Mounties of lore.)

The hockey player is more heroic precisely because he or she is so flawed, so human. Hockey players have to rise to the game; the game demands it.

—Will Ferguson, Calgary

A Few Words about This Book

ONE OF MY FAVOURITE WRITERS is Annie Dillard, despite what she once said about writers who write books designed for specific audiences or markets, which is: "It amounts to a wasted and sad life."

Well, I wasn't sad, or even all that wasted, while writing this book. Though writing a book for hockey players does sound a little iffy. I mean, the suspicion is not only that hockey players don't read, it's that they probably can't. But my equally strong suspicion is that this won't deter them. So if this applies to you—that is, if you can't read but have gotten this far—I salute you for helping me prove Annie Dillard wrong.

That rumour's all nonsense, that hockey players are dumb. I know of several hockey players who read really well. And Eric Nesterenko, while playing with the Chicago Blackhawks, actually published a book of poems. (To my knowledge he was never beaten up for it—at least not by his own team.) During *Hockey Night in Canada* interviews, Ken Dryden's lawyerlike mouth almost single-handedly succeeded in putting an end to that dumb-rumour, but it only half took hold. What I'm getting to in my roundabout way is that oldtimer hockey players only act dumb for a few hours a week, and they actually lead other lives.

I've played oldtimers with truckers, doctors, mail carriers, chicken farmers, Buddhists, retirees, dirt hippies, preachers, dot-com millionaires, policemen, wood cutters, drug dealers, sea captains, witches, and eighteenth-century explorers. I've never played against an all-gay team—that I know of—but that's probably coming. So, while as hockey players we may in fact not know how to read, in our other life we probably do.

THIS SEASON SO FAR

September

IN LIFE, nothing is so delicious as anticipating that next hockey game.

Well, okay, let's not exaggerate, there's that anticipation when, well, remember when you were nineteen and half the buttons were undone and your hands, hers too, were shaking and moving faster? That and, sure, I guess there's also the anticipation of food, when you're starving and the waiter slides that steaming plate of grilled garlic prawns under your face and you make an involuntary noise, and people from other tables look.

So sex, food, and maybe also shelter during a storm. But a hockey game is right up there.

Sitting in a schoolroom in Winnipeg, every Monday morning I would begin daydreaming about Saturday's game and I would not stop. That next game was basically all I looked forward to in life. (No sex yet, and I doubt there were prawns in Winnipeg in those days.) In the meantime I would read my Hardy Boys books, and go to Cubs, and watch black-and-white TV, and hang around doing stuff, but all I was really doing was biding time. Physically inert but mentally on fire, I was scoring goal after goal in my imagination.

Same when I started playing oldtimers, I would go to work, stay interested enough to not get fired, and feel a constant pull in my gut about the game that night. Home from work, I'd bounce a kid on my knee, and he'd ask me what I was staring at, and I'd say, "Nothing, Connor," and he'd say, "I'm not Connor, I'm Lise." My gear would be bagged and waiting by the door an hour early. I remember once I had a game and my wife, the tardy FeeFee, was late coming home. I recall pacing, and shooting fierce glances at the clock every ten seconds. She didn't show up with the car, didn't show up with the car, didn't show up with the car. She'd forgotten about my game completely and eventually it was too late for me to make the game at all. When she did finally get home, she said I looked as if someone had died.

So, after a whole summer off, anticipation of the *first game of the year*, well, that's usually a pretty fine bit of excitement too.

But not this year. I'm not sure why.

I got the call from Lyle yesterday. I was at the kitchen phone, standing in the open door to the deck. Outside, the warm September sun shone and the evening birds chirped in that melody we assume has something to do with human happiness. It seemed far too early in the year for this particular phone call, but apparently we have a practice next week, then our first game the week following.

I picture the practice. It's always the same. This single practice, which we humorously refer to as our training camp, will begin with a few three-on-twos. That's to make it seem like a practice, which is where you do drills to "make you a better team." Everyone will look horrible. Hardly any passes will connect, even from ten feet away. After five minutes of this ragged fiasco, Lyle will interrupt things and we'll split in two and have a scrimmage. We won't look any better, and passes still won't connect, but a scrimmage is more fun. Which of course is the whole point.

So another season begins, but not for me—not yet, if at all. Which likely explains my dramatic lack of enthusiasm.

I'll be missing this year's training camp, and the first games. My back just doesn't seem to be healing. I own a two-man kayak, a hog of a boat so big and stable you could probably stand up in it, throw your head all the way back and chug a beer. That information alone should explain the state of my back, but I'll supply a bit more detail. Camping the past summer with my family, I was on the beach and the tide was coming in, and in order to keep my kayak from being swept away I had to haul it up one hundred yards of sand single-handedly. Picture a guy digging in his heels, reefing on a twenty-foot craft that is sticking to the sand like Velcro. The guy is greying and paunchy and has no discernible muscles, but he's acting like he thinks he does.

That was two months ago. It no longer hurts to get out of bed, or walk, but in order to stoop to insert dirty dishes into the dishwasher I have to grab the counter with the free hand, and bend at the knees. There's no way hockey is in the cards for a while.

After talking to Lyle I paused at the phone, stood in the evening sun, and considered something. I stood out there for a while. A feeling has been growing over the last few years. Here it is: I have to admit to myself that I don't really care that much about playing. I'm busier than hell. I hardly have time to even think about hockey. I haven't really missed it since it stopped last April. And I've been missing it less and less as the summers go by. I called my brother Bub a few days back and his team hasn't started up yet but he feels the same way. His words, "I'm so not into it, but maybe I'll play," sound like my mood exactly. But my bad back lets me delay any decision.

There are tons of reasons why I should just hang 'em up. My chronic bad back is a big one. I have four kids, and one is twelve and he still likes to roughhouse with me, and another is six and she likes to "wrestle." My wife, the formidable FeeFee, sends me little guilt-out signals communicating that, if I screw up my back for good, my children will be deprived of a physically engaged father and grow up underexposed to the robust male side of things. (It's amazing how verbose her little signals can be.)

Plus, I seem to have health problems besides my back. No, not just borderline obesity and the cardio tone of a snail. No, in May I lost consciousness, in my office. Just went down, head on desk, for maybe five or ten seconds. I was on the phone to my wife at the time, sitting down. The amused FeeFee, when she heard me whimpering and slurring, "Don' hang uh, don' ha' uh," thought at first that I was fooling around, and later said that I sounded like Minnie Mouse. I regained consciousness, but then there was some odd visual stuff and some numbness, and one cheek is still a tad numb. Not to go into gory details, but I had to wear an octopus-like heart monitor home for a night, and I'm still waiting for an MRI brain scan, but there's apparently a lineup at the tumour machine so I have to wait till later next month. But would brain cancer be a reason not to play? No, it would be a reason *to* play. Which brings to mind the sonnet, "Gather ye rosebuds while ye may." That's all I know of it, but it definitely applies here, the translation going something like, "Chase yer pucks while ye can play." But at the same time, this incident has seen me become a bit philosophical lately, about how life is short and it could possibly and suddenly get way shorter, and I guess I've been staring at my children a little more than usual, and I guess hockey, along with money, career, the Jaguar I'll never afford, etc., gets put into perspective.

A third reason to hang 'em up is that hockey seems to make me drink too much beer. But I'll ignore this one. The fourth reason, that hockey is a kids' game, I have been ignoring for many years.

But I don't seem to miss hockey. An odd thought strikes me: what I do miss this September is the *feeling* of missing it. I miss that September eagerness to hit the frozen pond. That drive, that nutty little joy. And that almost animal urgency once the game starts. It's so much mindless fun to cruise out from behind your net, to lay down a neat pass, to maybe pop one in on a goal-mouth pass from your buddy.

I miss *wanting* that, and I begin to understand. Losing ability isn't the main mark of age. Losing desire is.

And it's funny, but Connor, my fifteen-year-old, seems to have strong opinions about me playing oldtimers. Of all my kids, he and I have always shared an affinity for sports. He knows the quiet joy of seeing the whole rink (in his case the soccer pitch) and laying down a good pass into the hole a guy's breaking for. For some reason he's stayed interested in my "career." If I score a goal, for instance, he likes to hear me describe it. He likes it that I can, on occasion, still stickhandle past a thirty-five-year-old. Maybe he's just humouring me, but I don't think so. Whenever he hears me talk about hanging 'em up, he scoffs, says, "No way." I'm not sure why he cares. Maybe it's that, once I quit, he knows his dad will gain fifty pounds overnight and he'll be the son of an instant codger, and maybe a cranky codger. I suspect, though, that he sees how much the game means to me. Chances are I betray something in the way I talk about it.

So, what the hell, I'm going to play. At least another season. Who cares about reasons. You know exactly what I mean.

But if we need reasons, maybe one good one is this: it feels great to use your body as it was meant to be used. Here's another: maybe, like an animal, if we don't use our bodies the way they were meant to be used, we go nuts.

I CALL MY CHIROPRACTOR for an appointment and I go see him the next day. The funny thing is, the bastard won't adjust my back at all. I made the mistake of telling him about my little pass-out in the office, and the persistent numbness in my cheek and lip. Since that tells him something about this nerve and that nerve, and since I'm also in the long lineup for a brain scan, he implies that I'm a potential stroke victim. Actually, what he's really implying is that *he's* a potential lawsuit victim. Apparently it's happened—a chiropractor cracks a neck and something dislodges and flies up to the brain and that's all she wrote. All I want is my lower back adjusted, but oldtimer health, it seems, is getting more and more complicated. He lets me hang out in his heated massage chair for ten minutes. It feels great. He closes the door because I sometimes can't help groaning. My chiropractor also plays oldtimers and we sometimes do talk about it, but since he looks exactly thirty-five and has a body like a triathlete and more energy than three regular people, we don't really have much in common except the rules of the game itself.

The next day I visit a new chiropractor, I keep my information simple, and he cracks my back. I'll see how it goes. Walking out to my car in the barely chilly September air, I picture the guys in the room, the beer cooler in its position of honour. There's a lively murmuring all around, and the occasional guffaw, as they share what they did on their summer vacations. Someone's asked Big Mike how the fishing was at Sooke and he's shaken his head and glared at the floor and told them the salmon are gone and gone for good. I bet that my right winger, one of the four Daves on the team, has some good stories about cruising the B.C. interior on his rebuilt motorbike. (Two years ago near Campbell River he hit a deer and broke a collarbone, but he was way more worried about his busted bike.) For sure Rich, our manager-coach, has begun pacing and giving us tips about putting it off the glass or on the tape. He's already started swearing about team bankruptcy and screaming *no way* because the guys have begun chanting *Free Beer!* and he's taken it seriously like he always does, even though the chant gets going pretty much every time we win, or lose, or tie, or even practise. I think that once, about five years ago, he caved and we had free beer—an act of mercy, since we were on the wrong end of an 11–0 blowout.

FINDING YOUR TEAM

FOR SOME GUYS IT'S EASY. For lots of you it's as easy as a bunch of guys deciding to form a team and work up a sweat, if only to justify some Friday-night beer. For some—and this is a common one—it's a case of already playing on a beer-league team,* wondering why you're losing every game, then understanding that you're all sort of old now and it's maybe time to airlift the team into an oldtimers league.

But for others, finding an oldtimers team isn't easy at all. For lots of guys, *admitting* you're an oldtimer—that is, admitting that you're addicted to age—is the difficult first step. I know it might seem odd to see age as an addiction, but it is. In fact it's the worst one, because it not only kills 100 percent of all addicts, but it's also impossible to quit. So we might as well just admit to

---

*This is the only footnote in the whole book, I swear, and it's only for those of you—you might be a wife, a girlfriend, or a spy from soccer—who don't know the difference between "beer league" and "oldtimers." Just think of oldtimers as being the senior division of beer league. Oldtimers have to be at least thirty-five, and slapshots are forbidden. So is "contact," though what that word means exactly seems open to interpretation. But in either category you will find leagues of varying ability, from ex-pro to complete hacker, as well as differing degrees of competitiveness—some leagues have playoffs and keep stats, for instance, and some don't. Oldtimers drink just as much beer as beer-league players do. But we tend to be more mature, if not stately, while drinking it.

it and then get on with having the best life possible. Which is why we now need to find a team.

Well, not just *a* team. You'll want to find *your* team. A team can be identified as "your" team if it meets two criteria: one, you want it, and, two, it wants you. These two conditions can be difficult, sometimes almost impossible, to find in one team.

We all have different stories about finding our team. Here's mine.

After playing my first oldtimer game, at age thirty-seven after a twelve-year hiatus from putting on skates, in a tournament with my brother's team back on the west coast (see "The Abyss"), I knew that hockey had to be in my life again. Playing those first games felt a bit like dunking a cold toe in the hot fountain of eternal youth. Playing again made me feel ten years old again—chasing a puck for no reason except that somebody else wanted it—and it was fun. Yelling involuntarily because you whacked a puck into a net. Wanting to catch and kill a guy because he has a puck and you don't. Basic, primal, animal, childlike *fun*. You all know what I mean, so I won't go on.

Home from the tournament, in Fredericton, I asked around about oldtimers hockey. Apparently it was alive and well in town—everybody seemed to know someone who knew someone who played it. I persisted, and tracked down some leads. I was told that there was a guy who worked at St. Thomas University, Al, who played oldtimers on a team that might need a body. I worked at the University of New Brunswick, and St. Thomas is a small school that's independent yet attached to the UNB campus—sort of like a weird uncle who lives in a shed in your backyard but who is never seen not wearing a tie.

I called Al and left a message. I didn't note the whole name at first, the "MacAdam" after the "Al," until he returned my call.

But hearing his voice acted as a kind of trigger. Because I did know that Al MacAdam was in town coaching the St. Thomas hockey team—the same Al MacAdam who scored over a hundred points one year on the Bobby Smith line with Minnesota, and later played with the Canucks. When I heard his voice, all of this information tumbled into my brain and crowded out the part that normally forms words. The conversation went something like this:

"A—Al? M—M—"

"Yes."

"Ma—Ma—Ma?"

"That's me."

"Who pl—pl—pl—"

"Yes."

"For M—M—M—"

"Yup, that's me."

"Then the C—C—C—"

"John called and told me you're looking for a team?"

I grunted something, not knowing how to tell him I wanted not just *a* team. I wanted to play on *his* team.

"It's hard to find a squad in this town, Bill. It's a pretty tight ship. But call this guy Arden. Arden Doak. I think they're looking for a guy or two."

"B—B—B—" This continued for way too long but it was the closest I could come to saying, "But let me play for *your* team. I'll set you up time after time just like Bobby Smith did and wash your car after the game if you'll let me play for *your* team."

"You want Arden's number?"

"O—O—O—"

That's my memory of it. I never did get to play for Al's team. And damn it, Al's team was a beautiful team to watch. I would eventually watch them from our bench as they kicked our ass. And

I watched them blow by me while I manned the point. I likely had a silly little smile of appreciation as they went by, their speed cooling my face with pleasant arena breeze. It was ridiculous that we played them at all. They not only had Al, but a guy who had led the American league in scoring only a few years earlier, and a goalie who'd played some pro, and a whole whack of good guys.

Anyway, I called Arden Doak. He has a way of yelling into the phone so that you have to hold the receiver a foot from your head, but I managed to get the info. He said they would "take a look" at me to see if I "fit in." Like a boastful idiot I told him I'd played junior and all of that, and he laughed extra loud and told me, "Well, *that* might be a problem."

To make a long story a little shorter, I'll just say that there are reasons why some teams have openings to fill.

The UNB Reds, soon to be named the Fredericton Stinkhorns (see "Team Names"), was an odd collection of humanity. Two ministers, one of whom also had a doctorate in fungi. Two professors, one a psychologist who studied dreaming, another who taught social work. A charismatic carpenter. A banker, this same Arden Doak who yelled into phones. Another guy who fixed up front-yard cars and bartered them in New Brunswick's underground economy. (He once traded a rusted-out truck for two barrels of fresh smelt, and ran those inland to a fish market.) A judge in criminal court who, when in the middle of a murder trial, would have a second beer. A farmer missing a big toe, a high school English teacher. Plus a guy who, under the guise of unemployment, bred and sold dogs. And several other guys who did mysterious Maritime things.

Anyway, a nice mix. I didn't know any of these fellows when I first walked into the room, of course. All I knew was that they were "taking a look at me tonight," and that, new to the

Maritimes, I didn't understand what half of them were saying. Hardly a word. I think a bunch of those friendly guys, speaking to me that first night, and on many nights to come, might have thought I was autistic, because I did a lot of staring back at them, not responding appropriately. Either that or they thought that I believed I was the King of France and would not answer to peasantry.

Let me explain. Some of these Fredericton guys simply didn't speak my language. No, they weren't Acadians. They spoke English, just not my brand. If you've ever watched the CBC news and heard a Newfoundland fisherman interviewed dockside for his opinion of government policy, you will understand what kind of English I was hearing. But it wasn't like Newfoundland dialect at all. Compared to the rest of Canada, the Maritimes have enjoyed a couple of extra centuries of existence, and it was a time when folks didn't get around much, living and dying within twenty miles of their village. As in pockets of Europe, dialects developed, wherein a fellow from Pickwick could instantly tell if the guy accosting him for spare change was from Grunge-on-Erin. Same with the Maritimes. Drive ten minutes out of Fredericton and people start speaking, for all intents and purposes, a slurred kind of Welsh.

I literally could not understand what half my teammates were saying when they were joshing and got up a head of steam. The guys I couldn't understand were typically from a bit out of town, and worked at blue-collar jobs. In those early weeks, when I made the mistake of sitting next to one, he might turn to me, smiling, and say this, really fast:

"Billy! So yer op an gin tuh nes for doon yup, eh?"

Quite afraid, suspecting I'd been asked some kind of question, I would smile vaguely and nod at my teammate, who now looked at me as if I thought I was the King of France.

I soon learned to enter and survey the room in order to pick a strategic spot, one where I had better than even odds of hearing English. I got in the habit of doing this until, about three years later, I realized I no longer bothered to do it. I sat anywhere, because I now understood everything that was being said. It had taken three years. Even odder, I could now speak like them. And, when talking to them, I did. According to my brother, whom I saw out on the west coast each Christmas, I'd picked up a bit of an accent myself. (He started calling me Cod Boy, but I didn't care. I was actually a little proud that I could speak the language of Loyalist farmers.)

Anyway, my new team took a look at me that first night. I was instantly at ease, once I saw how dicey a few of them were on their skates. And the few who skated well didn't seem to know when to pass, or to whom. Those who knew how to pass couldn't shoot. Our goalie, Dana, who had the prototypical old-timer's pot belly, couldn't get up after he went down. Basically, the UNB Reds were a classic shitty team.

Since I was already the King of France, I slowed down and didn't try too hard during my tryout for fear of being a show-off. I later earned my first nickname—The Franchise—but thankfully it didn't stick. Anyway, I saw that my new team fulfilled only one of the two necessary criteria. It wanted me to play for them. But I wanted to play for Al MacAdam's team.

It took me that same three years or so to grow to love these guys and to enjoy myself. How important was it, really, that half the guys you pass it to never score, or never pass it back? Because the other half of them did and, shit, the half that didn't were doing their best. And it's so easy to forget that there are always a zillion guys better than you are, on the many rinks of the nation. Easy to forget that, had I ended up on Al's team, wouldn't I be one of the players other guys are getting mad at?

Anyway, getting mad at a shitty oldtimers player is sort of like getting mad at the weather. Every oldtimers player is a force of nature—he isn't likely to hear you at all, and he isn't likely to be swayed by a bit of petty criticism in any case.

In the end, the UNB Reds turned out to be not that bad, and I turned out to be not that good. Maybe I just had to get the hang of what they were all saying.

Prime Time

SOMETIMES CHOOSING YOUR TEAM has less to do with getting in with a group of friends than it does with finding the ice time that suits your particular lifestyle.

When I heard recently from a friend back east that Fredericton was building not one, but two new two-rink complexes, I got really angry and regretted having moved to Victoria seven years ago. The thing is, Fredericton already had the highest ratio of indoor rinks to people in Canada, plus they flood their public tennis courts for kids' shinny and for couples to drift around on, holding hands. If they have the highest ratio in Canada, chances are they also have the highest ratio in the world. And they're building four more rinks? What it means, of course, is that not only will Frederictonians not have to drive their kids to practice at 4:30 in the morning, but, even more vital, their oldtimers will have the best pick of ice time in the entire world. If Fredericton had decent Thai food, I would definitely move back.

It's an important issue, ice time. Most of us know what it feels like to play hockey too late at night. You've had your day at work, and your home life, and probably some quality couch-potato time, and then you find yourself packing your gear and driving off to the rink at an hour when your body feels tricked because it thought it was going to bed. This is called "midnight hockey." It doesn't matter if it actually says twelve on the clock or not—midnight hockey is more a state of mind. In the room you get dressed in a zombie-like way, trading not much more than a grunt with teammates who also have to work tomorrow and who also can't believe they're actually here. But then you play—and it's not bad. In fact, it turns into some serious fun. Maybe *because* it's so late, and doesn't make any sense at all, you actually let loose and have a good time. You also understand that midnight hockey is for those of us who *love* the game.

You shower and have a beer. You're feeling better than you did when you arrived, but you're aware that you do have to work tomorrow. You finish a beer and agree with a few teammates that your adrenaline's going to keep you from sleeping for a while anyway, and the room fills with the sound of a bunch of second beers cracking open at once. And now, as if miraculously, some of the best discussions you've ever heard pop up all around you. You make an accord with no less than three guys to gather your families at the same lake this summer. Somewhere along the line you all agree to do the Beer Guy a favour tonight by emptying the cooler altogether, having decided that getting four hours of sleep is really no worse than getting five. Eventually you do barge out, suspiciously boisterous given the hour, zombie-like no longer. And now you notice the mismatched gang of hackers out there still toiling on the pond. Anywhere you go in Canada they're always there and they always look the same. Some have long hair, all are pale, many sport weird vintage uniforms, one guy with a Czech national team jersey with SMEGMA or DRZT on the back, and some with numbers like 99.9, or -2, or ?, and of course several of the ugliest guys wear 69. Some are skating insanely fast, and others look content to patrol a small area.

They have slack faces but betray an odd determination, much like chess players do, and you can tell that their love of midnight hockey is pure.

Leaving the rink, you pass an even stranger crew of gangly geeks making their way in from the parking lot. They're really pale, and knobby-kneed, and in even worse shape than you, and none of them say a word to each other, and sometimes weird smoke follows them in the door. You have no idea what these *after*-midnight guys are up to at all, except looking for a room in which to strap on wet gear that doesn't fit.

So when is the primest ice-time?

Five years back we had an excellent slot: eight p.m. on Thursdays. It was perfect—enough time to digest your light dinner, enough to help the harrumphing FeeFee with the dishes and watch *Jeopardy!* with her and then get Lilli ready for her bath. The one drawback was that after the game there was a bit too much drinking time, and it was easy to do enough damage to make Friday morning painful. So, nine would've been better. (You don't want to have to exercise self-control in these matters if your choice of ice time can do it for you.)

But our ice time got bumped to a ridiculous ten-thirty, the arena's explanation being that kids' games got priority. I imagine there was once a day when oldtimers were treated with respect, were seen as wise elders deserving honours of all kinds, but I'm afraid those days are gone. One option was to move to an eight-fifteen Sunday slot, which we decided to try on for size. We've been trying it on for four years now, and it's still an odd one. The hour is fine—it's the day that's weird. For one, sometimes it's hard to escape that big Sunday dinner. Though both the upright FeeFee and I were hippyish black sheep as young adults, we try to fool our kids by posing as responsible and traditional parents, meaning that on Sundays we try to get everyone to eat together.

Sometimes the only way to lure them is to stuff the oven with some gigantic piece of meat, or bird, and roast it. Then I help to eat it. And though I've sat swollen and sloth-like and burping on the bench a hundred times, regretting that Sunday dinner, it's hard not to eat what's in front of your face, especially when it's covered with my extraordinary gravy.

While Sunday at eight-fifteen is also early enough to be a dangerous drinking slot, it's proven quite safe, mostly because it's weird to keep things going and hit a bar on a Sunday night. I mean, I don't know that many of us Finishing Stars actually go to church, but getting faced on a Sunday night just feels somehow wrong. Sometimes we do, and sometimes we don't. But if you're like me, Sunday evening still resounds with the strains of *Bonanza* and *The Ed Sullivan Show*, and the only acceptable mood on a Sunday is a slight depression, because the weekend is over and school is tomorrow.

So we're still checking out that Sunday evening ice time.

Friday night is an odd slot too. Turnouts on both teams can be slim, mostly because "social activities" tend to take place on Friday evenings, and unless you're a single guy, hockey on Fridays is sometimes simply *not allowed*. Also, the problem with Friday evenings is that, to put it crudely, if you do play you'll likely end up too bombed to drive, or maybe even walk, and you have to spend all night in the dressing room, which can be a little ugly—though there *are* showers in the morning. But Friday nights are out.

Saturday nights? I don't think even the gangly geeks play on Saturday nights. I don't know if arenas are even open then.

BEER

FIRST OFF, in case anyone reading this section happens to be a prude, teetotaller, or scowling member of the moral majority, let me say that none other than Benjamin Franklin once said, "Beer is proof that God loves us and wants us to be happy." Benjamin Franklin actually said that. And that's all I need to say on this point.

No, here's more, from no less an authority than Winston Churchill, who reminded his critics, "Always remember that I have taken more out of alcohol than alcohol has taken out of me."

And one more: Have you ever noticed that the Stanley Cup is shaped like a huge, godlike beer bottle?

After the Game, It Is Important to Replenish One's Fluids

BEFORE THE GREAT BLOSSOMING of oldtimers hockey, any league that catered to the washed-up, no-longer-scouted, post-twenty-five-year-old hockey player was called a "beer league."

Beer-league players soon discovered that they had it way better than any other hockey players, including those in the NHL. In a beer league, the ultimate trophy, the only trophy that counts, is a brown bottle, and every beer-league player—even if he's just lost 17–2—gets to sip bubbly from it after every game. (Actually, these days I'm talking cans, not bottles, but cans are just bottles that don't break when thrown. Also, and more importantly, cans are bottles that cool faster in the Zamboni snow in the team cooler.)

So beer is the ultimate quest, the ultimate reward, and old-timers hockey is the ultimate beer league. Think about it: in oldtimers, though we all do a good job pretending, nobody *really* cares who wins. What happens out there on the ice can hardly even be called exercise—c'mon, admit it, the amount of exertion put forth has nothing to do with aerobics or weight loss or muscle tone but, rather, is calculated to arouse, but not go beyond, what might loosely be termed "thirst."

I think I can honestly say that a fair proportion of the guys in any given oldtimers room continue to play the sport because it allows them to indulge in guilt-free beer. As W.C. Fields told us, he used to keep beer handy in case he saw a snake—which he also kept handy.

All of this is why beer gets its own section.

The Beer Guy

The most important position on the team isn't captain, or star centre, or goalie, or manager, but the Beer Guy. The Beer Guy comes into the room prior to each game, pulling a cooler on wheels. The most striking thing about the Beer Guy and his Cooler (which also deserves a capital letter) is that when he pulls it into the room it is heavy, dragging its square ass and squealing its little wheels. But when he pulls it out, it has some-how magically lost almost all of its weight.

The Beer Guy is not only an important—some might even say sacred—position, it's also very difficult. It goes beyond heavily dragging in and lightly pulling out the Cooler. It also involves tallying the night's take, restocking the supply, managing all the loonies and toonies in the cash bucket, spraying the fucking cooler out with a fucking hose when it starts to fucking stink, buying ice (in those heartless rinks where the Zamboni guy doesn't save it for you in a Special Beer-Ice Pail), and, most of all, not forgetting that there's a game tonight at 8:45. All in all, the job involves not just physical strength and grace, but a grasp of micro and macroeconomics, a nose for hygiene, and a steel-trap memory.

Here's one story about a Beer Guy I know:

Loyalty

SEVEN YEARS AGO, when I first moved from New Brunswick to Victoria and found a team (The "Canadians"— see "Team Names, Bad"), I had a lingering suspicion that B.C. oldtimers were sort of, well, not as "professional" as those out east. That is, in B.C., hockey is not indigenous. It's hard to find those frozen ponds, frozen horse turds, etc. But seriously, it is an expensive sport here in the far west, due to the historical lack of rinks. And unlike Saskatoon or Saint John or Cornwall, way out west all the best athletes, like Steve Nash or Larry Walker, grow up to play the more fancy sports.

Suffice to say that I suspected my new western teammates to be other than bred-in-the-bone puck chasers. I expected them to say "fucking" as opposed to "fuckin'," and perhaps they would even excuse themselves after farting next to a new guy.

In any case, about halfway into my first western season we had a road game out in Sooke, which lies almost an hour's winding drive west of Victoria. (It occurs to me that Sooke might be the most western hockey road trip one can make on the entire planet, unless one continues, by boat, to China—which of course is east again, being close to Newfoundland.)

On my solo drive to Sooke that evening, flashing police lights made me slow up. I was on a winding road in the middle of the deep bush. I passed a blue car lying balanced on its side.

Its flattened roof and shattered windshield bespoke of a flip or two before it had settled. Poor bastard, I thought, and sped on, hoping I'd be in time to lace up before the puck dropped. I gave it no more thought.

We were short some players that night, but that's often the case on road games that involved a drive like this. It wasn't so much the distance or inconvenience as the fact that it was legitimately dangerous and immoral to have more than one beer in the room after the game and then drive that road. So you know, why even play?

Though we had to play short and double-shift and get more tired than most of us considered appropriate, a true crisis loomed: one of the missing players was the Beer Guy. In the pregame dressing room, and now along the bench, there were curses, and then plaintive murmurings, "Where the fuck's Neal?" "*Neal's* not here!" and even the head thrown back, pleadingly whispered, "Oh my God . . . *Neal!*" but I think that was me. Neal was the Beer Guy, and Neal equalled Beer. The word "beer" wasn't even mentioned. That he was one of our best defencemen and we were being pummelled 8–1 didn't come into it. No: waiting for us after our struggle was a dressing room crammed full of *no beer*. I mean, picture the Louvre crammed full of no art.

Scanning the bench, I noted the sagging shoulders and hollow, vacant eyes. It resembled a scratchy black-and-white documentary on refugees in 1930s Europe.

About ten minutes before the end of the game, I heard murmurs, then shouts, of a different sort. The helmeted bench now resembled wildflowers on a hillside turning their bright heads to the sun. Here came Neal, and he was pulling the Cooler. The Cooler was scraped and missing a wheel, and it made a little shriek as it was dragged. Neal was limping too. And his face was whiter than the ice.

Neal limped up to the bench.

"Hi guys," our Beer Guy said, too softly. He was staring off in an amazed, tentative manner that suggested he'd found himself on the bottom of the sea and didn't know how he'd gotten there or what to do next.

"Neal! Buddy! Where ya been?" Ten guys basically shouted this in unison.

"I flipped my car . . . what's the score?"

To make a long story short, Neal was in shock. He came to the room with us after the buzzer, still staring from his ocean bottom, and he told us, in a quiet little voice, how his front tire had caught the gravel shoulder and he'd flipped, he thought, a few times. How maybe his collarbone was broken (it turned out to be ribs). How the police had looked in the car and seen the scattered dozens of beer cans but found none open, so they didn't charge him. How he'd explained to them that he had to get somewhere tonight. And how they'd helped him fill the Cooler and driven him here to the Sooke Arena. Neal picked up his head at this point and remembered aloud that they might be still waiting for him outside, to take him to the hospital.

Most of the cans we drank from that night were dented, and because of this a few of them sprayed at us with that weird anger beer sometimes has. But I came to understand that oldtimers hockey way out west was the real thing, and not nearly as fancy as I'd suspected.

Food Signals from God

IT'S UNDERSTANDABLE AND TYPICAL that little kids don't like, say, acorn squash, even though it's kind of sweet and a pretty shade of orange. Little kids usually don't take to Chinese food, either, other than sweet-and-sour chicken balls. But as we mature, we not only begin to know what's good for us, we also gain the ability to *taste* what's good for us. Broccoli actually isn't so bad—in fact sometimes it feels kind of necessary, and we can taste that. Sometimes us guys find ourselves actually craving a salad. We sometimes pass on dessert, because we actually don't want it. We find that we sometimes actually *don't like* fast food. And as we get real mature, we begin to notice that big slabs of beef make us sluggish, if not downright tired, and should be avoided before a game. Filled with two or three pounds of beef, the best our bodies can do is finger-tap the TV remote, and even that gets noticeably slower. My point is that, as we mature, as we get older, our bodies begin to tell us the truth about food, as if we're receiving Food Signals from God.

Little kids can't hear these signals, possibly because the signals get scrambled trying to get past the Ritalin, so they keep hating what's good for them—broccoli—and want to live solely on what's bad for them—sugar and fat, preferably at the same time. This they can easily accomplish with a concoction that godless forces have dreamed up and called "ketchup chips."

Where am I going with this? Well, only that I'm thankful that, as adults, we are finally able to tell what's good for us simply by staying attuned to the signals God sends us through the loudspeaker that is our body. For instance, I now eat my wife's kale soup, which is deep green and fibrous and bitter, and I love it. I'll have two bowls, my body thanking me with amazed whispers of, "You *heard* me! You *heard* me!" with each slurp.

That I bring up beer (so to speak) at this point is inevitable. I mean, as a mature adult, attuned to God's signals, I am allowed and indeed encouraged by God to tuck into whatever tastes good, because that is God's Infinitely Wise Clue that it's good for me. If something both tastes great and makes you feel fantastic, like that fourth beer after a game (which is the first one you're actually aware of, the first three having gone down like raindrops into the Grand Canyon), well, that's a bonus. A gift, you might say, from God.

I *love* it that I've matured and finally know what's good for me!

It's the *delayed* Signals that confuse me a little. There are at least two, and I don't know exactly what it is God's going on about here. One is the morning after, that "hangover" signal, and I really don't get it. We've had a bit of fun, sure, but it's innocent and harmless, though maybe sometimes a little loud. But why does He think it's so funny to wake you up, one leg stuck to the bed, your head a truck horn going off, a cheap little Canadian flag taped to your cheek, and your wife glaring at a mysterious cut you can't remember getting? What kind of sick Signal is that? Even crueller is the sad fact that, in your twenties, this kind of hangover used to take you twenty-eight beers to earn, whereas now it only takes about five.

The other delayed Signal is, of course, the gut. The mysterious growing gut. I remember when I first started oldtimers at age thirty-seven, and with my elbow I nudged a fellow youngster on the bench at the sight of an older guy on the ice. He was a D-man with a gut that actually protruded out from his jersey at the belt line, showing hairy skin and a black hole of a belly button. We chuckled at him, but we had no idea that we were making fun of our future. And now, as I buy even bigger T-shirts, I have no idea which beer to blame my growing gut on. Which particular night of drinking? It's almost impossible to figure out. It's such a delayed Food Signal from God that it's a difficult one to act on.

More Food Signals from God

BESIDES BEER, us oldtimers have gotten smarter about what else we put into our bodies. Remember the time, the old days, when the idea was to have a great big steak before the game? I remember back in junior, being asked by the coach or manager or trainer if I'd had "the game steak" today. If I hadn't had a "game steak" I probably zipped by him too quickly to even hear the question, so full of zippy-light pasta-energy was I. If I'd indeed had the stupid "game steak," it probably took me several seconds to pick up my head and nod yes to him, and it would be the third period before I had worked through the sludge enough to take my meat rage out on someone, typically some little forward who dared poke his skinny little ass into the crease.

Remember those days? Before we learned to listen to the Food Signals and fell into the good habit of pasta and a salad four hours before the game? Do you also remember Gordie (that's Gordie Howe, for you youngsters who've just turned thirty-five) coming on TV to tell us kids that, before each game, for "real food energy" he ate a Jersey Milk chocolate bar? Maybe he did and maybe he didn't really eat one before each game, but back in those days we believed in TV commercials, especially Canadian ones, even if Gordie talked a little funny and never did seem all that bright. (Though he apparently does the *New York Times* crossword puzzle in something like twenty seconds and is a professional-level bridge player. Like Wayne, he just couldn't *act* very bright.)

We learned about the chocolate bar lie just by feeling the Food Signals in our bodies. I don't know about Gordie, but whenever *I* have a chocolate bar I become an edgy ten-year-old for about three minutes and then I want a nap.

And we learned about "game steak" in a similar way. I guess with steak the idea was "you are what you eat." In other words, since steak is cow muscle, if you eat some, you have enough instant cow muscle that that speedy little bastard on the other team will now pay the price if he tries to go around you like he always does. The flaw in this "you are what you eat" thinking is obvious. We are not hamburgers, and we have all eaten thousands, perhaps millions of them. Burger is basically ground up horns, udders, and snouts. We oldtimers are constantly showering with each other naked, and if "we are what we eat," the evidence should be there in the shower room loud and clear—but I can truthfully say that in the shower room I have seen no horns, no snouts, and hardly any udders at all.

Hard Beer

I'M SPEAKING, of course, about booze, that clear or tea-coloured fire-water that does on occasion find its way into the dressing rooms of Oldtimer Nation.

I'll tell you right off the bat that I'm not an imbiber of the hard beer. There are several reasons for this, and you can read about one if you ever happen to be in the audience when I'm playing in a tournament for my brother Bub's team, the Old Goats. The Goats keep an honorary jersey for me, number 19, and where the captain's C or alternate captain's A is customarily sewn on, my Goat jersey sports an I B. As I'll discuss later, a few other players on the Goats have odd letters—an S, and a B, for Spanky and Blowjob, respectively—but I'm not going to tell you what I B stands for. I'm just not. I have a wife and children. If someone pesters me enough I tell them a lie, that it stands for Ibuprofen, which isn't that bad a lie considering the amount I take for my back during tournaments. Anyway, it may well be the only two-letter jersey in the game—in the world. Suffice to say that I earned those letters after a night spent drinking hard beer. Apparently, near the end of the evening I took down a half-bottle like a thirsty kid draining his Mountain Dew. It happened at Cultis Lake, during a Chilliwack tournament, and Harley still has the stains on his mother's rug, I had broken glasses and some burns, and there was that eavestrough that got ripped off the cottage for the bonfire. You get the picture, and an understanding of why I stick to regular beer these days—or maybe a nice red wine for sipping on the beach with the meditative FeeFee.

The Team Bottle

MY BROTHER BUB'S TEAM has a team drink—white sambuca—and for tournaments they bring along a team bottle. Well, several team bottles, typically one for after each game. I don't know why, but I guess some of the guys feel that regulation beer isn't quite enough and they need that extra something—nudge, spark, glimpse of euphoria—from hard booze before they can get up the oomph to climb into their street clothes and comb their thinning hair. I used to need it, too, before I earned my letters and grew up.

Isn't it funny how some things escalate? At the annual Nanaimo tournament, my brother's team, after playing two games on the Friday, went through three team bottles of white sambuca in one sitting. I hogged extra beer, and watched them. It was ugly. The start was fine, of course—we had just come back to gain a tie after being down 4–1, so the mood was good. And some of these guys are respectable men—business leaders, a superintendent of schools, a dot-com millionaire, etc. But as the bottles got passed and chugged, and glistening chins wiped clean of that licorice syrup, the decibel level grew and grew, and what had begun as civilized conversation came to resemble a slaughterhouse full of goats having their guts slashed. I tried chugging my beer to keep up to their fun level, but there's no way my puny regulation beer could do the trick. I wanted earplugs. Near the end, just before we got dressed and headed out on the town to start the night's festivities, one of the more excitable players ran out into the arena, wearing nothing but his jock, to scream at both the teams on the ice for being selfish cocksuckers who never backcheck. (He is a defenceman, as you probably gathered.)

By the way, I did manage to catch up to the rest of the guys' fun level while using only regulation beer, so it is possible. You just have to be dedicated, and order two at a time.

Maritime Beer

BEER IN THE MARITIMES is actually rum. What the rest of Oldtimer Nation considers beer is seen by Maritimers to be something like tea, which you sip with your aunt on a Sunday visit.

Our goalie in Fredericton (see "Men From a Distant Galaxy") didn't drink rum during weekly games, saving it exclusively for tournaments. Because, for some reason, it worked on him like a magic elixir. It worked so well that Dana's tournament rum was actually supplied by the team. Friday afternoon, he'd take a pre-game warm-up pull. And Dana, a man who didn't stop a lot of pucks during regular games, would now, on rum, stand on his head and do the splits while up there, kicking out impossible second and third shots from five feet out. We'd win entire tournaments, not because of Dana, but because of Dana's rum. I think a lot of the guys wanted him to drink rum all the time, but Dana seemed to turn a bit yellow after tournaments, and I believe there came a time when he was forced by overly scrupulous doctors to quit Maritime beer altogether.

Weird Beer

YES, OF COURSE I MEAN POT.

But let me set something straight, so to speak. No matter what kind of pothead you might be, even some sort of Cheech or Chong clone, if you play oldtimers hockey your first beer-allegiance is to actual beer, real beer, the cold, wet brew in a can. No question. It just wouldn't feel right to clomp off the ice, hot, sweaty, and thirsty as hell, flop to a sit in the dressing room, and instantly light up a joint to quench the thirst. I mean, even scotch or banana liqueur makes more sense than that. (Actually, banana liqueur can be sort of perfect, especially during the playoffs really late at night.)

But sometimes a little bowl for the road can be better than yet another beer. We don't even have to get into the drinking-and-driving discussion, do we? Let's just go straight to the issue of you going to work the next day, with your hangover. Let's compare: there's the ordinary-beer hangover, where you wake up somewhere, naked and all cut up, rolling in ditch-weeds and gravel, whining for mercy and yanking at your hair. Or there's the weird-beer hangover, where you sit quietly in your chair for an hour or so, eating bags of salty things while you dream about pitching that old tent in a peaceful glen some warm day, still rather transfixed by last night's realization that the incredible shape of the female breast is itself the very image of God.

There was a time when pot and sport was a radical mix. This might not mean much to you younger people in this era when sports stars are synonymous with coke habits and giant earrings, but for those of us who grew up around the time when pot first insinuated itself into the dark, secret corners of sports, it does. Back in junior, in the earliest seventies, only a few of us smoked a bit of pot at the odd weekend party, and we had to hide this from the other guys. It was always a small joy when one of the straight guys joined us, being seduced over to the dark side, as it were. Maybe they saw that we were okay guys, and it hadn't seemed to affect our play, hadn't made us chicken in the corners, hadn't taken the edge off the shot, hadn't made the fighters less willing to drop the gloves. (Though, actually, I think it does do that. Maybe it's only laziness, but pot makes you less aggressive. And I also do think it affects a fighter's fistic ability.

Not the fighting itself: once the dance gets going a pothead is at least as lethal as a straight guy, if not more so—hashish is "the assassin's drug," after all. No, it's more that the pothead might study for a moment the fist coming at him, and wonder what it means, both in terms of imminent pain and the general state of violence in the world.) Anyway, it was fun watching some of those new converts to pot, especially those who took it *real* seriously. You know, those guys who, a month after taking that first toke in the parking lot, were leading Marxist yoga communes or weaving fests.

So it continues today, out there in the oldtimer parking lot. Typically, a team might have its little pack of guys who sometimes enjoy a joint for the road. They'll be out there in the parking lot having a last wobbly-pop and someone hauls out a fatty, and you can tell who isn't a smoker because he'll look down at his feet, or maybe roll his eyes at another non-pothead. The joint goes around, and the straight guys have to perform their duty of pinching it and passing it along. The neat thing is, sometimes the non-smoker pauses, as if weighing for a second the possibility that he's nearing death and hasn't yet experienced the dark side, then he mutters, "What the bejeepers," and takes a little puff. And so a rookie doper is born. A few minutes later it can be kind of sweet, hearing him giggle in that fresh, surprised way, and suddenly exclaim how *bright* and sort of, like, *gold* those parking-lot lights are. You feel a bit like you're fifteen again, except that the cold beer in your hand is legal now, while the weird beer still isn't quite.

Anyway, call me an old hippie, but I'd like to challenge all of you oldtimers out there who haven't yet had a taste of the weird beer to go ahead and do so. The songs on the oldies station on the way home, even Petula Clark, will sound different. But it's more than that. Let me say to you guys who tomorrow are putting on the ties and going up the office towers, especially you guys who *own* the office towers: those of us who smoked a bale of weird beer way back when, *we had more fun than you*. Simple as that. So there. So quit being a great big snobby chicken.

That's what I'm calling you, a chicken. Next time you see me behind the net, go ahead and elbow me in the face. What will happen is, I'll go down in a stupid bloody pile as usual, but all my pothead assassin friends will lose their minds at the injustice of it and dive on you, growling.

A.A., Eh?

MOST TEAM COOLERS contain a predetermined number of cans of a softer kind of beer, like 7-Up. Some guys just want to quench their thirst with that sweeter, lighter kind and then, after a shower, switch to a real beer to sit and socialize. But there are those guys who stick with the 7-Up, thank you very much, because a switch to the real stuff would prove disastrous. Basically, what's happened is, earlier in life they've had their share of beer—*more* than their share—and they aren't allowed to have any more.

If you're one of those guys who can't have a beer because it might mean the end of you, just know that, as oldtimers, we're respectful of that. And, if it looks like you can handle it, we'll give you a bit of a teasing. Just know that we're watching you. We've seen that little occasional glint in your eye, that flash of indecision and fear. Rest assured that we wouldn't let you have one even if you begged, or offered to pay double. (Well, actually, on our team, an offer to pay double would easily get you that beer . . .) We appreciate those times you've driven us home after we've had one too many and couldn't drive home and still consider ourselves responsible human beings. We also appreciate your lack of a hangover and your extra jump on a

Sunday morning during that tournament championship game.

We respect you because we understand you—maybe a little too well. Maybe we're afraid of what you represent. From what I can tell, most of us oldtimers are basically addicted to beer. We love it, and some of us might not play hockey without it. From the look of things, a few of us might just have to quit, sooner rather than later, and join you in the 7-Up line. Me, I've cut back a bit myself, making it a rule to never have more than one beer open at a time.

But it's nice to know that, if and when we quit the brown stuff, the team will still be there. So will the exhaustion and the bullshit and the laughs. It's nice to know that the guys will respect us but also make fun of us, and talk about it like it's no big deal, and put up with our stories about the drunk old days. And it'll be good to know there will be a couple of pops, actual pops, with our name on them, and that they'll taste good— almost good enough—going down.

Designer Beer

OUT IN THE COZY PARKING LOT of our home arena, we sometimes notice a few cars with the same few guys standing around, with a team cooler similar to ours at their feet. And a couple of times, when our cooler has gone empty, we've gone over to them and purchased a few of their cold ones. On both occasions, what they sold us were bottles of Corona, which is all that their cooler contained. On the second occasion I asked them in jest if that's all they ever drank on their team, and their bemused response was a simple "Yes."

I didn't know what to say. I felt speechless. Something was wrong, very wrong. First, hockey beer doesn't come from Mexico. Second, beer bottles aren't clear. Third, hockey beer comes in cans.

It's not the only time I've noticed something wrong with oldtimer beer selection these days.

Now, I happen to like all kinds of beer. Beer is something I've taken on as part of what has come to be called "life-long learning." So I've been educating myself: I've learned the difference between stout and bitter, I've brewed English strong ale in my basement, I know what "hoppy" tastes like, and I almost know what "wort" is. I enjoy a black and tan. I've tried this U-Brew and that U-Brew, and my latest batch is a robust and slightly mischievous IPA made from organic grains that I had to hand-grind on the premises.

I say all this not to brag, but to give greater weight to my suggestion that none of that *fancy-assed designer beer* belongs in a dressing room. It's just wrong. I'm not sure why, it just is.

And when's it going to stop? The most extreme version of designer beer, *wine*, has also recently been making inroads into the oldtimer room. Much as I love my brother Bub's team, the Goats, they have a disturbing spring ritual wherein, some time close to the end of their season, they actually have a dressing-room wine and cheese. Yes they do. Wine, cheese, and fancy meats. Now, mostly this is because one teammate is a partner in an upscale wine shop, and is generous enough to bring in, for free, a bunch of excellent stock for the boys to sample. But still. My brother Bub has described this evening to me more than once, and his tone is sort of disturbed, a little quiet and unsure, as he reports on the guys standing around in their smelly gaunch, one foot up on the bench, nibbling a corner of prosciutto and swirling, then sipping, an Okanagan cab-franc, nodding daintily, commenting on its nose, oak, and fruit.

It's all just wrong. And it's in the realm of possibility that if the next team scheduled to use that room got impatient and happened to peak in and got a glimpse of what was happening in there, the Goats might just find themselves in an old-fashioned donnybrook.

Maybe it has to do with childhood, with growing up. You know, with *tradition*. I remember being a rawboned and tow-headed youth cutting his teeth on 20¢ draft in the seedy taverns of both Toronto and Vancouver. I distinctly remember the taste—a combination of watery and, well, bad. It tasted like a living version of the dead smell wafting up out of the terry cloth. But it started to taste okay after a glass or two. I remember the rumour going around, that radioactive cobalt was used in it as a preservative, and, depending on who was spreading the rumour, that's why you got, or *didn't* get, a headache. I remember all sorts of neat stuff about that early beer, and also that most of the guys who drank in this sort of bar had faces that had apparently stopped a puck or two.

So though I'm not exactly sure of the logic, basic old-time beer is somehow intimately connected to basic old-time hockey, and it is for this reason that designer beer has no place in the dressing room. Room beer should be something mass produced by Molson or Labatt, it should be nationally advertised, and taste better after the first can. And it should be in a *can*. Everything else should be banned. Nothing brewed according to Bavarian Purity Law should be allowed in the door. Bags— especially those stewardess bags-on-wheels—should be checked for micro-brew contraband. No red ale or stout or brewed-in-small-batches porter. Not even pale ale or honey-brown-whatever should be allowed.

I'm going to shift gears slightly and suggest that even lite beer should be similarly banned. I don't care if you're fat—so am I. This ban is because lite beer tastes almost like American beer, and let's not get started in on that one.

THIS SEASON SO FAR

October

Yes, I think I want to play.

I wonder how the guys are doing, and if we've won any games. We tend not to win many before Christmas. I don't know why that is. But, most autumns, we look so bad and *are* so bad that anyone can beat us—a spilled bowl of goldfish could beat us. But then, after New Year's, boom, we look almost good, and we win a few. We actually smoke a few teams in the New Year. Yes we do.

Hey, I do think I want to play.

I've called my brother Bub and he's playing again. And though he's in rotten shape, and won't admit to liking being back at it, I can tell he does. The thing is, my brother never admits to liking anything. He was like that as a kid. And as a young man, in a rare confessional moment, he once told me, "If you hate everything in advance, you're never disappointed." Something like that. In any case, about playing oldtimers this year, he says, "The beer's okay after." Coming from him, that means he's having a wonderful time in all ways. And it's his dry way of summing up that old expression: I'd rather have a bottle in front of me than a frontal lobotomy.

So I decide to go and see the guys, catch one of our games. I time my arrival so that I won't have to watch more than five minutes of the actual game. Oldtimers might be fun to play, but it's not that fun to watch. One reason for this, of course, is the cliché: it's hard to watch because it hurts not to be out there contributing. The main reason, though, is that my team's so slow it's a bit like watching a bridge tournament. Also, we're still in the phase of the season when that bowl of goldfish walks all over us. Another reason for my strategic timing is that if I come for the whole game they'll expect me to stand at the bench and open the gate. If I don't, I'll look like a lazy asshole. It doesn't matter that I have a bad back. Nobody really cares about my bad back. They all have bad backs. If mine's good enough to let me stand there watching, it's good enough to open the gate for them.

Actually, the five minutes are almost fun to watch. Our Dallas-pattern uniforms are nifty compared to the other guys' orange-and-black throwbacks. The rink smells icy, like only a rink can. I can also smell that someone's walked by with a coffee. Certain smells stand out in a rink.

The guys are really into the game. No one notices me here at the glass. It's a faster game than I thought it would be. A few of our guys look like they've stayed in a bit of shape. My line scores a decent goal.

That is, what *should* be my line scores a decent goal. The guy who's stolen my spot is a spare I don't recognize. He looks pretty good and I'm man enough to admit I'm jealous. I'm man enough to admit that I would prefer to see my two wingers, Dave and Vic, yelling at their new centreman because he's stupid, selfish, and bad. I want Dave and Vic to suddenly see me, then leap up and skate over to high-five me through the glass. They don't. They score a nice goal on a pass from asshole, the interloper spare.

The buzzer goes, the Zamboni doors open, the teams shake hands. We lose 6–3, not bad for this time of year. A guy throws me the key over the glass and I open the door to the room. The guys troop in, coughing out my name, glad to see me.

Good to see the guys. Nice to have a beer in the room. It's so much better when you're sweaty and thirsty, however. A single beer is all I feel the need for. It tastes sort of warmish and too filling. The word "ambrosia" doesn't apply tonight, not remotely, and I wonder how it was ever possible to experience beer that way. Also, though we've had our happy hellos and a few guys asked about my back, talk quickly returns to stuff I wasn't a part of, the wacky stuff that just happened out on the ice. I stand near the middle of the room by the cooler and hear meaningless little conversations go on all around me. "You see Mike bat that thing out of the air?" "In the balls? You sure?" "No, last week he called a good game. He's an asshole but he called a good game." "*You* know, 27, that big guy with no neck. Fast guy with no neck. That guy. Yeah that's *his* wife, eh?" "No, Chris didn't blow that one, it went in off my skate. Chris only blew the other five. Right, Chris?" And Rich is pacing, telling us we've gotta start getting our passes on the tape.

I try to join in, bugging my winger, Dave, about the fancy new composite stick I see he's bought. (Me, I'm still a wooden stick guy. I survived the Easton metal stick era, and now I plan on surviving the composite era too. I always figured that, like chimps and some species of birds, our use of sticks proves that we are intelligent tool-users, but that's about it.) When I ask, Dave admits it cost him a hundred and fifty bucks. I ask him next if he thinks fifty bucks per goal this year is worth it and he throws an obligatory tape ball at me, but that's about it for me joining in the afterglow banter of the game.

I wave, leave, and a few guys grunt my name. I don't drag my feet in the parking lot, but I feel like it. I don't know what I thought it would be like. I consider these guys friends, and I hadn't seen them for six months, so maybe I figured there'd be a *conversation* or something. About what, I don't know. The war in Iraq? The looming bird flu? No. So what did I want to talk about? I look at what in my life is important these days. Last week, Lilli, my six-year-old, broke her ankle while jumping, was given the choice of fibreglass cast colours, and chose purple—and the ankle is healing nicely. I'd overheard my much older daughter, Lise, whispering something about birth control with the complicit FeeFee, and I got out of there fast, not wanting to hear any more. And a friend of my son Connor had nearly been in a knife fight, and I suspect this same friend of fooling around with drugs harder than pot, and I'm edgy that he's my son's friend at all. But none of this important stuff felt like dressing-room stuff.

I hadn't even mentioned to anybody in the room that I'm having a brain scan in a few weeks. Not sure why. In some ways I'd love to talk about it. I've been talking about it with the sympathetic FeeFee for months. I've been talking to *myself* about it non-stop. But it didn't seem right, there in the room, maybe because it wasn't a hockey injury. No, it was a *life* injury, an injury from that bigger game. That bigger game that we all play hockey to get away from.

Anyway, out in the parking lot, it dawns on me that because of my back I'll probably not be playing until I get the results of this test, and it's probably a good thing that I do wait. Because in the back of my mind I've had this image of me going into a corner with a guy, and we bash around a little bit, and this chunk of stuff becomes dislodged from one part of my brain and drifts over to another part. It takes about three seconds. The guy has grabbed the puck from me and scored, but I haven't noticed because I've started feeling really strange, I start whistling a song from childhood, then I talk like Minnie Mouse again, then I drool, and then it kills me.

It feels weird leaving the arena not tired. It's even weirder that my hair's dry.

THE GREAT ABYSS AND THE BIRTH OF AN OLDTIMER CAREER

I STOPPED PLAYING HOCKEY altogether when I was about twenty-five. I didn't skate, even once, for twelve years. I think of this period in my life as the Great Abyss. Then one day I emerged, blinking under the bright morning sun like that baby giraffe in *The Lion King*, and I started playing oldtimers.

My blind plummet into the Great Abyss began some time after I'd played in Europe and returned to Vancouver to play smatterings of senior, intermediate, and beer-league stuff. I was restless and didn't stick to teams. I played for Pharaoh's Retreat, and the North Shore Hurry-Kings, which were an offshoot of the infamous Shmyr Flyers. It's a bit of a blur, but I suspect I quit hockey outright after a last trip north to Alaska, which was a partially-collapsed-lung-and-drunken-horror-show, true, but it wasn't the sole reason I quit.

In fact, I didn't really quit. I just stopped playing. It's like jogging—you never hear of someone "quitting jogging," they just find themselves not doing it anymore. Likewise, I never decided to quit, not consciously anyway. I just stopped thinking about hockey, and one fall I didn't bother to make a phone call and get my gear together. It just didn't occur to me, didn't appear on my radar screen. As a matter of fact, for twelve years I didn't know where my skates were, or if I even had any. Nor did I care. As for gear, it just got left somewhere, and if it still exists, it's on its last stage of rot. I picture my SPAPS helmet (the Butch Goring kind) from Winnipeg, and Red Kelly's shoulder, elbow, and shin pads from my stint with the Marlies in Toronto. I doubt helmet plastic can rot, but I bet all the foam cushioning is gone to powder. I wonder where that helmet is now. Turned upside down, the SPAPS would make a good colander for draining pasta. You'd probably want to rinse it out first.

What did I do during the twelve years in the Great Abyss? I lived in Vancouver, Massachusetts, Toronto, Halifax, and Fredericton. I got married, had my first two kids, and stopped getting into much mischief anymore. I acquired a job, a mortgage, and pets. I managed to let youth go with a sort of long flick of the wrist, and was starting to welcome middle age and the wisdom and stability it would inevitably bring. But, without hockey, did any of this mean anything? I think we all know the answer to that. And maybe I don't remember much about those twelve years simply because there is no reason to remember.

Not only did I not think about hockey during those years, I scorned it. Saturday evenings, flicking the remote, cup of tea in hand, the *Hockey Night in Canada* theme music would play and my stomach would hollow out and then go sour—I'd snort and change the channel. (Picture a guy who has lost at love, and the expression on his face as he sees his ex flounce past and he hisses, "I don't need *her*." He doesn't know he's a pathetic husk, but to everyone else it's as clear as can be.) It was around this time that I began to appreciate soccer.

But even in the depths of the Great Abyss there were a few blips of light. One occurred about a week after my first daughter, Lise, was born. This was in Toronto during the 1987 playoffs. I remember because, one night, the three of us were in bed (me, the fatigued FeeFee, and the new, foot-long Lise), and I flicked on the TV. This TV was a twelve-inch black and white, a wedding gift from my wife's brother Steve, a film producer and gizmo wizard who couldn't stand it that we lived like cave-dwellers, lacking electronics of even this most basic kind. (I believe Steve had the first TV-equipped minivan on the North American continent, and after he showed it off at a family reunion, my deprived kids wouldn't talk to me for days.)

The TV was so small I could stick it right on the pillow beside my face while my two women slept. I kept the sound low, and was reminded how the really great hockey games can gain an intensity with volume turned down. It was a semifinal game seven between Washington and the Islanders. It was already in overtime. I watched and it was great. Now it was the second overtime. God, were those guys tired. I could really relate, having just gone through childbirth and everything. I mean, my wife was tired, and so was my baby girl, but I was *really* tired. But I could and would go the distance with this fatherhood thing, never giving up. Just like those guys on the tube. It was now the third overtime. Some of you fans know where this is going: I'd accidentally happened upon one of the longest playoff games in history. I don't even remember how many overtimes it went, four or five, but I can still clearly see LaFontaine, in glorious black and white, score that goal and sink to his knees. So tired were all those guys that it didn't look like the winners were any happier than the losers, or if they even knew anymore. It was a great game. But I didn't watch another one for quite a while. I don't know why.

There was another slight tear in the dark fabric of the Abyss a few years later, near Halifax. One winter a few families gathered at someone's Hatchett Lake property for a brunchy affair, and it was also to be a skating party. Owning no skates, I hadn't brought any, but the host had an extra pair that sort of fit, and the fun-loving and winter-clad FeeFee more or less insisted. I'd been dropping hints about my on-ice heroics for years, it seems, and I'm not sure she believed that I could actually even skate.

Now, one thing about my wife. The much-accomplished FeeFee had been a ballet dancer (see "Wayne Gretzky and the Battle of the TV Spines"), and as far as athleticism went, she was much more the professional than I ever was. I say all this in order to explain that she knew about and appreciated bodies and what they could do at the highest athletic levels. Also—and here was something I didn't know about her yet—when she watched a body perform at a strenuous and high level of athleticism, it made her really horny.

To make a long story short, the bundled and eager FeeFee watched me skate for the very first time. I launched myself out onto the black ice of Hatchett Lake unsteadily, but then did a few chugging strides. I circled back and came at her, and stopped two feet in front of her in the nick of time, sending up a modest spray of ice crystals. "Do that again," she said, her voice a sort of low whisper. So I did, and even though the lake ice was a tad bumpy, making me worry for my ankles, I added a tight turn or two, and skated backwards—only to spot an invisible loose puck, whereupon I stopped on a dime, chugged forward, intercepted the puck, and was now a fifteen-year-old on a breakaway. "Let's see a bit more of that," said the reddening FeeFee. She had long since abandoned our two-year-old daughter to whimper and flounder about in the snowbank. You can do the math as to when our second, Connor, was born, later the following year.

But none of this was enough to get me out of the Abyss. It was my brother who did that, with one phone call.

My brother had lived through his own dark age, one that, like mine, was filled with a similar mess of empty accomplishments. But he had fought his way out and had been playing oldtimers for a couple of years. Living on opposite coasts, we'd see each other at Christmas, but that was about it. Otherwise we'd talk on the phone, generally on a weekend if one of us had had a couple of beers, whereupon the sober one would patiently listen to a pile of bullshit. We sort of took turns being the sober one. In any case, on a few occasions he did mention he was playing hockey again, but in the low-key manner of brothers neither of us made any sort of deal about it. I'd ask how the hockey was going and he'd say, "I dunno, it's okay." Once in a while he'd have a juicy anecdote about a fight or a prank, or that he'd run into an old teammate of ours at a tournament. But never did he suggest that I should consider strapping on the blades again.

Until one spring. I was thirty-seven and living in Fredericton, and about to come out west on a little business. I was on the phone to my brother and, I don't know why, but Bub said, "We have an oldtimers tournament that weekend. Why don't you bring your skates?"

Oldtimers. Now, the word "oldtimer" is strongly familiar to most of us. Hearing this word, I bet I'm not alone when I can't help but picture an ancient western flick, where, turning a corner down there in the gulch, the sheriff encounters an old prospector with a beat-up hat, a long white moustache, a pick-axe, and a donkey with a huge dented frying pan tied to it. This prospector is always kind of short, dumpy, and in a good mood, and sometimes he limps. The conversation goes as follows:

"Howdy, oldtimer. Have you by any chance seen Black Bart hereabouts?"

"Mebbe. Who'm ah talkin' to, stranger?"

The sheriff aims his chest at the old guy so that the silver badge registers. The prospector sees the badge and spits a startling gob of brown sludge into the dust. Then he murmurs something suspiciously intimate to his mule.

So it was a little iffy to begin thinking of myself as an "old-timer," even for one tournament in faraway Vancouver.

I believe I simply replied that I didn't have any skates. There was a slight pause, then my brother said, "I think I saw them hanging downstairs at the parents'."

"My skates?"

"I dunno. Somebody's. They're Tacks. Didn't you wear Tacks?"

"Yeah."

"Well they're probably yours."

"Maybe."

"Yeah."

"Any of my old sticks in the garage?"

"How the fuck should I know?"

"Well fucking go *look*."

Anyway, my emergence from the Great Abyss sounded something like that. Rebirth often has an unexpected and modest face. Before I knew it, I was flying out to Vancouver, not thinking about business at all. Instead, I pictured my good old skates hanging in the parents' basement, and wondered how much a stick might cost these days.

And, to get serious for a moment (not that any of this book isn't utterly serious), I started to *dream* about the upcoming tournament. I started to dream about hockey, but never about playing the actual game. No, the dreams were about trying to get to the rink, and losing my equipment on the way. Or arriving there and having no gear, or no skates. Or missing the team bus and having to catch up to it somehow. In fact, in these dreams I never once saw ice or even a dressing room. They were always about me trying to get to the rink on time to get dressed. And in that unreachable dressing room sat my brother.

I was going to play with my brother again. I'd played with him in my earliest days of shinny in Winnipeg. Fifteen months older than me, in those earliest days he way bigger, faster, better, and he probably never passed me the puck even if I begged him, which of course you just don't do in shinny anyway. Then the organized team game separated us through peewee and bantam and midget, but when I was sixteen we played on the same junior team, the Vancouver Centennials. Two years of that, then he went to play in Europe and I went to UBC to play, but he returned to play for UBC for one of those years. Then we played together on the occasional beer-league team. By then we had the same friends, and we often lived in the same rented house. Went camping. We had always been close friends—most of the time, best friends. And hockey had been a big part of that. Now, apparently, I was going to play with my brother again, and for some reason I was already dreaming about it. I'm no child psychologist, but it no doubt had something to do with the time we'd spent in the crib together, babbling nonsense out of bubbly mouths and seeing who could throw their diaper ammo the farthest. Isn't a hockey rink sort of a huge crib? Oldtimer wives will tell you it is. And what's a slapshot but a mechanized flinging of one's diaper ordinance? I don't want to go any further with this analogy, so I hope you get my point.

In any case, it was going to be good to be in the same room together, pull on the same team sweater, insult each other about being fat and ugly, all of that. Compete on the same team. Go to war together. Pass the puck a bit but most of all show off for each other. No—most of all be proud of your brother if he got a breakaway or popped a goal. It would definitely be a situation where I would way rather see him get a hat trick than get a hat trick myself. Sort of like the feeling you get when you watch your kid perform. Sorry for the gush here, but I would have to say that wanting the best for someone else is one definition of love.

Well, I got to Vancouver and did my professional duties—not that I remember any of that, because I was here to play some fucking hockey. Pop some biscuit and bash a bit in the corners, maybe lay a perfect saucer pass and send my brother in alone. I arrived at the parents' place, probably said hi and maybe even hugged them, but I went right down to the basement to see if those were indeed my skates. They were. Old—ancient—Tackaberrys. Kangaroo leather. *Tube* skates! With blades capped by those white plastic protective knobs. Down there in the store room I kicked off my shoes and socks. (Like my all-time hero, Number 4, Bobby Orr, I wore bare feet in my skates. Still do.)

My face lit up, and the rotten old door to the Great Abyss creaked shut behind me, when that first skate slid on like—well, I was going to say "a glove." But since I'm a writer and allergic to most clichés, I'll instead choose a more accurate simile to describe my foot entering that skate, one that involves a penis, and an equally eager vagina. It felt *just* like that.

Enough detail. Let's get to the tournament itself, where I emerged from the Great Abyss for good.

I was unbelievably nervous sitting there in the room. All was déjà vu—the smells, the laughter, the wit and the bullshit tossed around, the bags unzipping, the sound of tape tearing off the roll, guys sitting around in their underwear. A few were old friends I'd played with before, and we had some fun insulting each others' aging bodies. (One of them, Mike, saw me undress and he burst out laughing. Mike's a surveyor and, having a way with precise calculations, he announced that, from the look of things, I'd eaten an estimated seventeen thousand hamburgers since he'd last seen me.)

Needless to say, I was in lousy shape. I've never been one for exercise. I *had* been walking to work, about half a mile each way, the luxurious FeeFee being too busy staying comfortable in bed to drive me. But the only thing physical about my job—teaching and writing—was pressing keys on my keyboard and lifting my coffee cup. Then getting up, crossing the hall, and draining the coffee. But there in the laughter-filled room I was confident I still had some muscle hidden somewhere under all that softness. My thinking was, since I weighed a lot, and since we all know that muscle weighs more than fat, I must therefore be rather muscular—maybe even in shape.

With my brother's help I'd scrounged gear, which was mismatched, didn't fit, and smelled like six different smelly people at once. Add to that my tube skates, which everyone in the room had a good chuckle at. The *coup de grâce*, though, was my glasses. For games I used to wear contacts, of course, but they had been lost in the depths of the Abyss. So it was glasses, which was fine, except that the previous night, over a few beers after my meetings, I'd somehow sat on them—or *somebody* had sat on them—and so they now sported white tape *exactly where the Hanson Brothers taped theirs*. Needless to say, I was a classic: beer gut, tube skates, mismatched, odorous gear, and taped glasses. Out on the ice I could be as shitty as shitty could be, but I knew I would be forgiven, and maybe even celebrated, because I was a classic.

We clomped out of the room and down the dark corridor in a ragged line. It was all so familiar, yet at the same time new and a little funny. I found it funny, for instance, that from behind, in these clean, bright uniforms and helmets, these oldtimers could easily be mistaken for a bunch of twenty-year-olds. It was also familiar and funny the way all clomping hockey players use their sticks on the floor like tall canes.

That first step onto the ice, though, was very foreign. Anyone who plays oldtimers knows this feeling every September, but take that feeling and multiply it by ten—then subtract thirty, add sixty, and then multiply that by your least favourite number.

That's how bad it was. I was in a bit of a panic because of how awkward I felt, and partly as a result of that, I dropped down to all fours. I think a few of my new teammates wondered what I was doing, suddenly dropping to all fours about five feet out of the gate. Well, fuck off, I was stretching. I was obeying the long-distance commands of the knowledgeable FeeFee, who knew everything there was to know about high- and low-performance bodies, and who had lectured me long into several evenings on the importance of stretching before I exerted myself in my first hockey game in twelve years. If I didn't stretch, she claimed, I would break a major bone any time I tried to touch the puck. Now, five feet outside the gate, feeling so foreign on my feet, I believed her.

I don't need to tell you that the first couple of shifts were ridiculous. Sort of hallucinogenic, for any of you who remember that word—or, more to the point, what that word actually felt like. In any case, I must have looked bad, because I was moved from defence up to a forward line, where I could do less damage. I think some of the boys were a little dubious about me at this point, because, despite all appearances in the room, I was still in their eyes "maybe a ringer," seeing as I'd played some good hockey in the past. My brother Bub, the team captain, had probably exaggerated a few of my exploits. But by now it was clear that I was not only no ringer but instead an albatross. Or, for you less literary types, a real shitty player.

But it did sort of come together and I had some fun. My arms and legs almost remembered how to work in unison, and when I passed the puck it generally went to the player I aimed it at, though maybe not too near the tape. I had some speed for about ten feet. If I mucked for even five seconds in the corner, though, my shift was over. And then, miracle of miracles, over the course of the three tournament games I actually popped three goals.

One took the form of me, an overweight ex-defenceman, bashing a rebound past a helpless goalie. On another, I deflected a point shot, just like a pro, except that the corner of the net I was aiming at wasn't the corner the puck went in. And on the third goal, it seemed that there were even shittier players than me out there, because I actually got around a D-man and snuck one in on the short side. I probably caused four goals due to my complete inability to backcheck past the red line, but I didn't harm the team too badly. And it was fun. We won our division in the tournament, and won a T-shirt, which I still have. And my brother did get a hat trick. His skating style hadn't changed since he was twelve, he still had that old speed, and it was great to watch him go.

After the last game, we sat slumped in the room, the cooler lid was lifted and cold beers went around. I think I actually rolled one over my red-hot forehead, like they do in TV commercials. I can't remember past the first beer, so I must have had a stupendous time.

Needless to say, I took my skates back to Fredericton.

THIS MORTAL FUCKING COIL

The Sound of Oldtimers' Hearts

THIS MORNING, as is often the case on a Sunday, I am awakened by the sweet face of my six-year-old, Lilli. She likes to crawl in with me and snuggle, I don't know why. I mean, consider the morning mouth, and the fact that until I have had my second coffee I'm spiritually ugly, if not down-right evil.

This morning, in the sweetest little voice, Lilli asked me, "Daddy?"

"Uhmmhmm?"

"Daddy, is a ladybug a beetle?"

To complete this perfect father-daughter moment, I told her, sagely, "That's right. A ladybug is a beetle."

To increase the perfection, Lilli laid her head on my chest and rested a moment. Then she said, softly, with a bit of awe, "I can hear your heart."

"Really?"

"Yeth." Lilli couldn't be any cuter if she tried, with that little face and its single, big front tooth, gleaming like a Chiclet.

"You know what it sounds like?"

"No, sweetheart. What does it sound like?" I had a sudden and profound sense of my mortality, of a noble, fifty-two-year-old heart that sounded like it'd been through the wars. It would have a stately and brave, but slightly weary sound, an honest, tough-yet-modest, Canadian sound. In short, an old-timer sound.

"It sounds like farts."

The worst part is, Lilli isn't laughing when she says this. It isn't a joke. She's a highly intelligent child. My heart sounds like farts.

Oldtimers' hearts sound like farts.

Old Injuries

I THINK THE MARK of a mature hockey player is that, somewhere along the line he has experienced the slightly puzzling sight of seeing bruises on his bruises. Otherwise, when you're an oldtimer, there isn't much to say about injuries. Except that almost all of us have injuries, almost all of the time.

Well, maybe there are two more things to say.

One, we do break easier at this age.

Two, our knowledge of injuries is now encyclopedic.

BY "OLD INJURIES" I don't mean injuries that are old, but injuries that happen *because* you're old. Death being the ultimate old injury.

Some old injuries are spectacular in their silliness. My brother Bub was, at an earlier point in his life, a winger with a mean streak and professional speed. While not quite a goon, he was known to hurl himself into corner after corner, and if a glove fell off and someone got accidentally punched in the process, well, that wasn't his fault. Anyway, this same tough brother—at fifty-three no longer quite as fast, and not very mean anymore—dislocated his finger during a game last year. Actually, he dislocated it *before* the game, in the dressing room. He did it tightening his skates. I'll end this story here, because it's too terrible and silly to continue.

Old injuries make you laugh and shake your head. It's either that or break down and cry, followed by permanent depression, because in your old injury you have just glimpsed your mortality. Not so much a glimpse as a pie in the face. Thanks, mortal coil. (I think "mortal coil" is a term from the Bible that has something to do with clay, and means "this body of yours that one day is going to die and rot—but not necessarily in that order.")

I suffered an old injury that almost rivals my brother's for silliness. One year not long ago, the season started on October 1, so on September 30 I decided to do some push-ups to get in shape. My plan was to begin with ten or fifteen and then add one every day for the rest of the year, because of course I was going to *do it* this year, get really strong and in shape for the first time since I was nineteen. By March or April I'd be doing hundreds of push-ups a set. Anyway, that first day I got to ten or maybe twelve, popped something small and innocent in my right shoulder, and didn't play hockey till January. Obviously, my mistake was to try to get in shape in the first place, but hindsight, as they say, is twenty-twenty. (Many oldtimers I know also indulge in this fantasy of a one-day "training camp" just before the season starts. Since the shoulder pop, mine now consists of a single five-minute near-fatal jog.)

I personally suffered another silly old injury, and I've seen it happen to others, so something really ought to be done about this one. It has to do with opening the gate. Sure, go ahead, laugh at the old guy who can't even open the gate anymore. But it's actually a serious problem. For one thing, unlike in the pros, there's no guy standing there and getting paid to open the gate. For another, some of us oldtimers choose to no longer "leap nimbly over the boards and land lightly on the ice," preferring instead to preserve some dignity and go in and out the gate, which is why it's there. (Who's the keener who first jumped over the boards, anyway? Wouldn't you like to get him? For making us gate users look bad? Shouldn't oldtimers hockey outlaw board-jumping like it did slapshots? I mean, seriously?)

I won't even bother to go into the old injuries caused by board-jumping. And I'm still on gate-opening here, which is at least as deadly. The sad thing is, gate injuries are caused by a player being *nice*. He's just sitting there on the bench, resting, drifting in and out of consciousness but otherwise enjoying himself, a couple feet away from the gate. A gasping teammate is headed off the ice, he's aimed himself at the gate, he wants it opened so he can get the hell off, he's gasping and can't even yell, he's desperate, almost dead, and it's your job—not only as a teammate but as a human being—to open that gate for him. So you *lean* over those two feet and *wrench* on that reluctant steel handle. Wrench, wrench, gasping teammate with sad eyes and shrapnel wounds is floundering ever closer, wrench, *wrench*, *pop*. Fuck.

I'm surprised that chiropractors don't chase oldtimers games the way American lawyers chase car accidents.

Have you noticed that none of these silly old injuries has anything to do with playing the actual game of hockey?

Another old injury I've witnessed in the dressing room could have happened at any level of the game, from peewee to pro, but an oldtimer dressing room is by far the most prone to this one. I was at a tournament with my brother's Old Goat team up in Chilliwack, a September tournament whose only stated purpose is to "get the rust out." (It's a horrible tournament, it really is, in that 90 percent of us do indeed "get the rust out," having not smelled a skate, or even a running shoe, since April, and the sweat that issues from our bodies at this tournament smells like rotten, over-fermented beer, which of course is just what it is. But then there's that 10 percent of players, the hockey-Eddies who have been playing for three teams all summer, and also jog—sorry, "run"—and are also probably high school phys ed teachers, or hobbyist cattle farmers who toss hay around with pitchforks the way Bobby Hull used to. Anyway, that 10 percent of in-shape bastards play this rust tournament like hot knives slicing through butter. (In case you didn't get the metaphor, we tubby 90 percenters are the butter being sliced through.))

Anyway, the dressing-room accident I'm on about involves skates and toes. Skates walking on toes. The injury I witnessed in Chilliwack involved a skate worn by a not-very-big guy, thank goodness, and a toe worn by a tolerant, forgiving guy, thank goodness. Anyway, the toe got stepped on, and the skate blade went almost to the floor. The toe—a big toe—was a dangler. It got cemented and stitched back on and the guy is still playing with the same grace as always (that is, a missing toe or two wouldn't have hurt his game much at this point anyway).

But oldtimers is more prone to this particular accident for two main reasons. One, most dressing rooms we get stuck in are built for peewees. Peewees we aren't—we are fifteen fairly fat guys crammed into a small space, where amongst the fat feet and hockey bags an inch of bare floor is hard to find. Two, also unlike peewees, after a game we are in a hurry, even a frenzy, to grab a cold can of beer from a Cooler posing in the centre of the crowded room, as coy as Annette Funicello in a bathing suit, and who can blame a guy, really, for stepping on living flesh trying to get to her?

Playing Hurt

SOMEONE ONCE SAID that life is one big injury that ends in death. Whoever said that is probably dead now, so my vote is that what he said no longer applies. I'd rather think of life as a great big weird game that ends at the buzzer. And I think that hockey players are good at the game of life because they know how to play hurt. When you're an oldtimer, playing hurt is something you just have to learn — otherwise you won't play at all.

Another thing about injuries, something that is known only to us oldtimers. It's one of those secrets old people have, the kind they blab on and on to younger people about, but no one really listens, so when you finally get old and learn about it first hand, it feels as if old people were keeping this a secret from you. The secret is (and if you're a young person reading this, you won't absorb any of these words at all): when you're an oldtimer, your body no longer heals. Injuries just sort of become part of your body, your mortal coil. I suppose they do heal, but so slowly you don't really notice the healing process. Long gone are the days when you could sprain a wrist, wince a few times, flex it, and whisper to yourself, "Three, four days." Gashes were clean scars in two, three weeks. Well, that kind of estimating is over. Unless you're counting in years, or — I'm serious here — decades.

The shoulder of mine that popped when I was doing push-ups one September in an attempt to counter all the beers and burgers I'd ingested over the summer? It's been years since that last fateful push-up, and my shoulder still isn't right. A doctor has deemed it a "subluxation," but that's just another fancy word for *old*. The shoulder seems to get about 5 percent better every year. I suppose whatever's happening in my shoulder could still fall under the definition of "healing," but it's a stretch.

This truth, that as oldtimers we no longer heal, came as a shock to me. I didn't lace on skates even once between the ages of twenty-four and thirty-six, and in those twelve years something dark and weird mutated within my body, something that took away the miraculous powers of cellular rejuvenation. The September I first started playing oldtimers hockey and stopped a puck on my instep, the bruise lasted so long—it was months and months—that I found myself forgetting the cause of the injury altogether. Instead I began to think I had a loud, easy-to-see kind of cancer. Now, every time I get a nick or scrape or bruise or pull, months go by, I forget the cause of the injury, and I realize that I have cancer. Different forms of it, in lots of places all over my body.

I'm pretty sure everybody sitting there in the dressing room thinks the same thing as they painfully tighten skates before a game: that they have eleven different forms of cancer, all over their body. No one mentions it. We make fun of each others' swollen guts instead. "When're you due?" being the most common. "Twins?" being the second.

To Hangummup or Not to Hangummup

TO HANGUMMUP MEANS, of course, "to quit my beloved game of hockey for the rest of my life." It refers literally to hanging one's skates on a rusty nail in the back shed. Once you've hungummup, you forget about them completely and spiderwebs are allowed to grow. If you happen to be Bobby Orr, someone will come along and steal them, dust off the webs, and sell them to a museum, but for the rest of us, those skates will just keep hanging from that nail until the laces rot and they fall to the floor. (And they will make no sound, because there will be nobody there to hear them.)

Hanginnummup usually means a lot to a guy. Sometimes not, but it usually does. It can carry an ominous tone, something along the lines of, "I'm so old now that my body can no longer play a game I enjoy."

You tend to hear the word at two different times of the year— right when the season begins, and right when it's about to end. When you hear it at season's end, it's usually a teammate, after a game, though he hasn't played for a month because of his back, which has been injured for the third year out of the last five. He's sitting there beside you in his street clothes, having a beer he isn't enjoying. He says—they always say it this way—"Ahhhhh, I think I might just hangummup." His face shows no expression whatsoever.

When you hear it just before the season starts, it's the same guy, on the phone. His back is better but he hasn't decided, and he says exactly the same thing. And you know that next week you'll see him lacing on his skates along with everyone else, and though he'll still be wearing no expression, you'll see that certain excitement in the way he moves. He's almost childlike, almost a little nervous.

Some guys are lucky enough to hangummup and not feel too bad about it. A guy on my team, Bernie, quit at the beginning of last year and, according to his wife, is quite happy about it. Bernie has been playing hockey since he could walk, she explained, and played all through childhood, and junior, and university (he and his twin brother played for Boston College), and then in various beer leagues, and, finally, oldtimers. Somewhere along the way he developed a bad back. According to his wife, Bernie doesn't miss it at all. In fact, "He's relieved to be out of it. He's playing a bit of golf now."

Maybe having that "bit of golf" to fall back on is important. It seems to soften the blow for some. Kelly, the other guy to quit our team last year—and I swear this is true—left to teach ballroom dancing on a cruise ship. He had to sign some sort of agreement not to bed any of the clientele, which for Kelly might be a problem, but otherwise I've heard he's having a painless retirement from hockey. Sometimes I think guys start sniffing around for a new hobby without even knowing why. Me, I've started to get a little bit too interested in Tai Chi lately, which feels suspicious. Am I searching for a valuable Eastern discipline that will nourish both my body and my soul, or am I scouting out a landing pad for when I hangummup?

We all know lots of guys who simply will not hangummup. They just won't. Lots of guys joke, only half-joking, about dying on their skates. And I predict that, seeing how many over-sixties teams there are now, this will become more and more common. It will be a new Canadian phenomenon. I predict that we will soon be seeing a stat in a *Maclean's* magazine that has oldtimers hockey sandwiched between prostate cancer and obesity as a leading cause of death in males.

The stat will be misleading, of course, because the simpler fact of the matter is that oldtimers isn't dangerous—it's just that some guys don't know when to hangummup. We all know guys who keep on going, long past their due date. One older guy on my team—our coach, Rich—also organizes an over-65 team, and each September he demands of each player a signed note from a doctor certifying that they've been okayed to play. Previously, too many guys lied to Rich about their health, and one guy falling dead at Rich's feet after a game was one guy too many.

What's weird is the *eagerness* to get back to playing after an injury. In Fredericton, after I herniated a disk, and went through months of agony and healing and ibuprofen and dragging a foot as I limped to work, I was told by my health professional that, "once the pain climbs out of your calf, and then hamstring, then buttock, and climbs *above the belt*, you can start skating again." Well, I started skating once the pain climbed out of the calf, and I was gritting my teeth and racing into corners with my buttock in full pain. This was a few years back. I think the pain is sort of over my belt now. Most of the time. And I'm not bragging here. I'd say that my story, and my stupidity, is fairly typical in this sport of ours. A good friend of mine on my brother's team, Mike, is so stupid that he's still playing after two back surgeries. To get the team bottle of sambuca down, he has to tilt his head sideways rather than throw it straight back, and he falls over now if you yell at him too loudly for a pass.

One guy on my team, Duane, an admirable scorer and drinker, has innumerable knee-operation scars, some old, some new. One of his knee braces was made by Bobby Orr's first knee surgeon, and it's the original medieval model, all pig iron and leather straps and buckles. Over the past summer, Duane snapped an Achilles tendon rounding second base during a coed beer-ball game, and he's back playing, noticeable limp and all. No way he thinks it's time to hangummup.

Another guy on my team—one of the four guys named Dave—is always injured. He's in his late fifties, skates as fast and as aggressively as a fast thirty-year-old, and gets approximately one goal a year. He *loves* hockey. Much of his body is bandaged or purple, and the placement of the bandages, and the purple, shifts around throughout the year. He's married to a somewhat younger woman who's into some alternative stuff. She's been spotted in the arena concourse dangling a crystal over Dave's naked, purple shoulder. Dave himself has told me about the relief he gets from what's called her "healing touch," which turns out to mean that her hands hover a few inches over his injury, not actually touching it. Clearly, as long as she doesn't hang up her crystal, Dave won't hangummup either. He simply doesn't know how. And why should he, when he's in love?

Though Dave's maybe a bit more colourful than most, I think I can say that my whole team is like that. Two guys have heart stents. (One guy—one of the four guys on my team named Bill—broke a wrist and had a heart stent put in two weeks later. He's back playing. At work his colleagues have a pool going, the main bet involving what will go next, and when.) One guy's had cancer. Another had a full-blown heart attack, and his brother and father both died of heart attacks at a younger age. We get dressed, and the row of naked white knees is marred by scars. Duane's scars have scars—his legs sport red crescent moons, pink hammers, and purple sickles. More generally, many of us have the profiles of pregnant women. Fifty-three-year-old pregnant women. Most of us are so physically ugly we should have our careers terminated on aesthetic grounds alone.

We won't hangummup. I know guys who would rather play hockey than have sex, and they haven't scored in a year. I know guys who have jeopardized more than one marriage because of oldtimers hockey, and they won't hangummup. We won't hangummup. We might end up a number in a column in *Maclean's* magazine, but we won't hangummup. Bernie's happy playing his bit of golf and Kelly's teaching the foxtrot somewhere off Belize, but *we* won't hangummup.

We're Not Getting Older, We're Getting Smaller

I SAW SOME *really* old people playing hockey the other day, and I can't decide whether it thrilled or scared me. Read this, then you tell me.

There's a tournament here in Victoria, the Playmakers', that draws teams from all over. It's popular for a few reasons—one, it's in April, so while the rest of Canada is buried under miles of ice, here in Victoria it's prime golf. Teams from Saskatoon and Calgary come with their wives, and while the guys golf the gals shop, and in the evenings they reunite for cocktails, the wives comparing their new Cowichan sweaters and the guys lying about their drives. Hockey games are scattered throughout the week. Another reason the tournament is popular is that the age divisions favour the older players—I mean the really older players, the true oldtimers. There's maybe only a couple of over-35 divisions, and a couple of over-45 divisions, but then they really start to calibrate things, with over-50, over-60, etc. There is even an over-70 division. Since there aren't many over-70 teams out there, and even fewer that travel as a unit to tournaments, this division takes in random players, from anywhere, and they are then divided up into teams. It's all fun, you get to meet new people, and there's no real team rivalry—though you wouldn't know it from the feistiness on the ice.

Well, I happened to stop and watch part of one of those over-70 games and, as I said, I was thrilled and scared. Because, well, these men were smaller than most men. They were, most of them, the size of boys. What I was seeing was a group of old men who had in common that basic reverse growth that occurs when the cartilage between vertebrae dries up and shrinks. I saw up close what happened to my father. At twenty he was six foot five. When I was growing up, I remember him giving me the once over every so often and saying through the side of his face, "Hey, you're getting taller than me." Well, he kept this up through his fifties and my twenties. I never got taller than six feet even, but there came a time in his later years when he said it and it was actually true.

It will happen to all of us, as it already had to these two teams of short men. But what I also noticed was that their strides were a little jerky, as were their arm movements. As well, if a puck slid up and went through their legs and beyond, quite some time (*one thousand one, one thousand two*) would pass before they understood what had happened and jerked their body around to begin the chase in a different direction. (Well, maybe they understood right away what had happened, but for that understanding to travel down their aged neural pathways all the way to the ankles took some time.)

What I'm getting at, and what thrilled and scared me, is that for a fleeting second these old men looked and played exactly like young children. The size, the uncertain skating style, the reaction time, the ability. Good God, I thought. Elton John immediately came to mind—not the pudgy tiara-wearing singer himself, but a song of his, the *Lion King* song "The Circle of Life." That notion of what goes around comes around. The phrase "second childhood." The adult diapers aisle in the pharmacy. I saw something huge out there on the ice during that over-70s game. If it had been you standing there watching these old men getting smaller, playing their way back into infancy, how would you have felt?

Well, Death

AS THE SAYING GOES, death is nature's way of telling you to slow down.

It's maybe a little funny that oldtimers can be abbreviated to OT. Which also stands for "overtime." Which sort of means "borrowed time." Which could also mean, in the context of this chapter, "You've been playing this game way too long, fool. When will you read the writing on the wall?"

When I first started playing oldtimers, or OT, my new Fredericton team was without a name. It had begun as an alumni team for the University of New Brunswick, whose teams were called the Red Devils, and so the oldtimers called themselves, appropriately, the Red Faces. Not a bad name (see "Team Names, Good"). But over the years the team had lost any players with any connection to UNB at all. Plus, UNB teams had just changed their name to the somewhat lame Varsity Red. (Fredericton is in the Bible Belt and, incredibly, the word "Devils" had been offensive to generations of some locals, so much so that sufficient pressure was brought to bear and someone who makes those sorts of decisions turtled under some big churchy fists.)

Anyway, we had a brief team meeting before our first game. "Do we need to change our name?" was the question, followed by, "If yes, to what?" These guys looked like non-serious guys suddenly looking serious. Good thing we were mostly naked and the door was closed, or Robert's Rules of Order might have walked in.

Being a rookie, and knowing nobody, I didn't want to say anything. Also, I favoured "colourful" names, something like the Island Hairies, or the Staggering Cyclopses, or something stranger still. I like the other team to think a little about what they might be getting into when they go into a corner with you. I would love to play for a team called the Feces, for example, or, for that matter, The Devil's Giant Human Dildos, but that just might be me. In any case, some of the guys knew I was a writer and, after a few grunts and shrugs and lame ideas offered up— the Reds, the Fredericton Reds, the Old Reds—a few turned to me and asked if I had any great ideas.

I thought I did. If the new UNB team name was the Varsity Red, and we wanted a nice pun on that, like Red Faces, proudly proclaimed our age and infirmity, well, I thought I was on to something when I smiled and said, "The Varsity Dead!"

No one said anything. A few heads went down. Most of all, no one laughed.

The guy next to me explained politely that, after their final game just last spring, in this very room, one of their teammates had come out of the shower, towelling off, and stopped right there—my new teammate pointed to a spot on the floor about five feet away—and dropped dead of a heart attack. (Actually I think the term used was "took a heart attack." I was freshly from T.O. and this was suddenly all very weird.)

We remained the Red Faces. Until we became the Stinkhorns, one of my all-time favourite names, and the team's resident wordsmith had nothing at all to do with that team name either—but that's another story.

ANYWAY, of all the injuries possible in oldtimers, death is probably the biggest.

Death does happen, and oldtimers do talk about it. We try not to bring it up when wives are present, though they don't seem to tire of bringing it up themselves, sometimes hopefully.

But the Big Injury does happen. During my nine years playing in Fredericton, I heard of perhaps seven or eight deaths in and around the region. New Brunswick's is a fairly small and tight hockey community, and when someone dies, lots of people in the dressing room know, or know of, the player. About once a year I'd arrive at a game and walk into the middle of a dressing-room conversation that went something like:

"Hear about Archie MacKenzie's brother?"

"No."

"He dropped dead in Moncton."

"No way."

"Which brother?"

"Kenny, Archie MacKenzie's brother. Dropped dead in Moncton. Last week. The Monctonian. The Sunday game."

"Jesus *shit*."

"Who's Archie MacKenzie?"

"You know, yellow helmet? On the Aces? That fast guy. Lane's brother, too. Kenny's the young one. Only forty or forty-fuckin-two."

"Lane's brother died?"

"Dropped dead in Moncton. Sitting there with a beer and *boom*. Tony Manno was telling a joke or something, and Kenny falls off the fuckin bench and plants his face. Dead before he hit the floor."

"Must have been quite the joke."

"Fuck off. We're talking about Lane's brother."

"And Archie's."

"Was he in shape?"

"Better shape than *you*."

"Who's Kenny MacKenzie?"

ODD HOW IT OFTEN happens like that—a heart attack, not during the fierce-breathing grit of the game, but after. Towelling off, or sitting there, having a beer. Apparently the phenomenon is just like that of the Type A executive who works like mad for years, flies to a beach someplace hot, gets the lotion on, flops down on his towel, opens his magazine, sighs a couple of times, then has his heart attack. It's the sudden relaxation that kills you, because the heart decides to join in and just sort of *really* kick back and take a break too. Seriously, though, they also say that, because of this phenomenon, it's important to "warm down" after a hard game by taking a few medium-brisk laps around the ice. Lately I've actually seen a few guys do this. I must say they look a trifle serious doing it. There's this special look on the face, a kind of inward gaze . . .

A CERTAIN DEGREE of gallows humour can be a good thing at this point. (A favourite writer of mine once wrote that, since we're all going to die, all humour is gallows humour.) On more than one team, after more than one game, more than one player has hustled off the ice after a game, in a hurry to get a beer in him "to thin the blood real quick."

There are other reasons it happens, of course. Being grossly out of shape can be the killer, but surprisingly not that often. For every heart attack that's the result of some lardy chain-smoker finding himself on a breakaway for the first time in two years, there's a story of a non-drinking fitness fanatic dropping dead after a normal skate.

One New Brunswick village, Nackawick, had two deaths one year. The Nackawick rink used a diesel tractor to scrape and flood the ice, and you could really smell it, especially if you were standing outside the dressing room between periods having a smoke, and there was speculation as to whether diesel fumes might have been a cause.

In any case, after a game, in a bar, talking to one player from a team which had had a player die on them a month earlier, the guy explained to me his new philosophy of sport. His new, slower approach to the game of hockey: "There are no loose pucks."

Dying with Your Boots On

I'M NOT SURE WHERE that expression came from, but I think it's cowboy vintage, and has to do with dying on the range (though that would be "Dying in the Saddle," wouldn't it? But doesn't that have something to do with dying while screwing?). Anyway, the phrase we want here is "Dying with Your Skates On." I have talked to more than one person who has expressed this desire. They didn't want it to happen any time soon, but that was how they wanted to go.

I had the privilege of playing with a wonderful older fellow, once upon a time. I won't mention his name on the off chance that he wouldn't want it mentioned. But he knows who he is, and so does everyone who's been lucky enough to know him. Eight years ago he was still taking his shift on left wing, going up and down the ice in workmanlike, Ron Ellis style, at age seventy-one. Now, I didn't hear his words personally, but some teammates had, and the idea expressed was that, when his time came, he wanted to be on the ice, playing a game. Surrounded by friends, no other worry in the world except trying to score a goal. It's one of the more reasonable deaths I can imagine, when I consider some of the deaths I've seen, or heard about. It's a death I'd be proud to witness. And it's one I might even consider for myself, if I have the courage, and if my back holds out, and if a team of younger men will continue to have me.

As for this player—let's call him Norm—at the end of every year he would formally thank us younger, slightly faster men for letting him play a regular shift. And when we thanked him back, for doing us the honour of playing with younger men and showing us how to get old properly, I believe we thanked him sincerely. It was maybe the only time of the year when anything serious got said in the room, and it always felt fine.

I last saw Norm some years ago now, at the other end of the country. I hope he's still alive, and playing. If he's not, I hope he scored a goal that night or, even better, set one up.

WHAT THE HELL ARE WE THINKING ABOUT?

We're Thinking about Ourselves

LIKE ALL OLD PEOPLE, oldtimers spend most of their time dwelling on highlights from the past. In an oldtimer's case, this has largely to do with hockey—that is, pre-oldtimers hockey. Often when an oldtimer pops his second beer, his skates freshly off and steaming before him, he leans back against the dressing room's cinder-block wall and a wistful look comes over his tired, old eyes. What he's doing now is thinking back on the days when he was young, and fast, and tough, back when he could pick up the puck behind his own net and skate through the other team and stick it top shelf on the dazzled goalie. In other words, he's lost in a world of egomaniacal delusion, but he's having a good time, so let's not disturb him.

I am going to indulge similar memories here. No book about oldtimers would be complete without memories, because, well, they're what we're made of. In fact, by the time you're an old-timer, memories make up 93 percent of whatever brain tissue you have left up there. In any event, when things start to drag a little for me in the writing of this book, just as it happens in real life, I'm going to let myself drift off into a memory. These memories will be scattered throughout, like nuggets of rebellious youth, like wild oats. I declare here and now that all of them are true. I will label them "Memory #1," "Memory #2," and so on so that you'll know one when you see it. Then you can either skip it, or run and put on some oldies background music to add to your nostalgic pleasure. Maybe The Carpenters or Roy Orbison if you're really old, but it should be something sentimental. I suggest the Beatles' White Album.

I'll stick a few memories right here.

Memory #1: Me 'n' Number 4, Bobby Orr

GROWING UP IN WINNIPEG, I played hockey most every winter night on neighbourhood outdoor rinks, and pretty much lived for the game. Occasionally I read a comic book, and I probably attended school, but otherwise it was pretty much all hockey. Each year an all-star team of ten-year-olds called the Winnipeg Colts was gathered to travel to a tournament in Brampton, Ontario. To be picked was every kid's dream, and I was lucky enough to get picked. It was a long and expensive train trip, and I remember selling candy orders door-to-door to raise money. I don't know why I remember this so clearly, but I do. I think it was my favourite part of the tournament—because it was driven by anticipation of what I was sure would be the best time of my life. I hauled around this big box of samples and people could order Licorice Allsorts, or gumdrops, or mints, and I'd take their money and write down their name and address, feeling important. I also remember the northern lights hanging in the big prairie sky, a green and pink blaze, and I will swear that they crackled and hissed above me. I don't know why, but they were not at all scary. Quite the opposite.

It was a great dream. We were picked from *all of Winnipeg*, and I hadn't even *been* to all of Winnipeg, and now we were on a train to Ontario—crammed two to a sleeping berth, but so what? (I was crammed in with my defence partner, and we were the two biggest guys on the team, and though that first night he pointed out these illogical logistics to me, giving me a tired shove in the process, I still didn't care.) On the way down to Lake Ontario, maybe on the second day, we stopped in Parry Sound. We got out of the train and took a bus into town for the sole purpose of going to Bobby Orr's house, to meet him. (I have no idea who arranged this, and had no idea then how impossible these arrangements probably were. I have some dim recollection now that somebody was somebody's cousin's friend.) I remember pulling up to Bobby Orr's house, a two-storey wooden one like all the rest of them on an ordinary street. There was deep, deep snow, but it was melting—it was far more tropical here in Ontario than it was back in Winnipeg. We had already sort of heard of Bobby Orr, though he was still in junior, but junior was the NHL to us ten-year-olds. In any case, that's how famous he was.

We were taken upstairs to the "trophy room," which was a room brimming with trophies on painted shelves built for that purpose. Bobby Orr was waiting for us in that room, shy as can be. I remember his voice. I was really nervous, too, since I was also a defenceman. I don't have much memory of his face, likely because I was last up the stairs and, along with a few others, didn't fit into the kid-crammed room. So I was sort of outside the door, listening. Bobby Orr explained what a few of the trophies meant, and he hoped we had good luck in the tournament. We went back down the stairs.

For years, I considered Bobby Orr my close personal friend. He was always my favourite hockey player, but he would have been anyway, since he revolutionized the game for us defence-men, and he was so beautiful to watch, skating that fast with no apparent effort, doing the Savardian spinarama so quickly and purely that nobody bothered to name it after him first.

And we had a magical connection, right from start. My sweater number on the Winnipeg Colts? Number 4.

Memory #2: Famous Close Personal NHL Friends of Mine

I'VE MET BOBBY HULL. I accomplished this by standing in line to buy his book and get it signed in a store in the Polo Park Mall, in Winnipeg. I was eleven or twelve. I think I took the bus there by myself. When I finally got to him, I couldn't speak. Here was the big, round, tanned smiling face that I'd seen on TV, and that graced more than a few hockey cards in the shoe box under my bed. In a surprisingly reedy voice he asked me my name. His smile looked genuine, though his smiling muscles, cut with two-inch dimples—like abs—had to have been pretty tired by then. He wrote "To Billy" in the book, along with "Best of luck," and it seemed utterly probable to me that this mountain of glory left-winger from Chicago would indeed be able to bestow luck on someone like me. Then he signed "Bobby Hull" in a sudden flourish, his elbow firing out, his famous wrist-shot muscles getting into the act a little bit. I wanted to stick out my hand and get him to shake it, like I'd seen a few other kids do, but for some reason I didn't. I think it scared me, because he was wearing a tight T-shirt, and those arms were easily the size of young pigs and seemed to have lives of their own.

I met one of Bobby's teammates a few years later. I didn't really "meet" him, but I spoke with him on my Christmas walkie-talkie while standing outside on our back deck in North Vancouver. My dad worked for Sears, and they had a new line of hockey gear, and defenceman Pierre Pilote was the NHL star who had his signature scrawled in gold over all of it. (I wore Pierre Pilote gloves, shin pads, and pants for a few years.) My dad had told me to go out on the deck and turn on the walkie-talkie at exactly twelve noon. He was up Indian Arm on a boat with other businessmen—and Pierre Pilote.

At noon I went out on the deck and turned on my walkie-talkie. Nothing happened except a lot of hiss. I pushed the button and said hello a few times. I waited five minutes or so and tried again. And so on. I think at about twelve-thirty I turned it on again, and out of the walkie-talkie came the instant roar of about ten men talking and yelling at once. They sounded excited and maybe a little drunk, but since they were responsible businessmen and it was only twelve-thirty, that certainly couldn't have been the case. Anyway, after I said hello the voices settled down, and Pierre Pilote's lone voice said, "So, Billy, you're a defenceman, eh?" His accent startled me, but he sounded genuinely interested, being a defenceman himself. (Actually, a smart, sensible, stay-at-home defenceman. An odd sponsor for a line of sporting goods, come to think of it. I recall that his name was scrawled over Sears golf bags as well. I wonder how that line did.) I said, I think, "Yes." Maybe I added "I am" to the end of that. Then there was silence, more hiss, a bit more shouting and laughing in the background, and someone not Pierre Pilote said "Okay!" and that was that. I said "Over and out," and turned off my walkie-talkie.

Memory #3: True On-Ice Encounters with NHL Stars

WELL, NONE OF THESE true on-ice encounters happened when they *were* NHL stars, because I never played in the NHL. Not that anyone who's ever seen me play needs to be told that. These on-ice encounters, two of which ended in injury, were with NHL stars-to-be.

First, I played against Mark and Marty Howe in a peewee tournament. Or even before peewee — atom, maybe? Tyke? Embryo? Anyway, Mark and Marty played for a team from Detroit. Marty had to be two or three years younger than his brother, so I think he might have *been* an embryo. I have virtually no memory of the game, or the two brothers, or how good they were, and I know they have even less memory of me. But I remember it was all we Winnipeg kids could talk about in the dressing room before the game. That, and whether or not their father would show up. He didn't.

In midget—I was living in Toronto then—at a tournament in Ottawa, I went into a corner with Denis Potvin, who was a little famous already, and he sort of knocked me out with a nearly invisible elbow. He turned out to be one of those players who, like Gordie Howe, are both great and dirty. Anyway, in the corner he tagged me with that elbow and I went down—more of a swoon than anything. I like to say he knocked me out. Saying "Denis Potvin knocked me out," I feel as famous as I'm ever going to feel. He did get two minutes.

Maybe a year later, in a regular league game, still midget, Steve Shutt broke my nose. He was still bantam, and we'd just heard about him in the dressing room, this young kid who scored goals like nobody else. He'd been called up from the Marlies bantams to the Marlies midgets. I was on the Toronto Wings that year. On my first shift, I grabbed the puck and started to lug it. I wasn't tough, and I had a defenceman's scoring touch around the opponents' net (your basic grunt-and-flail), but I was pretty good at lugging it. In the neutral zone, around a player I go and, *wham*, I'm on my knees bleeding, my nose cartilage separated from my nose bone. The whistle got blown only after I stayed there awhile and the blood-pool grew wider than a puck. The ref hadn't seen the stick come up. Of course not, it was Steve Shutt's stick, a future Hall-of-Fame stick, a stick so fast that no one has ever actually seen it in mid-flick. I think Shutt lasted a week or two in midget, then went up to Junior B that same year. He won the goal-scoring title for them and they bought him a beat-up old car, the joke being that he was too young to drive. Something like that, I never did get it straight. My nose sort of did get straight, though when I start to remember stuff like this it tends to start drifting towards one or other of my shoulders.

By the way, Steve, I got your number. I'm still looking for you. You still playing oldtimers? I hope you're extremely fat and I can catch you. When I do I'm going to rub my ugly, sweating nose on the back of your neck.

In B.C. in junior I played against Bob Nystrom, Gary Howatt, Eddie Johnstone, and a few other guys who went on to the bigs. At the time, these guys seemed pretty much like the rest of us and didn't really stand out. But I recall bouncing off Nystrom once. Picture a stern man in a hurry, running into a little girl he didn't see, and the little girl landing on her little bum. That's what it probably looked like.

Another real-life run-in? Once, as a paying customer, I was with a friend at a Canucks game, right near ice level, and he yelled at Tiger Williams—"Hey, Williams! You're ugly as a bag a hammers"—getting Tiger to turn our way and glare at *me*. Maybe I look like a heckler. I've since played against Tiger in oldtimers out here on the left coast, and he has behaved like a perfect gentleman. He probably thinks I'm really shy, the way I always avert my gaze—in fact, my entire face—whenever he comes near. (I hear bags of hammers have excellent memories.)

And I played with a few guys who went on to play a few games in the NHL as goons. I don't know why B.C. is so good at growing goons. It might be all this wood to hew and water to haul. Or the lack of schools. Once the railway comes through, maybe things'll change.

Anyway, I'm done name-dropping, and my modest proximity to these dropped names is as famous as I ever got. But it made me feel famous in some of the oldtimer dressing rooms that lacked anybody who had ever played much organized hockey, let alone been knocked out by Denis Potvin. But then from time to time a guy comes along who's played some real hockey, way more real than the hockey I played, and my fame shrivels just like—well, you picture for yourself how my fame shrivels up. But for a few years here on my Victoria team, I was at the top rung or two of fame, based on who I've played with, or been knocked out by—then, last year, a guy, Duane, showed up. Duane's not only been knocked out by more famous people than me, but he did some knocking out of his own. He knows everybody. When Pat Quinn comes to Vancouver to play the Canucks, this new teammate of mine gets a call to see if he wants tickets. He knows Bobby Orr. He knows which NHL star snorted coke at a certain famous three-day party and who didn't, because he was there. He's probably shaken Bobby Hull's giant hand. I bet Duane's tossed a beer to Wayne Gretzky. It's awful now, it really is. In the room, I'm permanently shrivelled.

Memory #4: One More Close Personal Encounter with an NHL Star

ONE SUMMER IN MY EARLY TWENTIES I was, let's say, "between everything"—jobs, girlfriends, cars, even places to live. I was house-sitting the grubby basement suite of a travelling friend, and for food and beer money I had a "job" where, from 1 a.m. till 4 a.m., I delivered the *Globe & Mail* to the coin-operated boxes throughout North Vancouver. Each night my brother Bub, who had a civilized day job, lent me his ancient, faded, rusted-out Rambler, unaffectionately nicknamed Piece-a-shit. I was always exhausted and especially ugly during this job, since I'd either just ripped myself up from a nap or desperately needed one, and my long hair always shot out sideways. And after expertly dealing with the first few boxes, I always had printer's ink on my hands and cheeks and forehead. Sometimes a finger or two would be bleeding from a wrestling match with a stubborn box that refused to open, key or no key.

One particular night I was loading a box outside a hotel nightclub near the Lions Gate Bridge. Parked under the covered entranceway was a white stretch limo, which seemed to cringe and inch sideways when Piece-a-shit pulled too near. I got out and keyed open the box, emptied the unbought papers, loaded in that day's edition, and cleaned out the quarters and slugs, dumping them into my filthy canvas bag. Finished, hearing the titter of approaching females, I stood up, and there was Harold Snepsts in a white suit and white silk tie, arm-in-arm with two of the most gorgeous women anybody has ever seen. I stood staring at the women, and at him. My jeans were ripped, my shirt napped in, my hair shot a foot sideways, my face was well inked, and I believe my mouth was hanging open.

Now, before I describe our transaction, first a little something about me and Harold Snepsts. The thing is, Harold and I had a history. Harold wasn't aware of it, but we did. I'd been out of serious hockey for a few years at this point, and for those few years Harold had become a kind of symbol for me. He symbolized this: about the same age, a fellow defenceman, he was in the NHL and I wasn't. He'd made it, and I hadn't. The thing is, I knew I was a better skater, passer, and stickhandler than Harold Snepsts was. I was. That a thousand other guys my age would say the same thing, and, not only that, could skate rings around me, and still hadn't made it, didn't matter. Deep down, of course, I knew I didn't deserve to be within miles of the NHL, but that didn't matter. What mattered was that Harold was in the NHL and I wasn't.

What did he have that I didn't? Well, he was bigger, could hit harder, and he could fight. (Now, I shouldn't shortchange Harold here just to make my point. I'll add that Harold—Harry the Hammer—could *fight like no other*, could make opponents religious, and could win games on his spirit alone. There were good reasons he was not only in the NHL but also a fan favourite. He was also by all reports a wonderful all-round guy. But I still have a point to make.)

It was monumental, meeting Harold Snepts in the parking lot. For some years, while I watched the Canucks on TV, it was this very man who had become my symbol of how life was unfair. I'd see him flail away in the corner, in my opinion rather clumsily clearing the puck, and I'd *tsk* and shake my head. I'd wonder again at my luck of being a nifty and smooth but, well, maybe a bit wimpy defenceman who happened to come of age during the Philadelphia era, when bullies won Cups.

So, anyway, it felt cruelly fateful, to be standing there in the middle of the night face-to-face with Harold Snepts, him all rich and shiny, me all poor and dirty, him with two babes and me with none, and no one looking like they were about to share. I guess I was staring a long time at the girls and mostly at Harold, my mouth still open. Harold looked like he was waiting for me to say something. One girl tugged on his arm now, the other checking me out sideways, the look on her face suggesting she thought I might be Charlie Manson's stupider younger brother. Harold was simply smiling at me, somewhat profession-ally, used to fans staring at him. But he looked like a genuinely nice guy, and I have no doubt he would've been kind enough to sign an autograph for me, or even suffer my opinion about the latest Canucks game.

He made the first move. Lifting his Freddy Mercury mous-tache a good inch or so, he grinned, and shrugged, meeting my eyes. It wasn't a scorning look, not at all, but neither was it sim-ply a friendly smile for the poor bastard doing his crummy job. It was an honest look, even a humble look. It said, "I'm lucky and you aren't." At this, Harold added a wave, and slid in beside his two friends, who had already found sanctuary in their car.

Me? I was too stunned, or something, to be friendly to Harold in return. I didn't wave back. I watched his white limousine as it drove away. Piece-a-shit didn't wave either.

THIS SEASON SO FAR

November

IT SEEMS THERE WILL BE a last season for me after all. It's late November, and I just played my first game.

I'm not sure why I played, but I did. I think my decision to play was based on my brain scan results. I'll keep things suspenseful for a moment and first describe the procedure. I'm not making any of this up.

First, understand that about six months have passed since I passed out over my desk, and I'm only now getting scanned. (And every time I watch *Sports Page* and hear another coach say about his injured player that "he'll go in for an MRI tomorrow," I start hissing through my teeth about our medical system.) I've enjoyed six months of visualizing tumours up here in my head—how big, what colour, it must be what's causing that bit of pressure behind my right eye, etc. I've been trying to shrink it, wherever it is, with beams of willpower. I've been thinking of my death, and my family, with deep wafts of sincerity and heart. The logical voice, suggesting that zero symptoms for six months likely indicates there's no tumour up there, largely went unheeded. No, I had a nasty little walnut growing, and tonight I was going to go get its picture taken.

I guess because I was nervous I drove to the wrong hospital— which nearly lost me my place in the tumour-machine line. I arrived just in time and was helped by a young, very attractive woman. She had a professionally kind, maternal, "You're a sweet sweet man and it's sad you're going to die this young" air about her. She kept lightly touching my elbow, or my shoulder, and her fingers lingered deliciously. Had I not been seconds away from the humming tumour-tube, I might have sprouted some wood and embarrassed myself through the flimsy green gown. Before I was strapped onto the bed-on-rails I was given a set of headphones and invited, for my listening pleasure, to choose from a surprisingly long list of albums. I chose *Dark Side of the Moon*, which, after looking at that contraption I was about to enter, I thought appropriate. I got strapped in, the phones snugged on, and Pink Floyd started their ominous bass riff and piano. The nice Lady of Sex and Death had a light hand on my bare leg as I disappeared up the tube. Anyone who's had a head MRI knows how deafeningly loud it is in there once the scanning starts. I didn't, and was pleasantly listening to music when, at the exact moment of the first song's spine-scraping scream, the machine's grinding roar started as well, and together it was the sound of a thousand human souls in a surprise freefall to hell. It was all too perfect. The effect on me was: this timing proves that there is a God, and God's saying, with a wink, "You're dead!" I would have shit my hospital gown, but, seeing as the gown had no back, I would've missed.

In a few days I got my results, or rather the persistent FeeFee did, by harping on the phone all day to some poor lab guy until he gave her a number to call, and then she badgered that next guy into saying something. And she was given the classic vaudevillean answer: "Your husband's brain scan showed nothing." Ta-*boom*.

As is typical in these life-and-death moments, my joy and relief were intense. But, also typically, brief. It was about a minute later that I stubbed my toe taking out the garbage, while the kids were fighting over the TV, and normal life had begun again.

And so had hockey. I no longer had any *serious* medical reason not to play. Only my bad back. And as for that, well, it wasn't in spasm, it hadn't just "gone out." No, it was a duller pain, residue from a herniated disc that flares up, and that had flared over the summer, outraged that I had dragged a two-man kayak. And now it was only brooding. But it wasn't getting worse, and I know enough about medicine to know that, if I had back cancer, it would definitely be getting worse. So my bright idea was to "try it out." Which means, in oldtimer-speak, take lots of ibuprofen and see if you can skate.

And that's what I did, last night. It felt as ridiculous as could be expected. We talk about "getting the rust out"? "Rust" is too mild a term to describe what I found in my body last night. Rust is a reddish, semi-hard coating attached to some otherwise sound iron. I hadn't skated since last March, hadn't run once, hadn't ridden a bike. Rust? What we were dealing with last night resembled something more like—well, picture a deep, dark cave, never explored by humans, with all these beige stalag-things hanging down and pointing up, and they're shaped like cones of dribbled fat but are hard as rock, and wet, and stained. And all around them are mounds and mounds—centuries worth—of guano, of bat shit. Yes, *bat* shit, and the black cave you're in is misty with falling urine, and you can't see, can't breathe and . . . Anyway, the point is, how do you hit a streaking winger with a decent pass when your body's in that sort of condition? Can't be done. After the game, during the first of many delicious beers, I was asked in all seriousness, more than once, if I was "a little rusty." They had no idea. Well, unfortunately, maybe they did.

But there is a season! Even if it's only last night. As a few sober friends of mine are wont to exclaim, I'm taking this puppy day by day.

And there was even a little bit of shine to the game. At first I was dismayed to learn that we were playing this great team, the Old Chiefs—a double oxymoron because they're all young and there isn't a Native among them. And, sure, all night they were blowing by me, and we did lose 10–2, but our team's general horribleness kind of swallowed up my more specific horribleness. And . . . I scored. I don't quite know how. I remember intercepting a pass, and then my hands did all this fast, clumsy, hard-to-see stuff, and somewhere in that blurred mess they shot the puck, and so clumsy was this motion that the goalie was completely fooled. (I'll likely use this strategy more and more as my career progresses.)

And I had a companion in rust. Duane, whose virtues I speak about in other places, also used last night's game to venture back out onto the pond for the first time since March. He had even more excuses for being shitty, the main one being his barely healed Achilles tendon scar. After last night's game, Duane took off his skate and sat there staring at his limb for a while, sipping a beer with contemplative patience. The scar was crude and huge. The flesh above it, up his calf, was white; the flesh below it was swollen and purple. Now, Duane and scars have a long history. He's had somewhere around a dozen knee operations. His upper body looks pretty decent and undamaged for an old-timer, but below the waist it looks like he's tried to run through some crowded wolverine cages.

Last night, Duane was even slower than me. The thing is, he scored our only other goal. Which proves one of two things: either we have a really bad team, or oldtimers is a really weird game.

BUT IT WAS DECENT being there in the room again. Big Mike, one of our noble veterans and generally the most pregnant guy on our team, had a classic little tale for us. (I should add that, if only half of Mike's tales are true, he's led what you might call an eventful life. He was in the navy, with the tattoos to prove it, and you don't even want to hear about some of the shit that happened to him in the Philippines.)

Mike had missed the last couple games while moose hunting in Alberta, an annual trek for him. Tonight's story got going when one of the team's four Daves thought to ask him if he'd gotten his moose this year.

"Nope," said Mike. He paused, appeared to lose interest, then added softly, "Got some dog, though." Mike kept undoing his laces, looking down. It soon became clear that he wasn't going to say anything more, which is exactly Mike's style, so eventually Dave asked him what he meant by that.

Mike finished one skate, then started in on the other. He didn't look up when he spoke. "Me 'n' my buddy, we came on three dogs running down some elk. *Trained* dogs." He kept at his skate, his face all red. It's hard leaning over when you're pregnant.

"You shot some . . . dogs?" Dave asked.

"Had to. The fucker. Wasn't even elk season."

"How'd you . . . you know . . . how'd you know they weren't just, you know, *dogs?*"

"They were trained. You could tell. And we found the fucker's pick-up. Gave him his dead dogs back."

"Jesus. You're kidding."

"Not kidding." Mike peeled off one long, wet sock, then the other. "Took the guy's plate number down, phoned it in, slashed his tires. Fucker's either in jail *right now*—or he's paid a fifty-thousand-dollar fine."

"Jesus. Fifty thousand?"

"They don't like poachers in Alberta no more." Shampoo and towel in hand, still a little feisty, Big Mike banged through into the shower room.

You gotta love stuff like that.

Getting dressed myself, I happened to notice that one of last year's regulars wasn't here. I asked the guy beside me, Vic, where Gene was.

"Cancer."

"What?"

"Gene's got cancer. Throat."

"What? Really?"

"He popped by in September, to say hi. He was fucking thin." Vic sat hunched over, tying his shoes.

"Oh. Well—but, I mean, how is he? Is he, you know—"

"Well, he was fucking thin."

"Is he, you know . . . Well what's the prognosis?"

"Dunno." Vic turned to me and raised his eyebrows, shrugging. He had finished with his shoes and was patting his wet hair. Strangely, as he did so he peered into the distance as if in a mirror, even squinting a bit.

"Jeez. That's really the shits," I mumbled, and Vic agreed. But that was all the information I was going to get about Gene. And likely nobody in the room knew anything more about Gene than Vic did, because Gene, when he'd visited, likely didn't tell them anything. Knowing Gene, I can see him standing there, smiling, tapping his foot, thinner, saying he was doing great and that he expected to be back playing by October. I remember when he had a puck-sized spider bite on his leg and couldn't play and he showed up smiling and told us about it and showed us. Gene was an interesting character who'd played his hockey at the University of Colorado. By far the roughest guy on our team, he took guys down constantly, straddling that line of what is a body check and what isn't, magically keeping to only a couple of penalties a game. Yet he claimed never to have been in a hockey fight. Nor did he drink.

I waved and grunted at the guys, grabbed my sticks, and left the room. Gene had cancer. Jesus, life went on outside the room. All the guys have these huge, complicated lives, just like me, and none of it gets talked about. We laugh and yell about the economy, maybe swear at a politician. You might hear, in a one-on-one chat, of a possible marital split, but that topic doesn't go anywhere—it's already too much information. I remember last year, when Jimmy, normally a quiet guy, told me about his problems with his wife, but only because it was kind of outrageous and entertaining. Seems his wife had "suddenly become a 'born again,'" and Jimmy, not religious at all, was having real problems with her trying to convert their two kids, save them from Hell. Jimmy was there tonight, dressing quietly over in the corner. I wonder how that religious problem is going.

No, oldtimers just don't want to find themselves in a deep and sobering talk, there in that room. Walking through the parking lot after my last season's first game, I recalled what one of the Daves and I *had* talked passionately about: last week's beer fest downtown, where the six-beer sampler cost only eight bucks, and how the oatmeal stout almost made Dave come in his pants. Dave had laughed beautifully as he said this, his eyes bugging out a little, as if in a slightly desperate search for a good time.

Throwing my gear in the car, my body felt pleasantly hollow, and there was breeze on my wet hair—a nice, familiar feeling.

OLDTIMERS AND THE THEORY OF NEGATIVE CAPABILITY

THE ENGLISH POET John Keats probably missed out on hockey altogether, but despite this he came up with some fine poems—he was the "Beauty is truth, truth beauty" guy—and he also thought up a theory called "negative capability." What he meant by it is, basically, the talent for holding opposing or contradictory ideas in your head at the same time, and being comfortable with that. Politicians use it when they say, "Violence is terrible," and then invade a country. Philosophers use it, saying, "That there chair is solid, but it actually doesn't exist." In particular the Beat poets of the American '50s liked to use negative capability while smoking weed and drinking rotgut and having sex with minors, all the while believing themselves to be models of sainthood. (They also used it in their poetry, but I'll save that discussion for when I write my book about oldtimers soccer.)

We oldtimer hockey players are constantly using the tool of negative capability. Any "mature adult" who "plays a game" shows a natural talent for self-contradiction. A fifty-five-year-old with an iffy heart who, with gritted teeth, chases a puck into a corner displays fine talent in the negative-capability department. As does an even older guy spending half a thousand dollars on new skates. Any oldtimer with high-ish cholesterol and semi-elevated blood pressure, who sits in an office by day and brings home respectable money to support both his family and his summer toys, but who by evening will kill for the puck and who bleats like a goat involuntarily when he scores a goal, who loses the game yet sits grinning like a village idiot as he guzzles beer, which mixes with sweat to glisten on his cheeks—this man shows a world-class talent for negative capability.

Playing Oldtimers to Stay in Shape

THE VERY NOTION OF "playing oldtimers to stay in shape" is the epitome of negative capability. Because a typical oldtimer is worried about having a heart attack, he doesn't skate all that hard, so during a game he works up only a one-beer thirst. But then in the dressing room that same typical oldtimer will kill this thirst with more than one. So the burning of a couple hundred calories is followed by the taking in of several thousand. Oldtimers find this equation, and these days most arithmetic in general, really, really depressing. Sometimes we are forced to go for extra pints and wings just to forget that this equation exists. I keep reminding my wife, the stern FeeFee, that I am playing this sport for exercise, increased virility, and longevity, so sometimes it can be hard to explain myself when I waddle in, reeking of beer and chicken grease, visibly fatter than when I left a few hours before.

I remember, one spring, being glad the season was finally over because I was getting so out of shape.

Going Nuts to Stay Sane

IT'S WELL KNOWN that in recent decades our pace of life has been speeding up. We're in a constant hurry to makes ends meet. Somehow, despite all these time-saving devices surrounding us at all times, there seems to be less time. It's also true that we're less in control of our lives. We can't tune up our own car anymore because there's no carburetor. The lineups at the hospitals are so long that the lump has gone elsewhere by the time you get somebody to look at it. There's less job security, we grow impatient reading about yet another famine somewhere, and the polar ice caps are melting.

That's all true for everybody, but we oldtimers have it tougher than most. We are typically straight, white, middle-class males who are perhaps just an eensy bit past the prime of life, and because of this we have special problems. One is that, gradually, for over forty years now, we have had our pedestal chipped away, until we find ourselves less than masters of the world or kings of our castles. Face it, boys, patriarchy has taken some hits. Anybody seen a TV show lately where a dad is *remotely* like the ones on *Leave It to Beaver*, *My Three Sons*, or *Father Knows Best*? Nope, just take a gander at the dads in *Malcolm in the Middle*, *Family Guy*, or *The Simpsons* (though Homer *is* my favourite fictional character of all time, next to Gully Jimson). As you may have noticed, we are in an era when middle-aged white guys are ridiculed with impunity. I think the idea is that, since we were the ones who ruined the planet, mocking isn't just allowed, it's encouraged.

So we're under extra stress, us oldtimers. Our bodies are not as supple, thin, or sexy as they used to be. Our abs are hiding under a truly startling layer of fat. We may even have Viagra issues. And there's that distant whistling—the Grim Reaper's callous tune—coming more and more clearly into earshot.

At home, who the hell knows what your kids are up to? They don't seem to have boyfriends or girlfriends anymore. It doesn't appear to matter that they don't know how to read. On their computer they are apparently typing *something*, and they are typing faster than we can think. Their excellent new posture at the dinner table might just be the result of some weird new drug we've never even heard of.

So I think it's safe to say that we oldtimers are under more pressure than women, children, citizens of southern climates, and anyone else on Earth in general. As a result, we've had to seek out extraordinary means of staying sane. And what we've found, of course, is hockey.

How many times have you finished a game, sat back against the cement wall, turned to the guy beside you, and said, "Phew. *That* felt good."

He nods, mumbles contentedly, "Gotta just blow it out sometimes."

You're both drained. In fact, the whole room is. You haven't even reached for a beer yet. It maybe lasts only ten seconds, but for that amount of time you are pleasantly drained of that day's bullshit. It's a bit like after sex, minus the woman, the orgasm, the afterglow, or the instantaneous passing out. But in both states you are incapable of thought. As a result, you have no worries. For a while, you are *sane*.

The reason why this small rant of mine is in the "Negative Capability" section is because, well, look at it: in order to stay sane, you must first go nuts. In order to flush out your cares, you must stuff your aging body into a plastic shell, put blades on your feet, and grunt and sweat and chase a meaningless black disc. You try to deposit it into a mesh cage, and if you succeed you roar with glee and rush at a guy in whose house you've never been, and you hug him and whack him on the ass.

Men Who Will Be Boys

IT'S FUN, ISN'T IT, to sit in a dressing room full of grown men—actually, overgrown men—and witness another overgrown man arrive and instantly burp? Because that's what happens. As soon as a guy walks into any dressing room, be he investment banker, Unitarian minister, grocery store stock-man, land surveyor, history prof, or car salesman, he drops his bag, stares off into the middle distance, and burps. He's probably been unconsciously saving it up all day. Later, after the game, in the ten minutes it takes to swill a couple of beers, the dressing room grows deafening with burps—the kind of burps I've always described as lumberjack burps, the kind eleven-year-olds love, forcing them up from the gut, happy and a bit amazed that what comes out sounds like the deeper voice of a man.

And I don't know, if it isn't negative capability, why is it that all oldtimers find it humorous when the high school principal leans and lifts half of his bare ass off the dressing-room bench and cranks himself in the direction of the investment banker three feet away, farting as loud as any eleven-year-old ever has? Both men wear the poker face of a running feud. Suffering the waft, the land surveyor nearby mumbles, "Who the fuck did *he* have for dinner?" And the Unitarian minister beans a random head with balled-up sock tape, for no reason other than he's in a good mood now.

You just don't see this kind of thing out on the street.

Oldtimers are professionals when it comes to negative capability, though they aren't great at explaining it. Especially not to wives, who for some reason can't get comfortable with the contradiction of their husband's coronary-bypass scar and his innocently demented face as he chases a loose puck.

But you oldtimers understand easily and are comfy as hell with it. You probably didn't even know that negative capability had a name. So the next time you enjoy it when the investment banker points his ass and gets back at the high school principal for all those years of humiliation, no sex, and bad marks, and you feel the reverberations along the bench in your own buttbone, and you find yourself laughing despite your otherwise shitty day, and you pop your third beer even though you're driving home, and in your own mind you remain a wonderful husband and father and model citizen, you are only enjoying negative capability in the way the poet John Keats meant you to.

I'm the Best Player on the Team But Nobody Sees It Yet

PICTURE THIS: your team's down a goal and there's a minute left. If your goalie is paying attention enough to notice the guys yelling for him to skate off for an extra man, he will eventually do so, but now someone has to jump on. Who? Generally it's your best player, typically a younger prima donna, probably named Jason, who already has three goals tonight—so it's Jason who jumps on. But what player on the team doesn't think that *he* should jump on instead?

Every player on any given team is identical in one respect only: everyone on the team thinks he is way better than he really is. It's true, and it's universal. Admit it. I mean, *I* think I'm better than I really am. And if you play hockey, so do you. It's hard to say why this is so. Maybe some guys think they're still as fast and strong as ever. Or maybe they simply have a wonderfully unrealistic movie of themselves playing in their minds at all times (I'm an excellent businessman, a fantastic father, a devil in bed, etc.)—and this movie has been running since high school. Or maybe, sitting on the bench and watching how slow and awful everyone else is, they can't help but assume they're better, since no one could possibly be worse. Whatever the case, everyone thinks they're way better than they really are. In fact, everyone pretty much thinks that they're the best player on the team. And moreover that, even after twenty years on the same team, nobody else realizes it yet.

The equally sad thing to report here is that everybody else on the team knows exactly how good you really are. You're the only one in the dark.

Picture a scene from an earlier time: some men and women with hair on their backs, huddled around a fire at the cave-mouth. Lolo, the prettiest female (she has fewer bark hunks in her hair and she has learned to work a charcoal stick around her eyes in an appealing way), is complaining that they have no lily bulbs to eat. At this, Ruck clambers noisily to his feet. The noise is his knee cartilage popping. Ruck has more grey hair than anyone else. (He's the only one over thirty-five, the only oldtimer.)

"Where hell think *you* going?" asks Splee, Ruck's wife. Splee is toasting the fur off a squirrel.

"We need some those lily roots," Ruck tells her.

"You mean *Lolo* want lily roots."

"We could all use some those lily roots."

"So why don't those guys go get?" She flips her head in the direction of several well-muscled young guys lounging in the shadows of the fire. Occasionally their eyes flick to where Lolo is squatting.

"Because no good at root hunting," says Ruck.

"And you are?" Splee's eyes widen, her sore-covered mouth curving up at the corners.

"Well, yes."

"Since *when* you good at root hunting?" Her smile rises more, and tears well up in her eyes, though that could be from the squirrel-hair smoke.

"I always been good at it," says Ruck. "I always been best-in-cave."

Now Splee and everybody else in the cave roars with laughter. The incredible thing is that Ruck doesn't hear them. Perhaps it's because he's already limping off on his root hunt. Or maybe it's the kind of thing that guys just can't hear.

Personal stats—like two goals in the last 193 games—have nothing to do with how good a guy thinks he is. Which is to say that *reality* has nothing to do with how good a guy thinks he is. In fact, the reverse seems to be true: the lousier a guy is, the better he thinks he is. It's some kind of twisted universal law. Look down any oldtimer bench. It's horrible but all too true that it's generally the worst players on the team who whine, yell at, and otherwise try to coach the other players.

"*Jesus!* Get it *out!* Just bank it off the fucking *glass!*" This from a guy who always coughs it up and who can't—*can't*—bank it off the glass himself.

"Who's got the guy in front?! *Who's got the guy in front?!*" This from the worst positional player on the team, the guy who runs around like two chickens at once.

"Pick up the trailer! *Pick up the trailer!*" This guy, who hasn't backchecked in over twenty years, now turns to address the bench. In stern, stentorian tones he says again, "Boys? We gotta go both ways."

These guys generally stand up to do their shouting and whining, and often there are more than one of them doing it at once. Their noise from the bench sounds like some kind of ugly ironic opera. There's no worse sound, really, than a sweaty fifty-year-old, with a big fat red face, whining about a game.

But that's only when you're losing. If you're winning, it's all good, there's no need to whine, and no need to decide which guy should jump on to replace your goalie, and everyone likes everyone else. All is harmonious, it's a fun game to play, and the beer tastes better. In all probability these are the two main reasons why guys really try to win: to silence the whining, and to magically make the beer taste better than birthday cake.

Old Guys Dropping the Gloves

SPEAKING OF NEGATIVE capability, what about fighting?

It's almost hallucinogenic to stand there watching two forty-five-year-olds in a fight. It's kind of hard to even register what it is you're witnessing. There's been a random high elbow, then that extra-eager pushing and shoving, and someone says, "Oh yeah?" and "So's your old man," and the two guys somehow remember how to drop their gloves, and now here they are trying to throw punches. It's hallucinogenic the way it is when you travel over dry mountains in distant lands, and a mile past the camel-ripe bazaar you witness a ritual contest where two naked men, covered in pink paint and dirt, engage in a slapping match with obscure rules, and the winner is awarded an upside-down chicken. Here, there's no dinner to be won, and you can't even hear the white oldtimer fists connect, fists that aren't doing any damage at all. The two guys are exhausted after three girlish punches. It feels even stranger when you realize that your teammate Ray is a high school biology teacher, and the other guy is that chiropractor they have on their team, and he's still wearing his glasses.

Well, maybe I exaggerate. Sometimes fights do break out between guys who can still throw them. Guys who used to enjoy it, probably a little too much. In oldtimers a small handful of guys still go looking for fights, and who the hell knows why. Habit, probably. Or it's what they've always been good at, so why not? Or they still get off being Feared by Everyone. Or they enjoy a residue of those hormones we all had in our Led Zeppelin days. Or, least likely, he's dragged his new girlfriend to the game and the fool thinks a fight is still the kind of stuff that can get you laid. (I dimly remember, back in junior, that winning a fight could get you laid. That is, after a tsking lecture and then maybe five seconds of icy silence, whereupon she can no longer stand it and, buttons popping, she throws herself on you, snarling with lust. Well, at least I guess that's how it might go. I do clearly remember how you very much *didn't* get laid when you *lost* a fight.)

In oldtimers, the truly crazy are soon gone, suspended for life. Each league has a few of them, coming in as rookies at thirty-five and leaving at thirty-five and a half, and the way they get suspended is typically legendary. Usually it's a serious-injury spear, or a two-hander over a head, that sort of thing. My favourite, because it looked so great and no one got that badly hurt, and because I actually saw it, involved a fist going right through a plastic full-face shield like it wasn't even there. I've also played oldtimer ex-NHLers, including two whose names are on the Stanley Cup, who for some weird reason still like to fight. It's as though, every once in a while, they have to check and make sure that Everyone Is Still Afraid of Them. It's quite bizarre, and probably has to do with something that happened in childhood. But to everyone else, an old guy fighting looks kind of gross, very much like the really, really old lady who has painted herself with a ton of garish makeup.

Come to think of it, and speaking of negative capability, maybe that old lady wearing the ton of makeup has a lot in common with every old guy wearing hockey skates.

But still on the topic of negative capability and fighting, have you ever noticed how the best fighters are often the nicest guys? Not always, but often. What is it with that? Are they ashamed of themselves, a bit sheepish because of their brutality, and trying to make up for it? I don't think so. Are they nice because they can afford to be? They aren't afraid of the world, so they can relax and be magnanimous? I think maybe that's more like it.

I like watching old fighters who no longer go looking for it and who are no longer called upon to fight much. But when a scuffle breaks out that they aren't involved in, a certain look comes over them, that of a mother hen. Their head goes up and they seriously scan the scuffle, making sure everything stays fair, making sure a teammate isn't in need of some protection. I like having old fighters like that on my team. You know that if someone jumped you from behind, they'd protect with the same ferocity they'd display protecting their mother from a home invasion. Teammates can be funny that way.

Still on fighting and negative capability, but this time about hockey fans: ever since I was a kid I've noted with amazement what happens, in the pros, when a goon gets traded. The goon is always the fan favourite. They love the guy to death, going crazy when he pounds a guy, feeling bad for him when he loses. Other teams' goons are, of course, the devil incarnate. I was living in Vancouver when Tiger Williams came to the Canucks from the Leafs. I don't know how fans do it, turning the devil into an angel almost instantly just because a guy's wearing the home jersey, but they do. Home jerseys are sort of magic.

The Oldtimers Path to Enlightenment

THERE'S TM AND YOGA and Zen and all the other Eastern mystical traditions, and there's a few Western paths to spiritual enlightenment as well. But I'm betting that not many people consider sports, particularly oldtimers, to be one of those paths. Well, it is. Every guy who plays oldtimers is on a serious spiritual quest, whether he knows it or not.

Every sports fan is aware of Phil Jackson, famous mostly for his days with the Lakers, but also for his somewhat mystical persona. Sportscasters have had lots of fun calling him a Zen master and whatnot, simply because he apparently meditates, and keeps his cool in an arena of seven-foot egomaniacal millionaire hotheads, and for years used his calming presence to prevent Shaq from squishing Kobe like a bug. Jackson also talks and writes about "the zone."

There are lots of ways of talking about this "zone." A friend once told me a curious thing about football and Eastern religion. Decades ago he played football for an American university. He was a lineman. Then the sixties happened, he became a typical experimenter with drugs, and after that a longtime student of Tibetan Buddhism, which emphasizes lots of meditation, including month-long retreats where you do nothing but meditate. My friend told me that, after years of meditation, which had provided him with tremendous insights and formidable spiritual experiences, one of the highest, clearest moments he had ever had occurred during a college football game, during a huge collision of bodies. Time stood still, he reports, and despite the explosion of heads and shoulders and the grunts and growls and thousands of fans screaming, it was incredibly intense, clear, and peaceful. He went on to say that, in this charged moment, he understood everything, but that words could never come close to conveying this understanding.

During her short ballet career, my wife, the professional FeeFee, experienced something similar during a performance in Chicago. It was opening night, nerves were high, hearts pumping, the lights hard in her eyes and unfamiliar. In this state of heightened anxiety, the emboldened FeeFee launched herself from the wings and flew to centre stage. She reports that, for maybe ten or fifteen seconds, she "became the music," and everything her body did was perfect and completely effortless. She was also completely clear of mind, so much so that she was aware, impossibly, of individual audience members breathing. She was awestruck by this experience and kept wanting it to happen again. It never did.

I had a similar experience in junior. I remember everything about it. We were playing the Cougars, here in Victoria, at the old Memorial Arena. I was on the blue line in the Victoria zone. We were killing a penalty, and we forechecked them into a mistake. One of their defencemen came out from behind his net with the puck and telegraphed a pass to a winger breaking out up my side. I pretended not to notice, but I already knew that he was going to make the cross-ice pass and I was going to intercept it. It was one of those passes that, had I missed, he would have had so clear a breakaway that he could have crawled in. But I picked off the pass. And at this point it got weird. No, not weird, the opposite of weird—everything suddenly made perfect sense. I remember so clearly: I had the puck and it was rolling, I took two steps in with it, went around a guy with ease, and let a wrist shot go from the high slot. Because the puck never sat down flat, the shot was wobbly, but I knew it was going over the goalie's shoulder, and it did. Somehow—and I know this really sounds lunatic—I was with the puck as it went in. That's right: my eyes kind of followed the puck as I shot it, and the effect was that the puck was only a foot away, even as it hit the back of the net. Somehow I followed it, guided it, in. I don't know how else to describe it. But the main thing was, everything was effortless, perfectly effortless, and also it was visually clear. The closest thing I can compare it to would be a car accident I was once in. Before impact, "time stood still," everything slowed right down and took on a luminous quality.

"The zone" isn't necessarily always this extreme. It can be much more ordinary, and happens quite a lot for lots of players. But it does have things in common with those experiences I described above. One, when you're in the zone, everything is effortless. Two, you can't force your way into the zone—it has to simply happen. Three, it has more to do with relaxing than it does with straining. Four, when a guy's in the zone, it looks easy. Five, when you're in the zone, great things happen. It might not look that great to anyone else; you might not go end to end and roof it. It might just be an effortless poke-check, or you might stickhandle your way out of a mess and then lay down a nice little pass.

I'm willing to bet that pretty much everybody who plays a sport with some degree of intensity has at some time or other experienced the zone. I don't think it's uncommon. And I'd suggest that someone like Wayne Gretzky is quite at home there, though he might not know it himself. It's possible that the zone explains how a skinny guy like Wayne can do what he did.

The funny thing is, the zone appears to be exactly what meditators are seeking when they meditate. Go ahead, read any book on meditation and check out how they describe the sought-after state: a heightened clarity, a stillness, a place beyond words, and effortless. It's what they refer to as "synchronization of body and mind." Eastern mysticism is not a purely psychological thing—it's only half mental, so to speak. It's mind and body together, in perfect union, and this is exactly what the zone is, too.

So I love it that the Zen retreatant sitting in his cave and the pot-bellied oldtimer patrolling his wing are seeking exactly the same thing, and that neither of them knows it.

ROAD TRIP!

Tournaments

MOST OLDTIMER ROAD TRIPS involve tournaments, where a herd of middle-aged men gather in a particular town or city for several days to play hockey. These men try a bit harder to win these particular hockey games, because these games "matter." Mostly, the herd is away from home for a weekend and attempts, en masse, to remember how to have some fun. This fun generally falls somewhere between having a few in the room and getting so drunk that you fall off the floor.

That's all fine, except that oldtimer tournaments are basically perverted. "Perversion" is not too strong a word. Typically, you play your first game on the Friday night. Win or lose, you drink yourself silly and, since you're out of town, you stay up all night. You play your second game Saturday morning. The basic perversion unfolds here, on the ice, Saturday morning, where you have two teams of middle-aged—no, suddenly *old*—men facing off against each other, severely hung over, no sleep, and now they not only have to "try," but they also have to pretend to enjoy it. It's perverted, it really is. It's also dangerous. Why are respectable middle-aged businessmen treated like this? Are pee-wee hockey players tortured in this way? Are they scheduled to play a game after drinking all night and getting no sleep, eating ribs and pizza at four a.m., after futilely flirting with strippers while tossing multicoloured shooters down their necks? No, they are not. And it's we who have the heart conditions, not them. It's perverse.

Why do we do it? None of us know. We've all tried explaining to wives (and also to strippers, between shooters) and all of us have failed. The prize for winning the whole tournament is sometimes an entire T-shirt, with a neon corporate logo on it, the kind of shirt you hesitate donning even to go upside-down under the toilet pipes. Or a cheap windbreaker that smells like Dow Chemical and cracks when you ball it up to throw at the garbage can. We all have quite a few of these prizes stashed away in drawers (some of us try to give them to the strippers).

Even more perverse, the *biggest* prize for winning your first three games is the bonus of getting to play yet another game, a "championship" game, on Sunday, and this after you have enjoyed your second drunken, sleepless night in a row. It's a bonus game in that you don't have to pay for it, and all the other teams only got to play three. Yay us! Before the championship game, I often look around the room at the wretched, grey, hang-dog faces and wonder how many would gladly pay what cash is left in their wallets for the privilege of *not* playing this bonus game. But, okay, sure, the bonus extra-hell free championship game for the T-shirt can actually be kind of fun. Basically, you have two teams who have both survived the weekend war, both on the ice and in the bars, and you're all tired and scarred and have lost seventeen pounds this weekend and gained eighteen back. You've come this far, you might as well give it your best shot. You might as well *go for that fucking T-shirt*.

In terms of perversity, though, I haven't mentioned the worst scenario. It's no joking matter. It's this: you've won all your games, or enough games by enough goals, and Sunday you're in the championship game in your division. You look on the sheet taped on the arena wall (next to the beer-garden door) and you see that

, for the championship, a team from Nanaimo. You
a few seconds, whap the side of your head, try to
t what city you have been in all weekend. You end up
asking a guy standing beside you. "Nanaimo," he tells you, and
you nod warily, remembering now that he is telling the truth. And
slowly a macabre image dawns on you: the men you are about to
do battle with might be your age and ability, but they live in
Nanaimo. They live in *this city*. They are not enjoying a road trip.
They have been home, eating salad and a modest amount of
pasta. They have taken their kids to visit an aunt. They have
played Yahtzee with the wife, and perhaps nursed a light beer
before watching *SportsPage*, and then to bed. You comprehend
this and suffer the sour nuclear flash of a condensed version of
what *you've* been up to all weekend, and you faint in horror and
exhaustion. The guy at your side who said "Nanaimo" catches
you easily. He's a player on the other team, he's seen it all before,
he was ready, and now he's smiling.

It's maybe the best feeling of all, though, if you go out there
and somehow suck it up, and beat that team who ate some pussy
salad and went to sucky bed. It's not about pride, or the T-shirt,
or corny Canadian courage. In the end, it's about rising above
all the perversity that is an oldtimer hockey tournament and
beating it at its own game.

Dads Gone Wild

ONE NEAT THING about road-trip tournaments, of course, is
you're away from home and you get to see that chartered
accountant teammate have more than two beers and act like an
idiot. Some guys do sneak off to bed, but most of us manage
some decent idiocy sometime during a tournament, and as a
result you see some hidden and unique sides to supposedly
respectable people.

At tournaments, we've all seen guys do all sorts of funny, crude, juvenile, surprising things. And when you think about it, isn't virtually everybody interesting and entertaining in some way? So why even single somebody out? There's one guy on my brother's team, Drew, whose hidden sides I first encountered at tournaments. Again, everyone's unique, but some guys are more unique than others.

It turns out we may have played against each other years ago, because he played for Alberta about the same time I was playing for UBC. Chances are we didn't, though, because Drew's a little unsure on what year he was doing exactly what. As we compared notes about university teams, he cheerfully told me he was dropping acid most days back then, "or maybe every day," even during classes and on game days, so dates run together in his memory. Talking about those acid days, his eyes sort of began swimming behind his thick glasses, taking on that awed, excited look that eyes do when their owners start remembering acid, even if all the times they took it can be counted on one finger.

Now, before you write him off as yet another lovingly-off-his-rocker middle-aged hippie, I'll add that Drew is a multimillion-aire geologist who, the last time I saw him, burned all the chest hair off a bemused teammate with a lighter.

Drew thinks he graduated, twice maybe. In any case, he ended up in grad school, but not for more than a few weeks, because he had a chance to turn pro down in Las Vegas, which was then in the International League. At that time, Las Vegas was pretty much a goon team in a goon league. I mean, picture it—an audience made up entirely of guys who look like Julian from *Trailer Park Boys*, squeezing the same rummer, except that these Julians all have wads of cash spilling out their pockets. And they're looking for a little blood between turns at the black-jack table.

Drew, who's about five foot seven, was the main goon on a team of goons in the league of goons. He fought three or four times a game, and otherwise cross-checked guys in the neck if they even looked at the goalie. I know that anyone who's ever played contact hockey won't be at all surprised when I say that Drew is one of the sweetest guys you'll ever meet. Kind and, before that third beer, soft-spoken.

He went on to become a geologist and did some good old-fashioned prospecting up North. Apparently he found some glittery stuff in the dirt and staked some claims. Long story short, now he has employees. And he plays oldtimers with my brother's Old Goats.

He's in his early fifties, Drew is, and though I've only played tournaments with him, I've seen flashes of the old Drew—the acid and Las Vegas Drew. Once, as we were drubbing a slower team pretty badly, the team found some shitty pride and began hacking us if we had the audacity to beat them to the outside. Suddenly the arena erupted with a horrible howling. It was a kind of bewildered outrage, a why-would-some-fool-do-this-because-now-the-fool-has-to-die sort of howling. There was Drew, centre ice, one glove off. Blood dripped from his thumb, and his thumbnail was bent back. He stood there, howling, searching for the guy who was going to die, and in his eyes was the weirdest look, in the end a mostly *amused* look. The ref hadn't even bothered to blow the whistle, because everyone had already stopped to watch. No one stepped forth to challenge Drew. Anyone he turned towards backed away quickly. The owner of those eyes was capable of anything. We all know what a bent-back thumbnail feels like, and this guy with the bent-back nail was howling, yet basically amused, and would be even more amused once he started helping someone die.

Eventually Drew settled, and laughed gently, and we led him to the room and got the thumb wrapped up in white tape. It was wrapped up about the size of a regular light bulb, and the same shape, and he had some fun with it in the strip bar later that night.

A couple of weeks ago I saw similar evidence of Drew's former glory. It was the Nanaimo tournament again, the Friday-evening game, and we'd just come back from a 5–1 deficit to tie the game 5–5. I don't know if it would have happened anyway, but an extra bottle of team sambuca came out of someone's bag and got passed around. Now, what's an extra bottle of sambuca when we're talking a dozen guys? Well, when you factor in all the beer going around too, and also that some of us don't drink sambuca (I personally haven't touched it since the last Cultus Lake tournament, when I earned that nickname I'm not going to tell you about), then that extra bottle goes a lot farther. Let's just say that Drew had a few more pulls than what's normal for him and, before we knew it, he had started a naked full-contact gut-butting contest in the middle of the dressing room. Things were pretty loud all around, with all the booze gone, the beer too. Everyone was roaring pretty good, as the next two greying, fifty-four-year-old opponents lined up at opposite walls, then ran full speed into each other's stuck-out gut. For some reason Drew had dubbed it a "wolverine" contest. From the vantage point of my computer, it all seems pretty juvenile now, and no doubt your vantage point is doing the same for you, but at the time it was pretty funny. My main point is that Drew, who has a decent-enough gut but is otherwise wiry and only five seven, easily won the contest, and he did so by more or less turning himself into a bull wolverine. He was frightening, his eyes behind those glasses the most frightening part about him. (Though when he gets excited he also sprouts an impressive blue vein in the centre of his forehead.)

Rumours about Drew may or may not be true. I do know he has this thing about not just wolverines but bears, which makes sense, given that, when he's not doing mega-deals, he still knocks around up in the bush. Once, while on an outing up north with his kids, his daughter had a run-in with a grizzly bear. Rushing to get between the bear and her, Drew yelled to his son, who didn't drive yet, to "get in the truck, floor it and drive straight over Dad," if the bear started to maul him, the idea being that he'd fit safely under the truck and the bear wouldn't.

Drew's bear stuff goes beyond that. He's told me, after only a couple of beers, that he'd like to "take on" a medium-sized black bear. "I could take him, I could take the fucker," he said, his sudden forehead vein betraying his otherwise calm manner.

I want to tell him, "Drew, that's why we play oldtimers, to get precisely that stuff out of our systems." That is, those of us who have any of "that stuff" left.

Drew's bear stuff continues. The year before I first went to the Cultus Lake tournament and earned my nickname, Drew outdid himself there. Let me clarify: Cultus Lake is not the sort of place to outdo yourself. Harley, a Goat teammate, has a family cottage there, on the lakefront, at which the whole team stays, crammed in bunks and foamies on the floor. Though it's B.C., it's anything but wilderness there at Cultus Lake—it's lawns, and crammed-together cottages, and no parking. Harley's family cottage is one step away from a doily-and-antique sort of affair. The immediate neighbours are quiet and elderly. There likely hasn't been a beach fire there in fifty years. Anyway, not the spot to "outdo yourself."

The year I arrived to earn my name, the boys were still abuzz over Drew's performance of a year earlier. Seems he'd surpassed his limit and cheerfully thrown up on himself. He was already naked, so no clothes were involved. A nuisance bear had been in the neighbourhood all summer, getting into whatever garbage it could. Hearing this, Drew brightened and, covered in tasty barf, declared himself bear bait and staggered outside to pass out. Some charitable teammates went out later and threw a blanket over him, but that's where he stayed until the built-in lawn sprinklers woke him up. He didn't attract any bears.

I think I got competitive with Drew the year I got my name. Maybe, hearing his story, I wanted to outdo him. I won't tell you what I did or what my nickname is, but suffice to say I too ended up naked, and needed new glasses, and ruined Harley's carpet, and the area saw its first beach fire in years. Some of Harley's roof had to be repaired. Apparently I took interpretive dance to new heights.

The year after that, both Drew and I were at Cultus at the same time. The games were all done, as was the team barbecue, and Drew and I sort of found ourselves sitting at opposite ends of the living room, beers in hand, eyeing each other. Who would win drunkest-fool honours this year? I sipped and pondered. I knew Drew was ruminating on the same thing, the same challenge.

As I pretended not to check him out, I noticed a funny thing: Drew and I were the only two guys here who wore glasses. Maybe we were overcompensating for our nerd personas, maybe not. But I noticed, too, that Drew's glasses were far thicker, and the eyes behind them way nuttier than mine.

Suddenly he was sitting beside me, telling me rather casually of the time he was up north and he had the urge to blow something up. For some reason, he said, instead of just setting a charge of dynamite or something simple like that, he decided to throw an open bucket of white gas into a burning drum of diesel. For extra effect he used a reverse, over-the-back of the head slam dunk to deliver the highly volatile fluid into the open flame. After ducking to avoid the worst of the fireball, he took a few moments to put out the spot fires on his eyebrows and beard before looking for something else to explode.

Telling me all this, Drew chatted casually, flapping a hand around on a loose wrist like some kind of English professor, as if describing a humorous mishap during his last visit to the bookstore.

It worked. There's no way I was going up against this guy. And as a result, neither of us got too bad that night. Harley's heirloom coffee table lost two legs, a guy broke a pinkie, and Drew—last I saw him before I went to pass out—was burning teammates' chest hair with a butane lighter. I could swear he shot me a look or two while doing so, as if to see if I'd changed my mind and was up to the challenge. I wasn't. I was also really glad I've never had any chest hair.

The Snoopy

I DON'T EVEN KNOW why I'm writing this, since pretty much every oldtimer in the world knows about Snoopy, probably more than me. I mean, one guy who spares for our team has been to the Snoopy eighteen times.

I also wonder about celebrating this tournament at all, since, well, shouldn't the world's ultimate, most famous, mecca-like oldtimers hockey tournament be held somewhere in Canada? I don't want to be anti-American here, but shouldn't such a tournament take place in, say, Gordie Howe's hometown? Or in Brandon, Manitoba, in the coldest heart of winter, on a series of outdoor rinks? In Plaster Rock, New Brunswick, there's an annual shinny tournament, held outdoors, on a shovelled lake, with no refs, no uniforms, no pads, no age categories, and the boards are two-by-fours that only keep pucks from getting lost in the snowbanks. The trophy is made of carved wood, and lots of beer and rum goes down. Now, that's the right idea, but if anything it's just *too* pure. It's like holding a folk music festival where all the musicians have to make their own instruments using only sharp stones and wood blessed by Druids. And shinny isn't really hockey.

But nor can anything played at the height of summer in California really be called hockey. For the rare reader who doesn't know, the annual Snoopy tournament takes place in Santa Rosa, California, in the height of summer. Some decades ago, ardent oldtimer and cartoonist Charles Schulz took some of his millions and built himself an arena to play in. The arena's design reminds one of the word "alpine," and the rink itself is kind of weird, what with its glass boards that aren't as tall as boards normally are.

In all fairness to the Snoopy, I have to admit to never attending it during its glory days, when Mr. Schulz was still alive and playing in it himself. In those days, it was even harder to get invited, likely because he was a gracious host and there were lots of fancy extras and freebies. I hear the wine flowed and the steaks were thick. Nowadays, since the Schulz kids took over, the bloom is off the rose. In any case it's more expensive, and the parking-lot barbecue costs.

It's still fun, though, if you have the bucks, and I'll stop griping about it after one last gripe. It's this: true oldtimers know that summer tournaments don't fucking count. How can they? First of all, the weather's all wrong. It's perverse, in fact. Especially in, good god, California. Also, as we all know, in summer there are two kinds of players: those true oldtimers who are instantly out of shape by May and who, come summer, have let their bodies follow a healthy instinct of relaxing and melting and spreading out like butter on a frying pan. The other, the *fake* oldtimer, is the hockey-Eddie who is in tip-top shape even in July, because he's been playing in three summer leagues getting ready to blow them all away at the Snoopy, and that is exactly what he does. Not that winning matters at the Snoopy, but it's a drag, it really is, to go down there for a week's wine tasting and get windburn from the Eddies flying by.

Otherwise, yes, it's fun. I apologize for besmudging this noble event. For one thing, it does take the wind out of even the Eddies' sails when, at the next centre-ice face-off, they realize they're up 9–0, it's the first period, and they're playing a bunch of smiling guys from New Jersey, their teeth all stained Merlot red, guys who clearly don't give a shit beyond spending an exotic afternoon with these serious fast guys from Canada. The other neat thing about it is that you sometimes bump into old old friends. (That second "old" is deliberate, because if you haven't seen them since midget, it's quite the shock.) Also, it's typical to head over to San Francisco to catch a Giants game—a doubly nice activity, since it's often weirdly frigid in the fog coming off the Bay, and it almost feels like hockey weather, and Canada, and it can even put you in the mood for your next game.

But for those of you who haven't been to the Snoopy and don't have the time or money or invitation, don't bother. Just go see the movie *Sideways*. It's exactly like that, only instead of two guys there's two hundred, and they're all like the stupid, funny one, who doesn't care what the wine tastes like and just wants more of it. They golf, they walk along roads in search of a restaurant or bar. They wake up with headaches but are generally pretty jolly. The main difference between the Snoopy and *Sideways* is that nobody, not even the stupid funny guys, is getting laid, because almost everyone brings their wives.

The Best Tournament in Canada

THERE ARE LOTS of really good ones, lots of bests. The most famous probably continues to be the Snoopy, which, as I've argued above, is wrong.

So, in all seriousness, I propose that the best and most famous tournament should obviously take place in Canada. It should be in some small place—a different small place every year. Places the size and temperament of, say, Cornwall, or Penticton, or Bathurst, or Moose Jaw, or Drumheller, or Corner Brook, or Sydney. It should be governed by the right people, some of whom are rich, so that the tournament doesn't cost much for players. I propose that the board of governors should be Pat Quinn, Howie Meeker, Dave Bidini, Tiger Williams, Tim Horton's widow, Merlin Malinowski, Rick Tocchet, Michael J. Fox, Jean Beliveau, Carl Brewer (consulted by Ouija board), William Shatner, and, of course, Pete Mahovlich.

It would be small, and entered by lottery. Three age divisions—plus-35, plus-45, plus-55—with a Good and an Awful subdivision within each. The prizes in the Awful division would be bigger. Teams would be helped with airfare. Beer in the room would be endless and free, and in the pubs all around town, beer would be a buck a pint, for everyone, for the duration of Oldtimer Week. Every restaurant and pub in town would participate in a best chicken wings, spaghetti, and Jell-o shooters contest, with the players casting ballots throughout the week. Neil Young and Colin James and Shania Twain would be well paid to come and play at the Saturday dance. If not enough single women were available in town, they'd be trucked in from neighbouring communities. *The Globe and Mail* would run daily stories about all the games, plus boxscores, on the front page, along with features on best party team, strangest jokes, and unsung backchecker.

It will be known as, simply, The Tournament. You can call any of the board of governors and ask where the first one will be held.

A Marvellous Tradition

THIS YEAR, playing in Victoria in the Pacific Cup tournament with my Finishing Stars team, I witnessed a marvellous tradition involving hard beer, in this case a fine brandy.

First, it's an odd tournament, with extra torture involved. After the three round-robin games played on Friday and Saturday, the two top teams in each division have to play a semifinal game early Sunday morning in order to qualify for the championship game later that same day. So we're talking *two* bonus torture-games. We're talking a bunch of fifty-year-olds playing five games in roughly forty-eight hours. Nobody likes this format except for the most obnoxious hockey-Eddie. It has something to do with making us feel good because we get not just one extra game for the same money, but two, and it feels more like playoffs, like real hockey. But, really, everybody hates it. Are you listening, Pacific Cup?

So we made the semifinal (actually, we won the whole damn thing—see "Ringers"), and this awful extra game took place at the Esquimalt Naval Base at seven-thirty Sunday morning. I really felt sorry for the other team, which was on a road trip from Vancouver and who, unlike us, a home team, were obliged to get really drunk the previous night. But it was horribly early for both teams. Largely because of our ringer, Murray, who had played for the California Golden Seals and the Houston Aeros, and who had never, ever gotten out of shape, we won. These games go by quickly, and it was only eight-thirty when we trooped into our dressing room, trying to trick ourselves into being happy that we had a championship

MIDNIGHT HOCKEY · · · 113

game to look forward to a few hours later. We hadn't settled into our seats to begin an unfocused stare into space, dreaming of breakfast, or bed, when the door banged open and the entire enemy team came clomping in. Of course the first assumption was that they had come to club us to death, but it was instantly apparent that they lacked sticks, or weapons of any kind. Instead, each guy carried two shooters, filled to the brim with an amber fluid. Each guy handed one of their drinks to one of us, keeping one for himself.

It was pretty fine. I don't think anything even got said, because it didn't need to. We all raised and clinked glasses with our new enemy-buddy, making brief but sincere eye contact, and downed some extremely smooth brandy. (I came out of hard-beer retirement for this one, but just for the day.) It wasn't yet nine in the morning. It sounds corny, but we all learned, again, that in this sport there are no losers, and that every guy you bash heads with in the corner could, in another life, be your good friend. And I was about to suggest that this fine tradition be made mandatory for all games in all tournaments, when I realized that the best part about it was the surprise. So I vote instead that we start surprising each other more.

Ringers, and the Surrey Red Army

SOME TEAMS HAVE a hard time finding a lineup to take to a tournament. Often this means only that lots of guys aren't that eager, and have offered the lamest excuses, ranging from vague mumblings about the wife's surgery to having to be at their long-lost son's surprise awards ceremony. Some guys can't even bother getting creative, and their only excuse for not coming to Spittoon Lake is that they have to wash their hair. So then you have to start phoning random guys on random other teams, asking if they know anybody who might want to play in Spittoon

Lake—and, by the way, do they have gas money? So, anchoring your defence, you end up with two bespectacled brothers named Ernie, both of whom are working real hard to get the hang of skating backwards.

For other teams, organizing a tournament lineup is a different game altogether. These are the teams that have exactly two lines—six forwards and four D. All of them are suspiciously trim. Two or three—the two or three who are unsmiling, all business, and look almost like real hockey players—wear socks that don't match the team jersey. These socks are the giveaway. These guys aren't brothers named Ernie. These guys are pickups. Ringers. It's almost a given—the teams with the most mismatched socks in their lineup will win the tournament.

Well, we can't blame these teams, can we? It truly is more fun to win than it is to lose. It's not a case of "winning the tournament," either. Nobody really gives a shit about that. It's just more fun to win, period. It's a state of mind. It simply feels better, on the ice, to be winning, and it feels better in the room after you've won. That's where winning really counts, there in the room, when you gobble up your first beer. After a win the beer does taste better. After a win, even though no one really cares, the room is instantly cheerful, the guys are giggling at the drop of a hat, and it's easier to love everybody, even the guys you don't like all that much. So if you have a hole in your lineup, why not stack? (I'm not talking about those teams—and we all know who they are— who tell their weaker players to stay home for tournaments, and actively recruit ringers. These teams shouldn't be allowed in old-timers tournaments, and their team managers are dickless bureaucrats who obviously got beaten up in the sandbox.)

Also, no matter how good you are yourself, it's more fun to play with better players. It's great to get open and actually receive a pass, and it's great to give one to someone who might actually beat a guy and score. Also, ringers tend to hustle a bit more in the corners, and do lots of extra work in general, in order to show that they are indeed ringers. Now, one danger with ringers is that some of them, after first ascertaining that the team does want to win, will next ascertain for themselves that the best way of help- ing the team win is to not pass to the weaker players, which might mean *you*. This is not a happy feeling, to be wide open and tapping your stick on the ice, and have the ringer see you, instantly assess your talent level, and then opt to go it alone. So ringers can sometimes be humiliating. And even though you won, in the room the beer tastes only marginally better than after a loss, and you refuse to laugh very loud at the ringer's jokes.

In any case it's natural to go with the best players available. We all do it. I don't think there are any teams who don't.

Well, there's one. The Surrey Red Army seems to have come up with a different strategy. I understand that they have a "good team" and a "bad team," and that they enter separate tourna- ments. This last Pacific Cup, we were slotted to play one of them, and we didn't know which one it would be.

It doesn't take long to find out. They look like they can skate okay, but suddenly the sea opens up and you're in alone on goal for no reason other than that no one seems to be try- ing very hard, and it's 3–0 five minutes in. Now we understand we're playing the "bad team," and we start noticing certain details about them. First, on the backs of their jerseys are their names, except that the names all read "McLeanov," and "Reganov," and "Smithtov." In the stands there are actual fans—mostly wives, but what appear to be brothers and friends as well, maybe twenty-five people all told. Our team has no one in the stands, and we live here. (Maybe everyone in Surrey is eager for any excuse to leave town, if only to enjoy three days of not having to worry about their car getting stolen.) The Surrey fans wave a huge banner—it has to be ten feet by fifteen—that reads "SURREY RED ARMY." They are drinking and cheering and mocking their friend or husband and having a great old time.

As were the players themselves. It became clear to us that this was the whole purpose of this team: having fun. Nothing was going to stand in the way of that; certainly not losing. Not even losing 14–1 would dampen their spirits. (One of the niceties of the Pacific Cup and lots of other tournaments is that "goals for" counts in the tie-breaking system. So teams like ours, eager to enjoy the two bonus torture games on Sunday, will try to score as many goals as possible against teams like theirs, leading to situations of absurdity and humiliation.)

But the thing is, the Red Army would not be humiliated. Another goal scored on them was cause for yet more fun. The D-man who lost his jock on our latest rush, or the guy who fell, or the sucker who put a cross-ice pass right on the tape of one of our guys, would be cheered and taunted in a celebratory way, and would take a bow, or do a pirouette, or some such.

Actually it was a piss-off. Once their strategy became clear, it made you a little mad. Their attitude—"You guys want to *win*? Really? Okay, go ahead and win. *We're* just having a good time!"—kind of rankled. It felt corny. It felt passive-aggressive. You felt mocked if you tried to score. They were making up their own rules, psychological rules, and the next time we went in on a breakaway, and their bench was hooting at the goalie, who then guessed like a soccer goalie on a penalty shot and went the wrong way, well, it made you kind of scowl. Because, the thing is, they had found a *different way of winning*. And so—shit— they did it, they beat us. And the beer didn't taste all that great after that game. But it never really does after a blowout, does it?

Memory #5: French Hockey with Al

THIS RECOLLECTION has to do with real French guys, not our Québécois kind, and it took place in France, which is where I lived and played hockey for a year.

My friend Al got me the hockey job in France. He is a character I need to describe. Al played on both my junior team and later at UBC, and he was the best guy on both teams. He didn't last either place, though. In a sense, he was too good. Too restless, in any case. He'd get sudden ideas about what to do with his life and where he should be. Al was maybe the smartest natural player I've ever played with. It was after being a late cut at a New York Islanders camp—where he was also too good and restless, I don't doubt—that he ended up in the French Alps, of all places, playing and coaching in St-Gervais.

He'd been playing in France a few years when, one fall, I found myself with nothing very appealing to do and he suggested I give France a try. Each team was allowed one "playing coach" from another country. (All of Europe was like that then. Only in Holland could teams hire more than one foreigner, which the rich teams did. Another friend, Donny, had played in Holland, on a team with a bunch of other Canadians, in Amsterdam. He described it to me: they were always either stoned or drunk, and women galore. They played hockey and got paid for it. Donny somehow survived paradise and is a respectable family man, and I hear he's now playing oldtimers.)

Al assured me there were lots of French teams in need of a new playing coach that year. The money wouldn't be bad, he said, even in second division. Even, he said, down in *La Ligue du Sud*, the Southern League. He snorted, shook his head, and smiled at the mere mention of such a pathetic league. But he told me to just grab my skates and buy a one-way ticket and he'd see me at the Geneva airport and we'd go from there. I shrugged and said sure. I had no kids, no job, no woman in my life. Utter freedom. It didn't even seem all that exciting, at the time. Can you imagine? That was the era.

When I landed in Geneva, Al wasn't at the airport, but that felt normal enough, Al being an extremely casual guy. I gathered my little suitcase and my skates and checked the crumpled scrap of paper with a hotel name scribbled on it and got a taxi. I found the hotel, and Al's room, and I knocked on the door. This was now exciting. I was in Europe, and I was going to play pro hockey—well, sort of. I'd be the only guy on the team getting paid, true, and the hockey apparently wasn't all that great, true, but I would be paid to play the game I loved. That I had no team yet, and hadn't played for over a year, and was sort of fat, and had come on a one-way ticket—none of these things felt like obstacles as I stood there at Al's door, hearing laughter from within. I banged again. The door opened, and here stood Al, naked, clutching a towel to his privates.

Let me explain Al a little more. He was six-one or so, and in great shape. We all had long hair back then, but Al had *really* long hair, almost to his ass. Not only was it the seventies, but Al, being half Ojibwa, was starting to explore his heritage a bit. Dark, muscular, hair to his ass—he looked like a version of Tarzan, or an intelligent Fabio. He looked at me, snorted, said, "You did it, eh?" To a female query, Al answered back over his shoulder, in French. Now, being half Ojibwa, in certain moods Al sometimes spoke with that sweetly deep throatiness some Native guys have, and when he spoke French he had that throaty tone in spades. It threw me a bit. It hadn't occurred to me that over these past few years Al had of course learned French. But it was the weirdest French I'd ever heard. He was fluent, but he had no proper French accent whatsoever. I realized he was speaking French with an Ojibwa accent.

There in the doorway, naked, Al spoke some more Ojibwa-French over his shoulder to his girlfriend, making her shriek with laughter. I could make out only a few words: *hockey sur glace* and *mon ami*. He said something more, and they both laughed again. What I picked out this time was *La Ligue du Sud*.

To make a long memory short, I had to badger Al to venture out of his love nest from time to time to phone over to France and try to find me a team. He told me there was no problem, that he knew everyone, that Papillon was still on vacation and would be back in Megève in a day, or that Leduc in Dijon was getting back to him tomorrow. A day later he'd tell me that those two spots hadn't materialized, but that Camille's team in Lyon was looking for a guy, and he had Camille's mother's number right there on his dresser. Things were getting dicey, as they say, so I told Al to give me the number and I'd phone Camille's mother myself. Al seemed to hesitate, so I kind of stuck my foot in the door and then got past him as he went to pick up the towel I'd snatched from him and tossed out in the hall, and on my way to the dresser Marie-Eve under her blankets gave me a smile and tiny wave with her pinky. There on the dresser was an empty mickey of cognac, a travel chessboard, and a *Herald Tribune*, but no scrap of paper with numbers on it. I ran and closed the door, locking Al out. In the end I let him in only after he promised, three times, to get dressed immediately and hit the phone downstairs until he found me a team.

Al was as good as his word, and it was just in time. A few hours later, while I sat in the room with Marie-Eve letting her practise her English on me, Al came to tell me that there were two jobs left in France: one in Dijon, the other in Toulon, and that he'd got me a tryout with Dijon for two nights from now. It was an exhibition game, Dijon against the French national team, and I'd play for Dijon.

"You didn't say anything about a tryout," I said, softly.

"They just want to have a look. There's no problem. Just pop a few goals."

I reminded Al that I played defence.

"Maybe play forward, just for that night. And pop some goals."

I asked Al how good the French national team was.

"They're not bad, a few Canadian guys who played American league, only one ex-NHLer." He listed off a few names I actually recognized.

I told Al I was in horrible shape.

"Well, maybe we should, I don't know, go jogging later."

I asked him if Dijon had a very good team.

"Nah, second division. You'll get creamed. But just, you know, pop a few. There's no problem."

"So, that other team, Toulon? That's, ah, isn't that—?"

"It's down south. *La Ligue du Sud.*"

I won't belabour the details of the tryout with Dijon, other than to say that Al did take me jogging, and it did no good. The three of us went to Dijon, where Al did indeed seem to know everybody, and where Marie-Eve had family, and a humungous family villa with stables and a maid and about a hundred acres. Al got me some gear, which I donned to face, with my Dijon teammates, the French national team. It was a packed house, maybe about three thousand. I was nervous, but I couldn't help but notice what I looked like.

Now, any guy who's played our game outside our country knows that "it's different over there." Even in the States it can be different. (I remember skating in a mall once, in Los Angeles, and the ice didn't seem like ice, and the air didn't seem to be the kind you were supposed to be skating in.) "Over there," things like tape, and dressing rooms, and skate sharpeners, and pre-game meals, and even fans—well, they're all different. Anyway, here in Dijon my stick, a Finnish club-like thing, was taped with blue electrician's tape. My helmet was one of those tiny Jofa things, and it had one blue lightning stripe painted (badly) on it. My shoulder pads were huge, making the Jofa and my head look even tinier, even tinier than Marty McSorley's, and my pants were small and tight and much too short. I looked like a hulking pinhead—giant shoulders, long, skinny legs, showing about three inches of thigh skin. I went out there and floundered around, doing my best. We lost 10–1 and it wasn't me who got the goal. In frustration I got their best guy to go into a corner with me and I bashed him, and even the home crowd whistled its disfavour. I had about enough money left for a train ticket to Toulon.

THIS SEASON SO FAR

December

I'VE PLAYED A FEW GAMES NOW, but only a few. A few games has not improved *my* game. I thought there were muscles hidden under this baby fat but I was wrong. I thought there was something called "muscle memory" but I was wrong about that too. I am in horrible shape and can do next to nothing out there. My bad back is stable enough—that is, I keep it doped into ignorance with ibuprofen, the oldtimer's friend, and it probably isn't even aware that it's playing. So I can't blame my back. I only have my entire body to blame. And my lifestyle. When I look at myself naked in the mirror, I think for some reason of underdone Yorkshire pudding, but with extra dents and some hair. I'm not trying to be disturbing, it's just the facts.

Mostly, it's not fun hearing that whining voice in my head. All out-of-shape oldtimers know this voice only too well. It's the one that goes, I *should* be able to beat that guy. I would *normally* make that pass. I *should* be backchecking at least once a game. I *should* have more than seven seconds of energy per shift.

I *used to* be able to play this game quite well.

I wish I could say "it's been great getting back" for other reasons, like the social aspect, but something about the team as a whole feels off. Over the years, this team has developed a whining element. We're all a little to blame, in the sense that part of the fun of oldtimers is to gossip about guys behind their backs, especially if they think highly of themselves. I doubt that there's a team in the nation that's free of this. And some teams are of course famous for their ongoing bad vibes—brooding, yelling, really nasty and infantile playground behaviour. Some of us have even witnessed—dare I say it—team fisticuffs.

My team is pretty good as far as team vibes go, except for this increased whining. A clutch of two or three guys are the most vocal, and I'll blame them. Maybe I'll let them off the hook a bit by saying that we all whine, but silently. They're just louder. What really grates about the whining is that it's constantly heaped on certain other players. Weaker players get picked on, sometimes ganged up on. What happens is—and I'll call the worst one Little Bug, and the next worst one Big Bug—one of the picked-on guys will make a bad pass and Little Bug, who happens to be sitting beside you, will turn his head slightly your way and say, "Fucker'll blame his new stick." If you snicker or in any way agree with him, you are now on his side, and the criticism picks up, and Little Bug adds, "Why does the fucker even bother taping it?" and so on, and with any encouragement at all Little Bug will escalate his badmouthing until it's, "Why don't we just all come earlier than him and lock the fucking door?"

Let's face it, what's *really* irritating about this criticism of other players is this and only this: if it was, I don't know, Sergei Zubov sniping at some guy to make his passes more crisp, it wouldn't be so bad, because Sergei Zubov makes crisp passes. If it was Scott Gomez whining that there's no one open out there to pass to, you'd tend to believe him. You get my drift. On my team, the guys doing the whining about Bart's shitty passes tend to be shitty passers themselves. Big Bug coughs it up in our end at least six times a game, yet he howls when

someone else does, especially when it's one of his pet pincush-
ions. I don't get it. We have a few emperors who lack clothes
on this team and, since I last played, they've gotten nakeder.
What I'm seeing is yet more proof that nobody truly under-
stands how shitty they are themselves. I'll include myself in
this, because it appears to be a universal affliction. But, c'mon.
Most of us, no matter what delusions we cling to about our
own ability, and no matter how shitty we think other guys
might be, at least we keep our poison to ourselves. Actually,
I've noticed that it's often the very best players who are most
magnanimous about the weakest ones. They seem to be able
to quite sanely see how everyone plays, and understand that no
one's going to change, except maybe get slower. They declare
to themselves, "This is the team I'm on," and make the best of
it. And maybe even have a good time, even though every second pass is in their skates.

But yes, okay, I'm pissed off and disheartened. I mean, you finish work, and your rotten day, and you take your bad mood to the
rink, where you want to have it beaten out of you by some manly
jostling in the corners, and maybe a self-satisfying deke or two,
maybe even a goal, and then some pleasant beers and dressing-
room hijinks and one belly-laugh and—poof!—your bad mood
has been magically lifted away. When the guys are bitchy with
each other, it's no fun on the ice, or on the bench, or in the room,
and you wonder why you're paying money to do this.

It's gotten worse, this whining, but something else is off, too.
The core of good players is gone. Some are injured, some gone
for other reasons, and we're getting routinely smoked. *Badly*
smoked. But it's more than the losing. Really, who cares about
losing? It's mostly the "feeling" on the team. I've never been on
a sinking ship, but I have a sense that this is what it feels like.
And I guess I'm feeling tempted to go the rat route.

I miss Bernie in particular. Bernie is maybe the only truly good hockey player on this team of ours, and to hear that he has retired because he no longer wants to play is rather depressing. Not just because we lose our best player. (He played for Boston College, and probably could have played pro but didn't, and, at fifty, he's the only guy on the team for whose skating I can still use the word "fast.") No, it's depressing that, on the ice, Bernie always *did the right thing*, had the best instincts, better than the floundering rest of us. So it's possible he'd also know, better than the floundering rest of us, when it was time to go.

George, our sponsor, isn't around either. George, our best D-man, a hulking Saskatchewan lad who, when he's in shape, can break up a rush and then go coast to coast and roof it, apparently has too much of a life outside of hockey. Business is booming, his company is expanding and hitting great cards on the turn and the river and it's keeping him in the boardroom late. Apparently he's come only once or twice this year. Our captain, Dougie Mac, is injured. Something about his leg. But there's something suspicious going on too, because Lyle tried calling him and his number's been changed. Has the captain fled his own sinking ship? Changed his number in case we came after him, like we were some kind of bug-eyed psycho who's stalking him? It wouldn't surprise me if he did. This whining has gotten *bad*. And Duane's comeback, like mine, has stalled. His Achilles tendon got all inflamed and needed a scoping and scraping out.

Still, I can live with this stuff. I can still enjoy oldtimers, despite the whining, the loss of four of our best guys, and the string of 13–2 shellackings. That's all bearable. What isn't is the discovery—and it's one that I seem to make every year!—that it's really not much fun when you're so out of shape. It's bad enough to be getting older, and to experience mediocre younger guys blowing by you with ease, but to be out of shape on top of that feels, well, shitty. It feels shitty knowing that, in even half-assed shape, you could have beat that gangly D-man and got a good shot on net. In shape, you could make that extra move and then get that pass over to the guy going in alone. In shape, you can still do a few good things. Out of shape, you can't do anything. It's just not as much fun being a lousy hockey player. I don't mean to be immodest here, but I'll suggest that it's even less fun for us guys who used to be sort of good. You know: if you never knew what it felt like to make that nifty move, you don't miss it. (To extend that logic a bit further, it must feel *real* shitty to be Wayne Gretzky right now. Though Wayne probably doesn't feel as bad as Number Four, Bobby Orr, whose niftiness must feel like a distant memory.)

And here I am, jeopardizing my back. Jeopardizing fatherly enjoyment with my kids. Lilli and I have this little game we play where I push her on the swing until she attains a certain height, and then she calls out, "You dropped a dollar!" and I ask her where, and she points to the spot right in front of the swing, and like a dummy I bend over, pretending to search for the money, and here comes Lilli and she boots me in the ass and I go flying. I act mad and crazy, and she laughs uncontrollably for the hundredth time. But here I am, sitting in a bitchy room with a pack of other shitty oldtimers, frustrated because we lost in double figures again, and I had no fun, got no goals, made no good passes, and I took so much ibuprofen I can't feel my gums. (Apparently when you snort coke and can't feel your gums, at least you're under the illusion that you're having a good time.)

I think I'm also mad at British Columbia. It's the middle of hockey season and close to Christmas, but there's no snow. It's balmy and wet out, and it feels nothing like either hockey or Christmas. Humbug. And the shopping frenzy has begun.

Though I don't think it has ever snowed this... should make snow mandatory for at least one week... Christmas. And families should come together on... Eve to decorate the real tree, under which at least 50 perc... all presents must either be homemade or exotic liquor. And I'd better get that new Hespeler Green Flash.

I do still want to play with my brother Bub's team in Nanaimo. They're a decent squad, and they're fun, and Nanaimo is the perfect town from which to flee after a debauched weekend. I want to look good in front of Bub and his teammates. I want to be a ringer, however unlikely that may seem at the moment. Okay, I'll modify that: I just don't want to be a weak link, an embarrassment, an albatross. That's enough motivation to get in shape, or at least less worse shape. It's something to aim for—to be in enough shape to do something good in Nanaimo. To have one more pretty good shift in my life, with my brother looking on. That's maybe enough to keep me going.

SEX, LIES, AND HOCKEY TAPE

IF YOU DON'T PLAY oldtimers and you just happen to be thinking, "Hey, raw steaming sex couldn't possibly have anything to do with a bunch of older fellows gathering to play our national sport," you would, of course, be wrong. Have you never considered what we do in that room and why we're in there for so long? Has no one let slip the secret about the special tungsten key that our "captain" keeps in his wallet, which, when inserted into the secret lock, makes all the hidden wall panels crank open, the spring-loaded Britney dolls fly out, the lights dim, and the disco balls descend from the ceiling? Have you wives never wondered how it is that your hockey hubby arrives home so tired and strangely content after what appears to be six or seven slow turns around the ice, listlessly batting at a puck?

I'm being silly, of course. Disco balls were renovated out of most rooms back in the eighties.

But it's true that sex does inundate the life of the oldtimer, just as it does the life of most everybody else out there. Though you could also say that sex inundates the life of a celibate monk, seeing as he works so hard to make sure that it doesn't. You know, it's that "Whatever you do, don't think of an elephant" thing. Imagine what a monk's sexual fantasies are like?

Probably similar to an oldtimer's.

Because, face it: for most of us, that's what it's become, a fantasy. I'm not talking about the healthy, normal sex at home with your long-term loving partner, which I'm sure is all very *nice* and everything, I'm talking real sex, the kind that happens when a hockey player meets someone pretty in a bar, and they fuck like crazy all night, and then the next day the hockey player coyly tells the guys in the room all about it, in a delicious series of witty hints, while getting dressed for the game. You know, *that* fantasy.

But at this point I'm aware that a huge chasm is opening up. Some of you, those in your thirties who are new to the oldtimer world, are saying, "Hey, wait a second, that's no fantasy, that's exactly what happened to Ray and Phil last week in Kingston. Except that we aren't so sure about the 'pretty.' Or the 'all night.' And Phil wasn't that witty, and his hints were just sort of, I don't know, *piggish*. And come to think of it, we didn't want to picture any of it, so we just told him to shut up."

So, yes, real sex does still happen in the oldtimer world. On road trips and during tournaments, some guys still do go hunting, and a few do still get lucky. (Though in the wisdom of old age, the term "lucky" is starting to seem very relative since, more and more, the woman we get "lucky" with looks a lot like our very own grandmother did when we were nine.)

In any case, this section is about sex, both the real and the fantastical, that we oldtimers, and pre-oldtimers, have sometimes enjoyed over the years. Rest assured, my eyebrow-raised FeeFee, that none of it has ever been enjoyed by me. One of my old coaches, long dead, once shared with me a pearl of wisdom that I have since learned to live by. He smelled of cigars when he said it, and wore a fedora tilted at an odd angle, had lots of facial scars, and wasn't too handsome to begin with. He looked like he knew what he was talking about, though, when he sighed and told me, "Kid? Just never forget that a good shit's better'n a bad fuck."

ver forgotten. This noble axiom has served me well,
ne out of many a painful complication come closing
nd I have to say that I sometimes pity my teammates for
their apparent lack of such skilful coaching in their early years.

Nasty Extramarital Sex: What Teammates Have Done It, What Cities They Live In, and Here Are Their Names

SOMETIMES ON ROAD TRIPS, especially tournaments, extramarital sex occurs. Now, any of you wives or girlfriends who are reading this, don't despair. Your husband or boyfriend has never engaged in extramarital road-trip sex. It wasn't him. You know it wasn't him. He just isn't the type.

But it does happen to some men who aren't your husband. This you should know. And therefore you should be extremely kind and grateful and sexually generous-as-can-be to your husband for not being one of those other guys. And if you try to be generous to him on Sunday evening when he gets home from that tournament, and he makes up a lame apology as he turns you down, it's simply because he really *is* tired from scoring all those goals he's just told you he scored. He really didn't have road-trip sex. Suspect him only if he returns from a road trip bearing roses. But even then he might just be thanking you, again, for letting him miss your sister's birthday to go play hockey.

Really, sex doesn't happen as much as a wife might think. Especially as their oldtimers get older. At thirty-fivish, some of the guys still have a wild oat or two left to sow, and we teammates occasionally see them working awfully hard to sow it. (Harder than they work on their backchecking, that's for sure.) But for the most part we are all far too old to have this kind of fun anymore. Plus, it's wrong. So we don't even try.

Or if we do, we go through the motions, much like the rituals of a long-dead religion. For instance, my team in Fredericton had a few guys who were still believers. Most of us would be at the bar—let's say in Moncton—and two or three guys would stand off by themselves, lurking on the edge of the dance floor, eyeing the women severely with that Clint Eastwood stare, as if *on the hunt*, looking on the verge of *asking a woman to dance*, as if that would ever happen, but their severely discerning eye somehow never does find *the right woman*, and so they lurk on, and on, resembling mere ghosts of sexual seduction as they hover like grey wisps, forever at the edge of so many brightly coloured breasts and butts bouncing merrily away. Actually, I do remember some actual dancing taking place, but typically a guy ended up with a woman who came up to his belt buckle, or the guy came up to hers, and the one dance was all it took to embarrass the hell out of both of them, and they turned away without a further word.

But sometimes, miraculously, sex somehow happens. There are lots of cool stories.

Some Sex Stories Are Like Fish Stories

THIS WON'T GET as crude as you probably think.

What I mean by "fish stories" is that sometimes, like a salmon, a story will get bigger, longer, and shinier with the telling and retelling. For instance, my brother Bub—who, like me, never lets the facts get in the way of a good story—has a favourite sex story he loves to tell about something that happened to him in—where else—Nanaimo.

I first heard it back when I started playing oldtimers and my brother had been playing it for a few years. He had some stories for me because he'd been to tournaments with a team full of thirty-five-year-olds, some of whom were single and some of whom didn't care if they were single or not. One night he was brutally roused from drunken sleep by some female lips molesting his own. Waking up, he recognized the demonic giggle of his roommate on the opposite bed. The woman kissing him was naked, and she had a tattoo on her arm. The TV blared, a joint smouldered in the ashtray, and freshly opened bottles of beer pointed at the ceiling. Bub was invited at this point to join in the fun, and the woman extended the invitation by performing some kind of gymnastic or yoga move for his viewing pleasure. Bub turned over, clamped two pillows over his head, and tried and succeeded in welcoming sweet darkness back.

I've heard the story in the years since, as my brother parlays it to new teammates whenever the good old remember-when stories come out, usually after we've emptied several tablesful of beer. Over the years, it's gone through some changes. In all fairness to my brother, he might be remembering new bits of truth. Because old age does that, doesn't it? Improve the memory for the long-term tidbits? In any case, I've heard him get woken up by a tongue rammed down his throat, and once he was woken by a nipple, and then it was a pierced nipple. Once, his roommate was standing there, a bit too close, with a hard-on. The woman's invitation evolved into her straddling Bub's face. The tattoo became a series of swastikas, and she had piercings in places unimaginable. The yoga stretches gave way to handsprings the length of the room. I think one time there were some oddly coloured condoms twisted into puppets, and shaving-cream adornments. (Well, maybe now *I'm* making stuff up. I can't really remember.) But the only thing that didn't change was (a) her being naked, (b) a tattoo, and (c) him trying to get back to sleep.

That's how it goes with some stories. But I swear I'm not adding to any of the stories that follow.

Anyone Can Be a Piece of Meat

WHEN I FIRST STARTED playing oldtimers, in Fredericton at age thirty-seven, I came to understand what it means to be what's called a "sex object." Now, anyone who's ever seen me in the flesh might be a bit dubious, but let me explain.

That first season, after a game, I followed a few of my new teammates to a bar. It was called Chevy's, and maybe it was a chain, because there was also one in Moncton. Chevy's was perfect for the oldtimer, no matter what the sport, or even no sport at all, simply because it catered to people our age. At Chevy's, if you were, say, forty-five, instead of feeling horribly like the oldest old fart in the whole establishment (which began happening to me sometime in my mid-thirties, so I stopped going to establishments), you felt right smack in the middle of the age range. What's more, the DJ played *your music*—early Stones, Creedence, Rascals, Motown, Beatles, lots of other stuff. All the old oldies. Neil Young and Santana for those who used to smoke a bit of pot, Kenny Rogers and the Bee Gees for those who didn't. But I have to say that even Kenny Rogers sounded okay on the big honking sound system. Anyway, it was a decent place to have a post–dressing room pint.

But when I walked through the door, it was instantly weird. I couldn't quite put my finger on why, at first. But it reminded me of places I'd been long ago—southern Egypt, for one; northern China, for another. Now, how could that be? I asked myself. What could this place called Chevy's, in New Brunswick, have to do with southern Egypt? Then I realized it was because I was being stared at. I was being stared at with unblinking, insistent eyes—about fifteen or twenty pairs of them.

The only reason I was being stared at was because I was under sixty and I wore pants. It likely helped that my hair was freshly "tousled," and that I looked flush from vigorous activity. The people staring at me were all women, all of them sitting at tables of women only, and these women were aged anywhere from forty to sixty. They were all hungry, wouldn't stop staring, and I felt like a piece of meat.

And I didn't like it. I suffered an instant revelation, a kind of trumpet bellow that blasted the teenager in me, the guy who is still pissed off at all those pretty girls I used to know and stare at, who despite my obvious suffering and yearning wouldn't go out with me. (Meaning, more importantly, that they also wouldn't let me climb all over them in a sexual frenzy.) Like everyone else of my gender, I have harboured this resentment for years. Imagine the paradise, I'd thought back then, getting constantly stared at by all these members of the opposite sex and being able to point a finger at whomever you wanted and then just going off and getting laid! Getting laid simply by saying two words: "you" and "okay"!

Getting stared at there in Chevy's, and then having to turn down lots of requests to dance, I understood that I could say those two words and get laid. It didn't feel that good at all. And I think I caught a glimpse of what it's like to be a woman who gets stared at and hit on, over and over and on and on, whether she likes it or not. Hunger, when it's aimed at you, makes you think poorly of the hungry. It didn't help that a few of them looked like an aunt of mine, a little like Kenny Rogers wearing too much makeup. Or that most were squeezed into incredibly tight jeans, and that some of these jeans really should have been using two chairs for support. (Not to be size-ist, but if you have a two-chair ass you should wear something loose-fitting and dark. I say this as someone with a one-and-a-half-chair ass.)

I did eventually ask a few women to dance, approaching a few of the oldest ladies, those obviously in their sixties. There wasn't much question of sex in the air, so we actually had some fun. I had particular fun dancing semi-slow with a neat older gal to Kenny's "Ruby, Don't Take Your Love to Town," which I believe is about a guy whose babe goes off hunting strange tail because he had his dick shot off in 'Nam. It felt good to be dancing with someone, encased in a musical robe of tragedy. And the dicklessness sounded fine.

But after that, whenever "So—where to, guys?" got asked in the room after a game, I'd always ignore calls for Chevy's and bark back louder about hitting the sports bar, where we could guzzle in peace and—as Naslund popped a nice one, top-shelf—stare hungrily, to our hearts' content, at the big screen.

Professional Road-Trip Sex

I'LL ADMIT with some sadness that the older I get, the less extracurricular sex I see taking place during road trips. I doubt it's because we're focusing more on hockey. I suspect we're just all getting a little . . . tired. And it's not that I want to see guys cheat on their wives, it's just that sex seems to be evidence of youth. And it's sometimes fun, isn't it? So I'm happy to be able to report some sex, even though it was paid-for sex, some time during one of the last several tournaments I attended. (For obvious reasons—namely, my personal safety—I won't identify either the city or the team. For added safety, and to become legally untouchable, I will also say that I'm making all of this up. While I'm at it, let me just say loud and clear that I'm making up this entire book.)

So, all right: recent oldtimer tournament sex. By the Saturday evening, we'd played three games and hadn't done that well as a team. But one player in particular did poorly. I'll call him Francis. Now, Francis didn't do *that* bad, no worse than the rest of us, but for whatever reason, he felt he had let the team down. Normally a dependable D-man, he'd let a few guys get past him this weekend, and he'd suffered a couple of comical cough-ups, putting the puck right on the wrong tape. So he sat there for way too long in his skates, brooding, while the rest of us were enjoying our showers and second beers. It was Saturday night, after all, and we were in a strange town for the night.

Francis was having difficulty shifting into postgame reality, which is that an oldtimers tournament is silliness at the best of times, and what a weird, even stupid thing to have just done, and at our age, no less! Obviously, what really matters here and now are beer, nachos, and, if there's no game on the big screen, then you pivot in your seat and watch the strippers.

So we went to the strip bar (actually, to throw more wives off the scent, I'll say we went to the *peeler* bar, which places us in Ontario.) There, Francis continued his sulk. Even after having pints and drinks forced on him, he refused to sit up straight and take notice of the delightful world around him. Finally, his defence partner got fed up and decided to buy Francis a treat to snap him out of it. Actually, I think the partner was more pissed off than anything. He grabbed Francis by the shoulder and squeezed really hard as he hissed at him, "Francis? I'm getting you a blowjob." From the way it was offered, Francis had no say in the matter.

Some of the boys happened to know that this bar was owned by bikers, and that sex could be purchased and performed somewhere on the premises. Now, I don't know how guys learn this stuff, but I'm always impressed that they do. I was also impressed by how quickly and discreetly negotiations were handled. A couple of guys (his D-partner plus another, fairly wealthy guy who was also disgusted by Francis's sulking) disappeared for minute or two, then they returned and whispered something to Francis,

who nodded seriously, rose, and went off down a dark ha
He had the determined, brow-knit look of a kid who was be
sent to the principal, and he was damn well going to tell his side
of the story. He'd enjoyed a lot of forced beer by now, and he
staggered a little.

The rest of us sat back and guzzled and watched strippers
and, to tell the truth, didn't think much about Francis, whose
sulk was now thankfully being attended to. We did wonder who
he might be with, and some of us moaned aloud at the thought
that he was off with Delilah, the blonde stripper with the face of
an angel and the body of, well, an angel. And suddenly Francis
was back. He plopped in his chair, grabbed a jug, and drank
straight from it. He wore the same severe expression on his face.
Catching up to him, a distinctly bikerish-looking fellow loomed
over Francis, put a hand on his shoulder, and said out of the side
of his mouth to the rest of us, his chainsaw voice having no problem cutting through the strip music, *"You boys keep him out
here. I'll tell you just this once."*

We all nodded eagerly and said, "Yes, sir," and when he
left we all turned to Francis. Francis was still in no mood for
talking, but eventually we pried the story out of him in dribs
and drabs.

"I guess they didn't like me yelling at her."

"Why the fuck were you yelling at her?"

"Well, she was yelling at me."

"Why the fuck was she yelling at you?"

"Because she's an idiot."

"Was it Delilah?"

"Yes."

Collective low moans. Several of us shook our heads in wonder and despair.

"Francis. Concentrate. Why was she yelling?"

"...ldn't let me touch her."

"...h her. I mean, I wanted to . . . *touch* her."

"...did you try to touch her?"

"I—I wanted to kiss her?"

"You tried to fucking *kiss her?*"

"She wouldn't let me kiss her."

"Why did you want to fucking *kiss her?*"

"Was Delilah naked when you were trying to kiss her?"

"Yes."

"And you wanted to *kiss her?*"

"Yes." Francis looked up at this point and almost smiled. His head wobbled a bit, and we could see how drunk he was. He slurred a bit when he said, proudly, "It took two of those giant assholes to get me off her. But I got her on the shoulder!"

By now the defence partner and the other financial backer of the transaction were yelling various things at Francis, about not investing x number of dollars so he could fucking kiss somebody's fucking shoulder. Francis shrugged. He wouldn't apologize. He did look a little happier, though. Somewhere in the tussle, it seems, he saw himself performing well. Finally playing a good game.

Francis's defence partner pointed a finger in Francis's face and said that the next time he played badly and decided to get depressed, he was going to tape the suicide hotline number to Francis's wrist and just shove him out into the snow. It being Ontario here, where there's lots of snow.

The Irresistible Make-out King

OKAY, WE ALL KNOW THIS GUY. It doesn't matter whether he's single (he often is) or married (he's often on his second or third wife). He's the guy who starts yapping as soon as you get in the car, bus, ferry, or plane, on the way to the tournament. He's yapping about the last time, and that waitress he met, or that guy's sister he was introduced to, or even that stripper who was eyeing him last year. He's sitting there, a truly slimy smile on his face, and he's wearing a nice crisp shirt. If you leaned over and smelled him, no doubt he'd smell like some sort of manly flower, pollen just oozing out.

Now, none of us oldtimers are against anybody getting laid. Even if it means committing the sin of adultery. I'm sure even our hard-core Christian teammates would agree, and say only, "Hey, it's none of my beeswax."

The thing is, that excited, pimped-up, studly hustler is *making* it our beeswax because he's not shutting up about it. He's not going to shut up all weekend, and you're going to have to get used to that smile. After half a day of it, you want to accidentally drop your burger all over his shirt. After that Friday-evening game, when guys start voicing the question, "So where we hittin' first?" and one side of the make-out king's top lip rises in a little smile, and he mumbles smugly, "I've got plans," you want to attack him. Just once, I wish we'd coordinate the attack and hit him with a prearranged intervention.

"What's that you say, there, Ernie?" asks the team captain.

"Ooo, I've got some *plans*," Ernie repeats, pleased to be able to elaborate, both eyebrows rising, leaving slug-trails as they do. You can smell his cologne through his game stink.

"We've been talking," says the captain. "I've gotta say, we're worried about you, Ernie."

"What?"

"It's clear," says a well-respected little guy who never says much, "since you talk about it so much, obviously you're covering up some severe sexual dysfunction there."

"Huh?"

"At first," says another guy, a law partner, "we thought you were actually gay, and in denial, but now we know you're not even gay, but a deceptive virgin."

"What?"

"An *evil* deceptive virgin."

"What the fuck?"

We soon have Ernie weeping and repenting, and we get his pretty wife Gail on the phone so that he can profess his love to her, and afterwards apologize to us and promise never to annoy us again.

That'd be so nice.

I've come to understand that team Romeos are just like those team tough guys who are always letting you know how tough they are. It doesn't mean they aren't tough, but they aren't nearly as tough as the guys who don't talk about it at all. Actually, come to think of it, the guy who brags about how tough he is is often the same guy who brags about how much he gets laid.

There was this one guy, I won't say where, who was an incorrigible make-out slime, and maybe the reason behind this rant of mine. I'll give him one thing: he worked like a dog at it. And, well, if a guy's that hungry for some strange tail, then who am I to judge his appetites?

It's just that he drove everybody crazy. Here was his pattern. Friday night, he'd do some serious prowling in the bars. Smelling like a musky violet, moustache trimmed, chest hairs tufting out of his crispy shirt, he'd work like a sly dog until he (rarely) got lucky the first night or (almost always) came away with a phone number or two, scrawled on a napkin. The next day, Saturday, he'd show up in the main room. By "main room" I mean the hotel room frequented by the most guys. We're all quite quiet, being hungover, and typically watching golf. We sit and lie on floors and beds, nudging aside the empty pizza boxes and drying skates. A few guys nurse their first rum and Coke. The room has an iffy, herd-like smell. One guy's fading into the bed, trying to go back to sleep, and he occasionally moans by way of telling us to shut up, seeing as we're now onto rum and Coke number two, and we're har-harring because someone's made a risqué Mormon joke at Mike Weir's expense.

Meanwhile, Ernie has slid into the room. He looks already showered and scented, and his shirt is a new one and crisper than the last. He pretends to watch about thirty seconds of golf, and now he's on the phone. There's a tattered napkin on his lap. He asks, way louder than necessary, "Hi, is Edna there?"

What follows is an hour or two of high-pitched slimy whin-ing and wheedling.

"I know, but why won't you come out?"

" . . . . "

"But that's okay, no I won't."

" . . . . "

"No I won't."

" . . . . "

"I know, but why won't you come out?"

" . . . . "

"But why won't you come out?"

" . . . . "

"Well I can bring a couple friends then." At this he looks up at us and nods vigorously, as if we're hanging on his every word and this is the best thing we've heard all year.

" . . . . "

"So why won't you come out?"

His wheedling and whining shows us what his first wife went through and what his current wife goes through now. After twenty minutes, the phone dripping with slime, he gives up on

Edna and dials the phone again and this time asks for Morag, or Cattywampus. And the wheedling begins again. Guys start leaving the room.

In the dressing room after the game later that night, Ernie says nothing and, if possible, is even more smug than usual. The next morning, he makes sure we all see her leaving his room. I don't know how he manages it—I suspect he makes her leave several times, because somehow all of us always see her leave his room. Her name is something like Ovaltine and she looks like a smuggler's parrot.

Once, while someone like Ovaltine was exiting down the hotel hall—and I swear this is true—our team captain asked Ernie in all seriousness why he didn't just masturbate.

The Funniest Thing I've Ever Seen

THIS ISN'T ABOUT SEX as much as thwarted sex.

Call me juvenile—the chastising FeeFee does almost daily—but the funniest thing I think I've ever seen involves the dumbest of stupid pranks. I was playing for the North Shore Hurry Kings at the time, and it was perpetrated by a teammate named Mike. It was a Saturday night before Thanksgiving, and there was a small turkey thawing out in the fridge at the house where I lived with Bub and a couple of others.

Now, Mike was a big guy, a middle-linebacker type who could "relax" and gain a quick hundred pounds, and then lose it almost as quickly. He was generally in the relaxed mode, and possibly as a result of this didn't get laid as much as some of the guys he hung around with. (And I'm talking about the early-post-disco era, where everyone's twenty-seven and no one's married, and if you owned a Hawaiian shirt and had ten bucks to drop in the bar, you could get laid.) He was also a bit weird for the women. Think of *Animal House*'s Bluto, but a bigger Bluto, and a Bluto who one day would be caught naked in public in some foreign country. The other thing about Mike was that he didn't like other guys having fun, or sex, when he wasn't.

This isn't really a story, so I'll cut right to it. We closed down a bar and a group of Hurry Kings, including the studliest few, came back to our house. Two carloads of surprisingly attractive young women from the bar were also on the way, mostly as a result of the studliest Hurry Kings' gruff and silky words to them. They were either stewardesses or a softball team—I can't remember now. Actually, I think they were a stewardesses' soft-ball team. A good combination, we all thought.

One carload arrived, and Mike didn't like it. He didn't like how the tone of the living room suddenly changed from "us drunk guys having lots of fun" to "you guys trying to be serious and interesting." He didn't like it that women had all that power. Gone were his partners in shooters galore and pig-squeal con-tests, and in their place were urbane wimps checking their breath in their palms and trying to leave early with a chick.

Mike stood by the front door to greet the second carload, which was just pulling up. I suppose I was nervously checking my breath and working up some material when, amid the clicks of girl-shoes stepping pertly up the walk, and Mike's cheerful greetings, the screams started. I arrived at Mike's side just as one girl turned from him and vomited. Others ran back to their car. From inside the house, everyone was throwing questions. Beside the vomiter, one girl just stood and stared at Mike in horror.

Not at Mike, exactly. At his penis. What Mike had done was go to the fridge for a prop, the turkey neck, which he'd attached with safety pins to hang out of his open fly—like a monster dick, like ugliness beyond all imagining. It hung there, about a foot long, a bit of brown flesh showing but mostly all sickly yellow-grey-white skin, with globs hanging from the end, which dribbled down into the evilest little point of yellow, glistening fat. The staring girl's expression said, "I didn't know they could *look* like that."

I don't know which was funniest—the turkey dick or Mike's smile, which was beaming, toothy, and full of sincere joy.

The other carload of young women left too and, not long after, so did the studliest Hurry Kings. It was all some of us could do to keep them from attacking Mike. But Mike, he couldn't give a shit. He continued wearing the turkey neck for a while—it flapped against his knees as he lined up the shooters, food colouring, and cheese—until some time during the night it came off, I don't recall how.

TEAM NAMES

Team Names, Bad

BESIDES BEER, one thing an oldtimers team has in common with a teenage rock band is that, sure, it's sort of important to be good, and to know how to use the equipment in your hands, but it's *way* more important to have a great name. It's even better if you're wearing your great name on your chest as you run a guy into the boards. Young punks in rock bands don't often get to do that.

Not everybody agrees with me about names, apparently. Not about my favourite rock band names (my all-time fave being Bardo Liars, "bardo" being a Tibetan after-death state, like purgatory, where it's *impossible* to lie, so if you *could* lie, and while being questioned by God, no less, well, how cool would that make *you*). And guys don't always agree with me about team names, either.

Here in Victoria I currently play for a team that for thirty years was called the Canadians. How boring, how lame, is that? How generic! I'd rather be called the Humans, because at least that might be cause for debate.

If your city happens to be a provincial or state capital, there is an oldtimer team in it called the Capitals. Probably two, in fact, and probably some late Tuesday night the Capitals will play the other Capitals. Or, if someone in your capital city felt a little debonair while selecting the name, it might be the Diplomats. Or the Senators. Now, my brother played for a team called the Senators for years, and they were a great team, winning most tournaments they played in, and they were a great bunch of guys, earning several "Best Party Team" awards at these tournaments they won—a rare feat, basically because they won despite being the most desperately hungover, if not drunk. The Senators had the usual excellent loonies and true originals on the team. But in the name department they were severely challenged.

Even worse are those stupid dangerous animal names: Tigers, Bears, Hawks, Cougars, Sharks. These animals are all famously fearsome but, really, who cares? These dangerous-animal names stopped instilling fear in opponents, I don't know, maybe hundreds of years ago. I mean, I don't care that the chest of the guy coming at me has the word *Cougar* on it if the guy is forty-two, wears glasses, and does my taxes every April. If that same chest said Sick Armadillo, I'd think twice before getting in his face in the corner. If it said Happy Snails—or, even better, *Escargots de Merde*—I'd think three times. And by then, of course, his biscuit is in my basket.

All I'm saying is, let's have some new animals. And don't get me started on teams named Flyers, Bruins, Leafs, Rangers, etc. I won't even go there. Leaves, I wouldn't mind. Dead Leaves, even better. Buds, okay, but my position here is that every merely okay name is a missed opportunity for a great one.

Team Names, Good

YOU HAVE TO REMEMBER that I'm the writer here, the word guy, so I know what's good.

For instance, I suggested that Buds is an okay name, mostly since it's the common in-joke about Canada's supposed team, the Toronto Maple Leafs. Bud Lites is even a bit better, since it keeps the Leafs pun but also says the team is weak, which is always the cool, self-effacing thing to do, plus it might get the team a sponsorship, by a beer company no less, and there is nothing cooler than that. Bud Heavies would be a bit better name artistically, though the sponsorship might be jeopardized. But think about it: it has at least four puns operating, plus the team is calling itself both tough *and* fat, both of which are pretty decent. Another decent, but maybe over-clever beer name is the Draught Picks. Also in the decent category are names like a Richmond team's, the Seagulls, which acknowledges a common bird of the region while at the same time describing their breakout tactic. (Actually, they're awful to play against because they backcheck like crazy, so the name is also a ruse, which makes them cheaters.) Cute names like the Polliwogs are also decent.

Decent, but not great. I would love to someday see a sweater with Touch Me I'll Have Another Heart Attack on it, but I'll agree that it's long and the sports store would likely charge too much. Same with Old Farts with Big Parts, which my brother Bub floated to his old team as a possible new moniker. He tried the Prunetang on them too, to a similar result. But lots of funny old-timers names have to do with a proclamation of virility (I wonder why that is?). There's the Pollinators, and the Purple Helmets. And the slightly obscure Lewinski's Big Cigar. Some teams are plain old adventurous, and there are some quite bizarre names out there. I've seen or heard tell of the Dung Beetles, the Wounded Moose, and one of my favourites, Soup and Fish.

But it's an art, isn't it? One of the cleverest team names can be found out here on the rainy western seacoast: the Fogduckers. As is the noble team the Vasectomites. These names deserve applause. Another Vancouver name, Friends of Jesus, I have to include in my hall of fame since my brother told me they were dirty, rascally fuckers who were using the name ironically.

There are others. In Winnipeg, a slightly edgy team calling itself the Whispering Doves deserves our respect for some disturbing subtlety. Slightly less subtle, but funnier, is an RCMP team named the Fighting Hedge Sparrows. There's a Toronto team called the Well Hungarians, which is in its own way perfect. And we should applaud the lunatic Flapping Dondalingers.

The team I play for now, the Canadians of so many years, has a new name, and it's decent enough. It was born at a team meeting I missed, so I can take no credit. It's one of those names that's a clever take on the sponsor's name, which in this case is the Finishing Store, an upscale home-improvement company owned by one of our defencemen, the strapping Saskatchewanian. Our team name is now the Finishing Stars. With it came new uni's, the Dallas Stars pattern, so the pun works with the sweater, too. Good job, guys. I understand a lot of beer went down that night, and I'm thankful that something decent came out of it.

My previous team, the New Brunswick team that was originally the UNB Red Faces, also changed names, about two years before I left. It's one of the best names I've encountered in the oldtimer world, and I'm intensely proud of it, though I had little to do with that one either, other than when I enthusiastically cast my vote in its favour. Our team had (maybe still has) a very old fellow playing on it, a septuagenarian (a guy in his 70s, for those of you not good at math). He was so old that he played with the University of Toronto Blues in the era of one-piece sticks and rovers. Anyway, he was not only a good lad, as they say in New Brunswick, but also a minister, specializing in weddings, and also a mycologist, a scholar specializing in mushrooms. He was also something of a flirtatious old bastard. In other words, a very well-rounded guy, if not a full-blown renaissance man.

We had rotten sweaters, just "UNB" printed on the front, giving off the stench of a bunch of boring bureaucrats. I think the logo also made the farmboys, who hated anything to do with the local university, take runs at us—a doubly awful experience because we had nothing to do with the university in the first place. So we were ripe for new uni's, and right about this time a teammate won the lottery, coming out of an office pool with about a third of a million. Good lad that he was, he coughed up for a set of sweaters and socks, home and away. Now we had to think up a name.

We went to the bar after the next game, fuelled with a purpose beyond thirst. A name. A team name. A name! Who, we asked ourselves, *are* we? By what term did we want the world to know us? Waiting for that first tray of jugs, we as a group no longer knew who we were and felt beset by an odd existential malaise. Our eyes flicked this way and that, warily, and none of us liked it much.

Someone asked the gentle old U of T minister mycologist, whom we'll call Norm, what he thought might be a name we could use. Norm sat back for a moment, pleased at being asked. He began to speak.

"I sometimes walk in the woods," he said, and then stopped talking.

"Yeah?" said one or two guys, after half a minute went by.

"I go into the woods to look for mushrooms."

"Yeah?" Followed by, "Looks like we need another round."

"It's part of my old job, actually. Did you fellows know I'm a mycologist?"

We knew. We also knew he'd sometimes been seen out in the deep bush, dressed in gumboots and a suit and tie, probably hunting mushrooms just before, or after, conducting a wedding. Or maybe searching for the wedding, there being a fair number of dirt hippies living in our area.

"I came upon a peculiar species the other day. You don't see it much." Then he spoke some Latin, maybe ten syllables of it. The waitress who was putting down our pints gave him a look that was more irritated than anything. "It's long—about this long." He put his old palms about nine inches apart. "And it's shaped like—well, it's shaped exactly like an erect penis." Now the waitress smiled, happy, I guess, to be back in famil-iar territory.

The guys laughed a bit at this, entertained in that way we're entertained by anything having to do with dicks. By now we had forgotten the purpose of his story.

"But it's a very odd fungus because not only does it have that shape, and not only is it all pocked and ugly, but it smells. And, well, it smells just like . . . shit." He gave the word "shit" all the weight and dignity only an ordained minister can.

We laughed some more. Now we were into a whole 'nother favourite arena, from sex to shit. Life was good, and it was maybe beer number three.

"And it has a strange name as a result. This peculiar fungus is called a 'stinkhorn.'"

I'll cut to the chase here. Yes, we became the Fredericton Stinkhorns, and our new jerseys—forest green for home, a weird grey for away—were emblazoned with those words, plus, below the name, a picture of, for all intents and purposes, a nine-inch, pocked, erect penis.

Needless to say, the debate that night was intense, almost violent. The forces of ignorance, the faction that preferred we be called the Buds or the Flyers or the Capitals, almost won out. I must say I grew loud. I jeered at the anti-Stinkhorn peo-ple and I yelled at them. I called them stupid, because they were. Tonight, in this bar, art was in danger of being thrown into the garbage. In the end—the rum shooters had something to do with it—truth and art won out. The anti-Stinkhorns found themselves mumbling in a kind of agreement, their eyes confused, swimming with beer, on their faces a look of handing over their car keys to a stranger and not knowing why. It was great. The first time they pulled on the new jersey, their faces wore that same look. That was great, too.

Our opponents treated us with instant confusion and respect.

BAD BAGS

REMEMBER THOSE TV COMMERCIALS about smelly hockey bags? They were good. The one I liked best was the guy walking down the sunny sidewalk, hockey bag over his shoulder. The guy's smiling, birds are chirping. As he passes, birds drop dead out of the trees, an old lady faints and collapses, etc. We can see now that his hockey bag is partly open, and God it must stink. And we all nod knowingly. As with all the best ads, I can't even remember what it was advertising.

Anyway, there are some pretty bad bags out there. Maybe you own one. Maybe you're one of the guys on your team who has a famously bad bag. Every team has one or two, and usually their bags are simple examples of slovenly male behaviour. That is, of hockey gear absorbing years of beer sweat and never— *never*—getting washed.

Sometimes a bag is so bad you sort of grow an instinctive hatred for the guy. You find yourself walking into the room, sussing out who's sitting where, and then deliberately not sitting next to bad-bag guy, him with the piss-coloured fumes rising from his gear. Sometimes, sitting there next to him, it smells a bit like a personal insult, this incessant sourness wafting up beside your knee. Like bad breath, it colours everything he says to you. He might turn his head your way and express some pleasantry about the weather, but what he says stinks. His bad bag changes everything.

Sometimes it's so bad it smells like the guy must have some kind of really serious disease. How can such cesspool-rot come out of a healthy, living body? He must be terribly sick inside. Imagine what fun a scientist with a really powerful microscope could have if he pinched up a chunk of the guy's long underwear (the chunk would just come off in his fingers, of course) and stick it under his lens. Actually, maybe it wouldn't be fun for the scientist at all. He could still smell the underwear chunk not far from his nose, and under the lens it would look like his worst nightmare come true: a sudden jungle of steaming, festering, wild monsters all jumping at his face, smelling like violent death.

It's probably not always internal organ failure that makes a guy's bag smell bad. Sometimes it's just practical. Sometimes, for instance, hockey gets played in spring, or even summer, and so a bag full of wet gear gets thrown into the trunk of a car. Where it sits. Let's say the car is black, and absorbs lots of heat. And let's say the guy in question tweaks his knee and doesn't play again for three weeks. Or goes on vacation, enjoying his month up at the cottage. You catch my drift. What's happening in that trunk is identical to what happens on the Galapagos Islands whenever an ocean iguana eats. Ocean iguanas were originally land creatures, who adapted (that is, they adapted if you don't believe in God) to the bare rock islands by plunging into the ocean to eat seaweed, which they weren't equipped to digest. So they fill their bellies with seaweed and drag themselves back onto land, crawl up the black rock, and just lie there. The tropical sun beats down and turns their bellies into an oven, their food cooks and gets absorbed, and they survive another day. Basically, this is the chemistry of our bad-bag guy's trunk. The smell of which convinces you that God does indeed exist, because in the dressing room, when bad-bag guy opens that bag, what hits you in the face are none other than the fumes of Hell.

I'LL CONFESS that I'm a bad-bag guy, but one with some creative flair. That is, mine doesn't smell bad constantly, but only on special occasions.

One October, Kelly (the guy who's now teaching ballroom dance on cruise ships) brought in a bunch of brown paper lunch bags each crammed full of kiwi fruit. Kelly had had a bumper crop, and we each got a bag. (Take that, you bastards back east: we play hockey and then pass around homegrown kiwi fruit!) I had a bite of one between beers and—sorry, Kelly—it wasn't all that sweet. Which I guess is why I just stuffed the bag into the skate compartment of my hockey bag and then forgot about it. It was the following March when a weird little waft alerted me to something. Now, picture what a paper bag of kiwi fruit goes through during five months in a hockey bag. Imagine how many smushings and bashings, how many temperature changes, how the fruit would mutate from jam to shit to crust, jam to shit to crust, over and over again. Suffice to say that, when I pinched something up between thumb and forefinger, what it resembled was a hardly recognizable paper bag in which several fruity rats had died some years ago. Teammates—those with a sense of humour—congratulated me on my new status of best bad-bag guy of the year. Others edged away unsmiling.

I store my gear (and sometimes I even take it out of the bag and dry it) in our store room. It's a decent store room—I even installed a fan to exhaust dampish hockey-gear smells over into my neighbour's yard. So when I spread my gear out to dry, I expect it to dry, and even be somewhat sweet smelling when I next stuff it into my bag. But I have cats. Two cats, one of which "likes" my gear.

One game last year I sat there in the dressing room opening my bag and, *boom*, my face got knocked back by a hefty waft. The guys to either side of me also shouted in disgust and bum-shuffled away from me as far as they could.

I guess I must have been in a hurry, because for some reason I hadn't smelled anything as I packed my gear. But a cat had pissed in a knee pad, basically filling up all the foam. I played with it that night, wet cat piss rubbing its way into my leg all night. When I got home I sprayed it with the hose, but the next day it still smelled. I soaked it in an empty garbage can, using strong soap. It still stunk. In the end, I had to throw the pad out in the rain, spraying rug shampoo and Drano on it, and I left it out there for over a week. You can still smell cat if you stick your nose right in there, but at least the boys aren't yelling at me.

On my brother's team, another bad-bag guy had a wasp's nest growing in his gear one fall, and the first time he laced 'em up a wasp flew out of his bad bag and tried to sting him. I heard of another guy who, opening his bad bag in the dressing room, coming out of a year's retirement, had to kill the dozen baby mice nesting in there.

Go ahead, all you good-bag guys, scorn us bad-bag types. We scorn you right back, but harder. You know who you are. You're the guys with gear that's washed. Even your *bags* look washed, the KOHO or Labatt's logos crisp and unfaded. You stick your skates (after drying their blades with that cute, special little towel) into the proper side pouches, which the rest of us use for road beer. And inside your big, clean bag you have *more* bags: one holds all your fancy shower stuff, like sandals, because you're scared of athlete's foot, which the rest of us know is only a myth, because collectively we've showered barefoot in team scum for a thousand years, and no one's ever caught it. And your fancy mini-bags contain not only shampoo but rinse (here I mumble "girlyboy" and leave it at that), and even a comb, for your hair, which is absurd, because you're only going home to your wife. Another bag holds special pre- and postgame fluid containers, which you will drink at specified times after your single lite beer. Another little bag holds various vitamins and ginseng and bandages and witchy cures, because you are far too afraid of death. Yes, good-bag guy, the rest of us are watching you and we scorn you. At home, you probably rinse your can opener after each use.

I don't have to add that most good bags are also stewardess bags, with those wheels and extendo-handles. I don't care how old you are or how bad your back is—those bags are poofy, girly, and should be banned. Call me Cherry, but the only oldtimer who should be allowed to use a stewardess bag is a goalie, and only if he plays with a shitty team and is routinely tired from stopping fifty shots a game. Some of us have discussed making it a rule that all oldtimers be forced to return to actual duffle bags, those faded olive-green sacks with the drawstring opening at the top. If you can remember those, and are currently using a stewardess bag, you should be ashamed of yourself.

Memory #6: One Hundred French Guys and Me

In France, after my humiliating tryout in Dijon, I said goodbye to Al and Marie-Eve and hopped the next train south, to Toulon, to La Ligue du Sud. The hockey there was apparently of a hopeless quality—like juvenile, said Al.

But at least Toulon needed a player. And at least I wouldn't have to try out.

Al put me on the train with several bottles of wine, for which I was just starting to acquire a lifelong fondness, and so, when I got off the train six hours later, I was in dire need of some food, and bed. I grabbed my suitcase and my skates and entered the town of Toulon. I could smell the ripe Mediterranean somewhere near. The town was cobbled and old, with narrow streets, and smelled pissy in that old-European way. Walking, I entered a part of town with streets so narrow that no cars could pass, and it looked dark and dangerous, as if a real pirate, as opposed to a Johnny Depp pirate, might lurch out of a doorway drunkenly and take a slash at my throat. (This old part of town, I later learned, was called *Cheecago*, because it was basically lawless and run by gangs of heroin merchants.) I decided that this was the perfect place for a fine French meal. Luckily, the word "restaurant" is the same in both languages, so I entered the first one I came to. Because there was no way any French restaurant could be bad.

I had enough money left for a hotel room and this one meal. I pointed to the cheapest thing on the menu. How could any food, in France, be anything but fantastic? This cheap thing would likely be the best thing I'd ever eaten in my life. I sat back and counted my blessings. I was about to land my first job in professional sports. I would be something of a celebrity, maybe even a hero. No matter that the hockey would be bad — if the hockey was bad, I'd look even better, be even more of a hero. And here I was on the Mediterranean, which meant warm water and palm trees. And palm trees meant bikinis, and bikinis and heroes were kind of magnets for one another, weren't they? This *Ligue du Sud* was paradise. Al knew nothing about France, or hockey.

My steaming plate arrived, and while I recognized the rice, and the string beans, the dimpled sausage thing in the middle looked all wrong. Also, and even worse, it smelled all wrong. It smelled really, really bad. It smelled like — well, like some hung-over grandfather guy had just shit on a plate and slid it under my face.

I turned away and took some breaths. I had shared an elegant meal with Al and Marie-Eve and I had learned from the cheese tray that the most elegant things could smell like a goat's ass but still taste rather good. This must be one of those elegant things. Not breathing, I took my knife and fork, cut a little wedge of what I was almost certain was a big intestine, and brought it to my mouth. I put it in. I chewed. I started breathing again, which allowed me to smell, and taste.

Not that I've ever eaten shit before, not in the literal sense anyway, but I knew this tasted just like shit. I gagged. I spit it out. Then groaned and swore. I sat breathing slowly for a while, then waved for my bill.

THE NEXT DAY, completely broke, I found myself in a suburb called La Garde, which meant "the guard" and referred to a gnarly old castle that stood rather dramatically on a little hill in a farmer's field right outside Toulon. (I was to learn that the village of La Garde was pronounced La Gar-DUH, because the *e* that was silent in the rest of France was, down south, down in *La Ligue du Sud*, pronounced loudly, and as a DUH. The word for shit, *merde*, was therefore pronounced *mer-DUH*. This kind of pronunciation made everyone down here, even nice old ladies, sound aggressively stupid.) The rink in La Garde was the only one in all of Toulon, which at the time was a city of about a half-million, and the main NATO port on the Mediterranean. The rink was kind of spectacular for its restaurant-bar, which ran along one whole side of the arena, closed in by smoked glass. Great place to watch a game, I figured.

In my pidgin French and their pidgin English, and with lots of hand-flaps and a little shouting, the team owners and I came to understand that the playing coach they hired would not only play and star for the *Toulon Equipe de Hockey sur Glace*, but also coach their youth teams, and in general run their program. The money they offered sounded fine—I'd actually be able to save some for travel later—and they were throwing in a free apartment, because a guy named NayNay was away, or in prison, I couldn't tell which. I asked if they might just consider throwing a *voiture*, any model, into the deal, but they stared at me blank-faced. I knew it would take a while to crack the mystery of French humour.

So everything sounded fine. I asked them, "When do I start?" and they pointed to a fellow about my age, wearing a Leafs jersey, sitting in a corner of the arena bar, by the window, who I noticed had been casting little glances my way. I'd just assumed he'd been stealing glances at the new Canadian hero. Now I noticed that, like me, he too was clutching a pair of skates.

Side by side, down in the penalty box, Phil and I laced up and got to know each other before our head-to-head battle royale tryout. Public skating was in progress: young French girls zipped past doing spins or hops, and old couples glided slowly, bound together in a weird skating embrace where they held each other's hand behind their backs, a thing I'd seen only in weird old movies. Phil and I were about to join this fray, and compete with each other, on skates alone, while the team owners watched us from behind that wall of smoked glass. I was wishing now that my hair was shorter.

Phil was from Winnipeg. He was just travelling around, he said, and was in the area and heard about this job and thought he'd give it a shot. Trying not to sound like a worried asshole, I told him I was here *only* because of the job, and I think I slid in something about a one-way plane ticket, and no money, and perhaps even something about having been made to eat shit only just last night. Phil was a nice guy. He laughed and said I probably shouldn't worry, he was more or less fooling around, giving it a shot. I saw now that the skates he did up were indeed rental skates. I asked him who he'd last played for, and he said he'd never really played organized hockey. I relaxed a bit. I'd been ready to do something a little desperate, like put gum on the bottom of his skate blades, or something even more Tonya Harding-esque. (Though Tonya was still whacking fellow toddlers in the sandbox at that time, I suppose.)

And though Phil did prove something of a klutz on skates, and I did win this second humiliating tryout without much effort (just to make sure, I did a couple of extra-fast laps to impress the bigwigs behind the glass, and didn't knock down too many kids or old people, I don't think). In fact, Phil was such a bad skater that he would have easily been the worst player on the team, even this *Ligue du Sud* team, which is saying something. Phil was to stick around Toulon for a couple of weeks, and we became friends exploring *Cheecago* together, and I got around to asking him—delicately, without revealing how bad a skater he was—just why it was he thought he had a chance of getting hired by this team as their professional, playing coach? His answer—Well, I'm from Canada, eh?—startled me. Then I thought it was a fine answer, after all. What more does a professional hockey coach and player really need, except to be Canadian? (Though it turned out that Phil was a little strange in other ways. He was by profession—I swear this is true—a hypnotist, and was taking a break from his practice to tour Europe, making some cash on the side by helping people quit smoking and such. He had a certain wistfulness around women, and I kind of wondered about a prairie hypnotist let loose amongst the French beach set. But I never saw anything untoward. Phil did offer to hypnotize me once, saying, "I can help you with your personality, if you like." I asked him what was wrong with my personality. He appeared somewhat surprised that I didn't know, then told me he thought I was, well, pretty dull. Now, let me admit that my personality *is* a bit flat. I know you likely find that hard to believe, what with all the madcap wit in these pages, but I have to confess that, in person, extreme dullness is my curse. In fact—I swear this is also true—in grad school I wrote a novel about an autistic guy who couldn't feel emotion, and my prof supervisor thought it was autobiographical. Yes, he thought I was autistic and bravely writing a book about it. That's how dull I am. I don't try to be. Actually, I think I'm quite funny in person. Maybe the problem is that my brand of "funny" is so dry that people have to *hunt* for the funny. Also, when I don't really care if someone likes me or not, like Phil, I don't even try that hard to be dry—I'm sub-dry, and my humour flakes apart before it even gets to a person. But I digress horribly—this is about hockey, and Phil's offer to fix my dull hockey personality pissed me off, I guess, because that night in a Cheecago restaurant with him I drank more than I usually did and was anything but dull. I grew quite animated, though my memory is dim. Maybe too animated, because that's the last I saw of Phil.)

But I was hired. I was the new playing-coach of the *Toulon Equipe de Hockey sur Glace* of *La Ligue du Sud*. Our league consisted of Nice, Marseille, Aix-en-Provence, Briançon, and a few others. I was given keys to my new apartment and, when I explained my penniless state, an advance on my first paycheque. Clutching my little wad of francs, though it was maybe only twenty bucks, I was *a professional hockey player*.

I was also the coach of their program, and I showed up at the arena for *la training*, two days later. I was excited to meet my teammates, who would become my buddies, the guys I'd go into battle with. I assumed I would be assigned a translator, perhaps an assistant coach. But down in the bowels of the arena, in the dressing rooms and public-skating lace-up areas, I found no translator, and no assistant coach. I found none of the owners, either. Instead, in various rooms, kids of all ages, from eight to eighteen, were climbing into their hockey gear. I asked where the Toulon team was. To this question I got identical responses: a kid of maybe ten would point to his chest, nod vigorously, and say, smiling, "Toulon!"

I eventually found a guy on the senior team—that is, my team. He was dressed in muddy overalls and dumping a duffle bag of artichokes onto the floor of the largest dressing room. People were stuffing them into coat pockets or hockey bags to take home for later. The fellow—his name was Dédé (DayDay), and he spoke fair English—introduced himself as a peasant, which was the local word for farmer. So my first teammate, Dédé, was an artichoke peasant. I asked him why he wasn't dressing for our first practice.

"The senior team, it does not practise."

"It doesn't? Why?"

"There is no need. We are very experienced."

"How'd you do in your league last year?"

"Eight."

"How many teams in the league?"

"*La Ligue du Sud* it has eight teams."

And so on. It also turned out that the senior team didn't practise because there were only two players—and now me, making three—who weren't employed in the French Navy, on a submarine, and out at sea. Except for games. (I never did find out why almost every player on the Toulon team worked on a submarine—the same submarine—and why the sub docked on weekends. It was one of those French riddles, and there were lots of them.)

In a kind of fog, I got into my gear, not quite knowing why. Eventually I found myself out on the ice—along with everybody else. There were a hundred hockey players out there—Toulon's entire hockey program (other than the team I was supposed to coach and play for, that is).

I asked a random little kid why he was here today.

"For our first training," he said, "with our Canadian coach."

I asked another kid, five years older, the same thing, and got the same answer. Apparently there was no league. Or uniforms. Most of them had sticks. Some of them could skate extremely well. This was the program, and I was its coach. I had no whistle. When I skated to centre ice and yelled, some of them stopped, but most of them didn't—this was France. I was Canadian, my skates were on, and so although my first impulse was to be polite, my second was to get violent.

THIS SEASON SO FAR

January

CHRISTMAS HAS BEEN ENJOYED and survived. The reason I bring up Christmas is because Christmas is inextricably linked to oldtimer hockey in three ways. One, there's a break in the schedule so you get even more out of shape. Two, there's the increased consumption of specialty beers, notably those dark, 8 percent kinds. Reason number three is gravy.

Like lots of oldtimers, I make an excellent gravy. We let the others—wives and aunts and people like that—handle the minor stuff, the brussels sprouts and the cranberry sauce and the weird orange potato–marshmallow crap, and we let them throw the turkey in the oven and turn it on and announce that it should be ready by five. But the actual *cuisine*, the gravy, gets left to the person who truly knows, who has an intimate way with, fat. That person is typically the oldtimer of the house. I won't give my gravy secrets away at this point, because I'm in the early stages of writing an oldtimer cookbook. Suffice to say that it's excellent, and uses dashes of fresh lemon juice, Chardonnay, Bengal curry, goat milk, unbleached flour, fresh cracked pepper, balsamic vinegar, plus—of course—the blackest giblet scunge scraped from the bottom of the turkey pan. So good is my gravy that my family and friends tend to forgo the other stuff and just chug it desperately, letting it run over their faces like marathon runners gulping water at the finish line.

Needless to say, since it's mostly fat, gravy slows a guy down for a while. Gravy is funny that way. It begins as solid turkey fat, gets melted down and eaten, then becomes oldtimer fat. It's your basic transfer. But the point is, it can take a number of games to work off. Flushing with beer—the regular, non-Christmas kind—helps.

Also on the Christmas front, the world junior tournament was great again. You can't beat a close international game. I love it when Canada's down 3–2 in the third and we start throwing our bodies at everything that moves, and the other team finally coughs up the puck behind the net, generally due to common-sense fear that they're going to die, and then some freckled mucker from Moose Jaw stuffs it in *right through* the goalie, to tie it up. Good old Canadian hockey. Then we score a beauty, a three-way pass worthy of the old Habs, to win. Love it.

Back to oldtimers. Midway into this month there was a tournament I'd long been dreading: the Pacific Cup. We Finishing Stars enter every year, and every year I dread it.

It's in Victoria, so there's no road trip involved, so most of the fun is gone. It just feels like a bunch of games crammed into a weekend. Also, most of the teams are really good and they have their way with us. Lots are prairie teams, here to get a break from the Canadian winter, which, I'll take obnoxious pleasure in reminding everyone, we don't allow here. The prairie teams typically come mostly to golf. They also bring the wives, so the drinking quotient tends to be modest, and we aren't guaranteed that we'll face a hungover team in the morning, which is the only reason I can see to enter a tournament in your own town. We generally have to play the dreaded Saskatoon Pic-a-Pops, who are a well-oiled machine, look as healthy as Mormons, and get up at sunrise for eighteen holes of golf and then have no problem thrashing us a couple hours later. So good are they that they wear practice jerseys—numbered, but no logo or name on the front. It's frightening. It's like playing ex-NHLers, or guys from a maximum-security prison, I can't tell which.

The other reason I dread the Pacific Cup is because of the whole Christmas-gravy thing, as discussed. And this year I'd skated maybe six times since the previous March, so I wasn't sure I'd worked off *last* season's gravy yet. And this season's gravy had transferred what feels like triple the turkey fat to my ass and, for some reason, my face.

But we got a good team together for it. Big George took time off from amassing money to show up, and our wily captain, Dougie Mac, healed just in time. Bernie didn't come out of retirement, but he did come to watch a couple games and have a beer in the room later. Plus my main linemate, Dave, has just turned fifty, and since we're in the plus-50 division, he should have by rights been hopping and dangling like a rookie out there. In all, our lineup was quite solid. A couple of our weaker players didn't play at all. (I'm not sure what's up—did Lyle have a hand in this? Are we starting to stack our team? Make cuts? I'm not sure I want to know.)

The most glaring part of our lineup, though, was a ringer. Now, Murray isn't your typical ringer. A typical ringer is a guy who's maybe about as good as your other best guys, and who helps your team with a goal-a-game contribution. But Murray was the ringer of ringers. A D-man, he played NHL with the California Golden Seals (remember the white skates?), and WHA with the Houston Aeros. Now, there's lots of ex-pros floating around oldtimers, but they tend to be as fat and slow as the rest of us, and are identifiable mostly by their bullet passes and genius down low. Murray, though fifty-one, is a just-retired cop who has never stopped playing and has never not been in shape. He has abs, and he flies. In the shower his legs look like a nineteen-year-old speed skater's, and if I was a pro scout they'd make me horny.

It turned out to be weird, though, having Murray on the team. It was thrilling to watch him pick up the puck and go coast to coast, beat their D-man to the outside and get a hard snap shot on net. Murray's still a true D-man, though, in the sense that even in oldtimers he doesn't quite have the hands or the timing to make a move on the goalie and roof it. But his skating is world class, and he can rip it. We scored nineteen goals in the five games, and Murray got eight of them, mostly on end-to-end rushes.

I haven't even mentioned the defensive part of his game, which was of course stellar. So, basically, he ended up winning the tournament for us. But the victory felt off, I guess because it wasn't "us," wasn't our team that did it. So in this regard ringers are questionable. In fact, after the final win, the feeling in the room was downright hollow. A few guys remarked on it later. It's different if your regular team digs down and busts ass and somehow wins. That feeling is great. It's certainly different than knowing that you merely grabbed a better ringer than the other teams did. The thing is, we *maybe* could have won without him. Probably not, but there was a chance.

And the tournament felt off, for me, in another way. It was an ego thing, the curse of a guy who used to be good but now isn't, mostly because he's in such rotten shape.

The thing is, like any ten-year-old, I wanted to impress Murray. I wanted him to know I was one of our team's best guys, and that I was a scorer on the team. I wanted him to know that I had played junior and university, and could have made it all the way if only I'd worked out a bit in the summer and taken things more seriously and caught a break and, you know, "tried."

Mostly, I wanted Murray to see that I was *a guy worth pass-ing to*.

But I wasn't. I was just another slug. I did end up getting five goals myself, mostly because, despite my two layers of turkey, I still possess a decent shot. But I was just another slug to Murray. I remember one play: it was in the final game and I was carry-ing the puck up the left wing through the neutral zone. I was fresh off the bench and had some rare wind and I was going to go in and do something dangerous this time, yes I was. Suddenly, just as I hit the red line, *whoosh*, Murray blows by me, a full head of steam. He nears their blue line, lays his stick down, and gives me a little look-back, so I send him the puck. He goes around their D-man and gets another good shot on net, but it was weird—I'm skating as fast as I can, but I'm so slow that my own D-man breaks by me and I have no choice but to hit him with a pass!

I'm that slow now . . .

And playing with a guy like Murray hammered home how relative this oldtimers game is. I mean, *anyone* can be the star if he plays with guys who are shitty enough. And *anyone* is shitty if he plays with a bunch of stars. I guess I didn't like the feeling of being shitty. I mean, *that* shitty. Being made to see clearly that I am that shitty. Thanks, Murray. And thanks, Time.

The tournament also felt a tad sour because of the whining, which didn't take a holiday for the tournament, but actually escalated. If a certain guy made a really bad pass, certain other guys would actually *yell at him in anger* from the bench. We are now officially on the verge of becoming one of those teams that might suffer a humiliating fist fight on the bench.

I now realize that *I'm* whining. I'm whining about the whin-ing! See what whining does to a team?

But I want to see what remains of my hockey career in a positive light. Even though I resembled a slug out there, I do know from experience that those five intense games over three days will translate into a bit of shape down the road. I felt no bounce out there, no jump, not a bit, and I'm beginning to wonder if I'll ever have jump again, but five games in three days might be the ticket. We'll see in a week or two. All I really care about, anyway, is getting a bit of jump for the Nanaimo tournament with my brother Bub's team.

And another bit of good came out of the Pacific Cup. My back wasn't horrible, mostly because I pounded it into stupidity with ibuprofen again. Still, by game five it was pretty sore and very stiff and I suspect my skating style resembled, more than anything, an Ent—one of those giant trees in *Lord of the Rings*. Afterwards, my style of crouching over the beer cooler to obtain a cold one caused a spare D-man, Doug, to laugh and ask, "Lower back?" He went on to tell me that over the years he's tried absolutely everything for his back, from acupuncture to exercise to herbs to traction. And by far the best thing for it, he told me, turned out to be an inversion table. A what? I asked. He said, "Remember when Richard Gere hung upside down by his ankles in *American Gigolo*? That." Doug added that they were on sale at the superstore near him in Colwood.

So I've just bought one. You don't actually hang by your ankles completely upside down. It's a table you lie on, and you can angle it anywhere from a little upside down to a lot. The idea is that, instead of letting age and gravity compress the discs between your vertebrae, making you increasingly shorter and older-looking and bent over with a cane, you use gravity to reverse that process, which results in making you look exactly like Richard Gere. I haven't tried it yet. I wanted to, but the severely compressed FeeFee grabbed it from me and strapped herself in as soon as I bolted it together, so I haven't had a chance. But I'll let you know. Especially if my wife turns into Richard Gere.

And it's all for the Nanaimo tournament. I've talked to my brother. He tells me they have a couple of new guys off the Friends of Jesus (or FOJ for short—see "Team Names, Good") who are really good, and he hopes they come to Nanaimo. He sounds in worse shape than me. He enjoys his Christmas treats even more than I do. On the phone his voice sounds a little squeezed and honking, like an actual fat person. He still smokes and, of course, drinks heavily at tournaments. Great—in Nanaimo I'll have to worry about him dying. You really don't want to die in Nanaimo. I have an image of us staying up all night, as usual, and then playing in slow-motion agony the next morning, and me hitting him in the foot with a badly hungover pass, and him briefly shrieking in pain while looking at me in wonder, and then going down, dead. He'd laugh at that one. But he'd agree that it's still probably too soon for either of us to die, entertaining as it might be.

OLD MEN SHOWERING NAKED

Practical Jokes or Practically Jokes: Outrageous, Juvenile, and Sickening

I DON'T MEAN TO get your hopes up with a subtitle. Basically, the whole idea of middle-aged guys in a shower room, soaping up, is ridiculous, a sobering kind of sight gag. Nature's cruel joke, if you will. But it not only looks real funny in there, it sometimes also *sounds* real funny, because lots of funny stuff gets said. I don't know what it is, but get a bunch of guys together, dress them up in colourful outfits and steel feet, exhaust them from chasing some black rubber, give them a few beers, and they start saying and doing funny things. This section is intended to be extraordinarily funny—and as a result, it probably won't be—because it's *about* funny. Much of it is also extraordinarily juvenile. I've looked it over and seen that most of it is about shit, pain, or sex, usually sexist sex. I have no excuses.

The Wittiest Room in the World—But You Had to Be There

IF BEAUTY IS IN the eye of the beholder, then humour is in the ear of the listener. What's more, the problem with wit is, as they say, "context is all." What they mean by that is, if I tell you a guy in the room farted and we all laughed like crazy, you'll assume we were drunk imbeciles and wonder why a professional writer such as myself would even report such a thing—until I supply some necessary background detail.

Doesn't it change things when I explain that the farter was a fifty-eight-year-old mail carrier named Philip who, in all the years he's played oldtimers, has famously never ever farted before? And that he was in fact *anti*-flatulent, would get mad at farters in his vicinity, coughing in disgust and shaking his head and even turning a little pale? And that Philip not only never let wind, but he also never scored, yet he had just scored the winning goal tonight. And, finally, that Philip had also, just today, worked his last day at the post office, and was now officially retired? Doesn't all that detail change things immensely? Because here we are, after the game, and it's boisterous, and someone mentions that, hey, Phil scored a rare goal on the very day he retired. There's a minor cheer in the room, then a lull, and then Phil farts. It's a modest toot, and Phil wears a little half-smile of irony. There's shock before the room erupts. We've all had a couple of beers, we all get it, it's perfect, and in this particular moment it's the funniest thing any of us has ever experienced.

The thing is, in a dressing room, you encounter "the funniest thing we've ever experienced" a couple times a week. You sometimes get a handful on any given evening.

It's not always farts. Ninety percent is, but some is the wittiest, most abstract, wise, and existential mirth I've ever heard. I have to say it feels kind of artificial, even hopeless, to try to describe some of the funny times. Too often, you simply *had* to be there. Too much of it is untranslatable. Often a good riposte rises magically out of the energy, the spirit, of the room. Sometimes it's just the way a guy does a double-take with his eyebrows.

And lots of times the joke depends on prior knowledge, as it did with the story of Philip retiring, scoring his goal, and farting.

Or if I'm sitting there in the room one September with St
and Mike walks in, and Mike sports a severe new beer gut, it's
funny when Steve says to me, "Shit, knocked up again." But it's
funnier when you know that Mike used to be even fatter, and
that he lost a bunch of weight for three or four years, and he's
just freshly gained it back. It also adds to the picture if you could
see Mike, and imagine him as a woman being impregnated.

So these are some of the insurmountable obstacles I face in
this section. But like an old blind dog I'll try mounting them
anyway. I'll also try to keep it as juvenile as possible, for a
change. I'll just add that some of it's just stupid and corny, some
of it's only weird—but all of it's true. Some of you might see
friends here, or maybe a mirror.

Shit Wit

THERE'S AN OLD FRIEND of mine, a guy we called Black
Mike because of his hefty mood swings, who was disgusted by
shit. Now, sure, *everyone's* disgusted by shit. The few cave dwellers
who enjoyed rubbing it on their forehead probably didn't get to
mate a lot, so shit-disgust has probably helped determine our
evolutionary success, and thank Darwin for that. In Black Mike's
case I'm talking about *abnormal* disgust, the kind that makes a
person turn pale and leave the room if the topic of poo-poo even
comes up, which can happen when boys pop beers and things get
a little, shall we say, casual.

In one Canadian city there lived an abnormal oldtimer like
this, a fairly nasty guy I'll call Vlad the Impaler. He was abnormal in lots of ways, only one of which had to do with fecal
abhorrence, a topic I'll return to shortly, since shit is how Vlad
got his comeuppance.

Vlad was not the nicest person. Or, put it this way: he was an
arrogant dickhead who liked to throw his weight around, or

ts of guys think it's part of the game to stick you

ay with it, but only a very few take this habit

aturity, and oldtimers. Vlad was one. His spe-

ɔu on your ankle pain-bone (actually his spe-

cialty was to show you that your ankle *has* a pain-bone). His other specialty was to stick only those guys he knew wouldn't chase him around the rink to hurt him back. Vlad was also the player-manager of one of the longest-running teams in town, and he ran it like a little kingdom. He picked the lines, he cut guys who didn't pass to him enough. If he could suck up to and seduce five ringers, he'd quite heartlessly tell his team's five least talented guys that they couldn't come to a tournament. That sort of guy. Lots of guys wouldn't play with him on principle, but he had great ice times and he kept things organized, so enough did.

In any case, since he bullied in the room as well as on the ice, there came a time, after a few decades of such behavior, when virtually everyone on every team in town, including his own, hated him and wanted some kind of general revenge. Being the gentle sorts that oldtimers are, rather than gang up and take revenge by clubbing Vlad's ankle pain-bone until he was dead, his team decided to more cleverly exploit his weakness, which, if you recall, has to do with his aversion to shit, an aversion everyone on his team knew about. This is a classically dumb and corny gag.

A guy on Vlad's team, Kenny, had famously bad gear. Whether because of superstition or laziness, Kenny's underwear was stained and ragged, and he was always ribbed for it. Kenny didn't mind—quite the opposite, because he was a little wild, if not imbalanced. Vlad the Impaler was more disgusted than most by Kenny's underwear, and his comments lacked any humour. After one game, they waited until Vlad was in the shower. In on the plan, Kenny went to shower too. Meanwhile, a generous gob of peanut butter was applied to the appropriate spot in Kenny's underwear, which was well positioned on the wall hook. Kenny made sure he exited the shower right about when Vlad did, and he followed Vlad to where they sat side by side, also part of the plan. Towelling off, approaching their spot, talking about the game, Kenny stopped and squinted at his underwear, saying, "Really?" He went up to it, asking incredulously, "Did I—?" Vlad, of course, is watching as Kenny puts out a curious finger, scoops up some peanut butter, and puts it in his mouth, mumbling and shrugging, "I guess I did."

Vlad the Imapler tripped over a bag on his dash to the toilet and he didn't make it in time.

I APOLOGIZE for calling any of the above "wit," but it rhymed with "shit" and made a decent title.

Five Minutes for Driving

THE NEXT BIT ISN'T TOO WITTY either, but it's one of the funniest things I've seen, on or off the ice.

I'll call him Viper.

We were an infamous intermediate team—"intermediate" meaning beer-league for guys who still want to play some semi-serious hockey. It's "senior" for towns that lack senior teams. Also, in intermediate there's a ridiculous amount of hitting and fighting. We were infamous because the majority of our guys enjoyed the hitting and fighting part maybe a little too much.

In any case, Viper was an oddity on our team for a number of reasons. For one, he was the best fighter on a team of good fighters. For another, he was easily the worst skater. But mostly, he was odd for the paradox he embodied: he was the lousiest guy on the team but the only one on the team who'd been drafted. (I don't want to get more specific than this, because I don't want

Viper to come and get me. You won't, will you Vipe? I'm mostly praising you here, I think.)

Viper did score a few goals for us, largely because he could bash away at rebounds with impunity, and sometimes when he carried the puck the two opposing D-men would part like the Red Sea. If any poor enemy D-men took him out as they were supposed to, then they also had to fight him, and lose. Viper was easily the best fighter I've ever played with. He had fists at least as large as his head, which was actually kind of small and a poor target, and he had that patient style, much like Tie Domi's, where he'd let five ineffectual punches graze his head before launching a few of his own. He wouldn't turn his head like Domi, but rather would bob and weave like a boxer, or a snake. His punches could inflict actual damage and injury. He loved the whole process. He would fight in practice if anyone felt like it. "Feeling like it" was apparently signalled by getting too close to him in the corner and actually touching him. In one practice, Viper beat up one of his good friends pretty badly. But there was no animosity afterwards, not at all, such being the friendly nature of our national game.

Our team enjoyed lots of brawls, and a dilly took place near the end of a second period. Both benches had emptied, and the ice was scattered with (a quick calculation) sixty gloves. One fight would sputter out, then another would start. Jersey-less guys cruised around looking for more action. Most guys were just hanging onto a counterpart, fists clinging to a jersey neck, talking about stuff but making sure they held on. One linesman had Viper, the other linesman the other team's tough guy. They'd both fought a couple of times and were done. Eventually the ref had the timekeeper blast the siren to end the period, then again a minute later. Still there were pockets of guys wrestling, tugging jerseys, guys taking a breather then starting up a fresh ruckus. So the ref told the Zamboni guy to drive on and start flooding.

The gates opened and the Zamboni crept along the boards towards a pile of guys. The driver stopped five or six feet away. He waited awhile, then honked, waited some more, then revved his engine. No one moved.

Except Viper. He ripped himself free of the lineman's grasp and flew to the Zamboni, where he reached up, grabbed the driver by the lapel, and dragged him down. He began pummelling the Zamboni driver with one fist, holding him down with the other. He hit him a couple of good ones but, incredibly, he also delivered those light, shortened speed punches goons use to show the audience they're winning because of how many punches they're getting in.

The driver made no attempt to fight back, and the three zebras and a few players dragged Viper off. For one thing, this remarkable spectacle worked to stop all the other fights. Everyone, lots of them laughing now or just shaking their heads, began the process of finding their own gloves and sticks. Eventually everyone went through the gates to their dressing rooms. The driver not only got up, climbed aboard, and finished his flood, he also never did press charges. I love this game: even the Zamboni drivers are in on the spirit of its violence, whereby it's all fine and legal if it takes place on the ice. (That is, legal until the era of McSorley, Bertuzzi, et al.)

But I see that yet again I've failed to supply an anecdote that contains anything resembling wit, which is the topic of this section. Unless reverse wit counts: apparently, Viper was dead serious when, after the brawl, he clomped into the dressing room and said, quietly, "That guy could have hurt somebody."

Untranslatable

I CAN THINK OF literally tons of cool one-liners that had the boys in stitches but, again, you really had to be there. The time a guy found a crumpled and forgotten team photo in his bag and threw it in the trash can, and another guy delicately plucked it out and stowed it in his gear, saying his wife was out of town and he "needed some porn for later." It was riotous at the time. It would help if you could see the team — aside from being collectively ugly, we're also grey, paunchy, and wrinkled.

There's the shampoo in the gloves, the tape on the skate blade, the stick blade plunged in the pissy toilet for luck. There's the secretly-shaken-then-politely-handed-over beer. There's the insulting each other's wife, mother, or ability to play hockey. There's the bullshit fantasy girlfriend you met last weekend, and how drunk you both were, and later you noticed the little camera, so you're probably naked on the Internet now — thank God your wife isn't into computers much or she'd see that you *can* get it up twice.

There's the guy with the buggered knee who came along to the tournament anyway, thinking he might play, but drank all day instead. He stood out at the bench to open the gate until it became clear, even to him, that he was gumming up the works, so he just stood there. During play he had to piss badly, but he'd have to walk across the ice to get to a bathroom, so he decided to use the garbage can — a huge old oil barrel — that sat between benches and in full view of thirty-odd spectators. He was decent enough to turn his back on the crowd, but he had to go on tippy-toes because the oil barrel was so high, and he fell, fully exposing himself, hurting his knee worse, the golden arc of stray piss a thing of beauty.

There's the image of the huge D-man, at another tournament, who'd forgotten his skates, but such was his passion to play that he wore the only skates anyone could find for him, about two sizes too small. He was in agony, and between shifts he couldn't sit on the bench but had to pace behind it, and on the ice his skating style now resembled a cross between a ballerina *en pointe* and a running baby.

None of this is much more than startlingly juvenile, considering our age, and I'm even more startled when I recall how, not that many years ago, two of my teammates, who were respectable citizens except when on the road at tournaments, tried to take advantage of two nice-looking women by pretending to be a friendly deaf-mute simpleton and his case worker. Ethically disgusting from the word go, their plan degenerated into pleas to "devirginize" the poor man because it was his birthday, and then the bar was lowered again, when it became clear their ruse was winning them no nooky, to a few drunken gropes and slaps and shouting.

There's the guy, yet another D-man at yet another tournament, who got almost fatally drunk the night before, but we forced him to play anyway because otherwise we would have had to forfeit due to lack of players. It was about the third shift when an opposing winger had the puck and came bearing down on him, getting by him easily. The D-man, actually trying to check him, couldn't move his feet but he vainly pivoted his body anyway, the vomit shooting from his wire cage as he did so.

None of this is what you'd call witty, but it does soften the hard edges of the day.

I was playing in this one tournament with my brother Bub's team and we won. We were sitting around, gently inhaling our beers, our glow a bit brighter from victory. A surprise bonus arrived when, along with the winner's box of Labatt's Blue windbreakers, they also delivered to us a giant party platter of meat: rolled-up ham and roast beef and pastrami and cheeses and olives, along with those neat toothpicks with the red plastic tassels on one end. It's the only time I've ever seen a bonus meat platter at a tournament, but there it was. It got plopped down in an empty spot. Soon enough, the guy whose spot it was returned from the shower, vigorously towelling off his face, and sat on it. He screamed when his bare ass got intimate with all that cold deli meat, and this was funny enough. But it got instantly funnier once we saw the potential. The thing is, Parker was out of the room getting his expensive cigar. Almost nothing needed to be said. Several of the boys took turns sitting bare-assed in the meat. But understand that these new asses were postgame, pre-shower asses.

And while these asses are taking turns going meat to meat, here's something about Parker. He's a generous and decent guy, who long ago played junior and then in Sweden, but who, like so many of us, has gotten rather portly. Parker, though, has grown an old-fashioned, elegant, Jackie Gleason kind of portliness. He favours gigantic cars and hefty cigars that cost more than a case of beer. He'll suffer an occasional lager but prefers martinis—martinis with a hard-to-find brand of gin. After games he combs his hair, applies unguents to it, and uses talcum powder in his various fissures. His pants have creases, and I doubt he even owns jeans. I could go on about Parker, but to sum him up for good and all, he also sometimes wears these sock things—I don't even know their *name*—these little mini garter belts that go around each calf and daintily hold up the dress sock below it. I think I've seen them in movies, when they want to establish that the guy's a billionaire, and it's weird to see them worn in a dressing room. But that's Parker, and he was wearing them the night of the meat platter.

Parker returned from retrieving a giant cigar from his car. He struck a pose to light it, with one foot up on the bench, which hitched up a trouser cuff, which allowed us to see one of those little garter belts. He puffed his stogie. Now, Parker is not above relishing a bit of praise, and the boys had decided to praise him for the pretty goal he'd scored today, helping the team to victory. (For a Gleasonesque man, he scores bushels of goals. He still has the hands.) The captain delivered a little speech about Parker's goal, and his valued presence, and Parker listened to all this, properly touched. He was presented with his platter of deli meats, which he began to sample, because he does love to eat. He ate a curled ham, and some turkey breast, and a wee hunk of smoked cheese. Then a—what's this? It wasn't until he plucked and stared at the pubic hair that the room, as they say, exploded.

Nicknames

WHILE PLAYING UNIVERSITY HOCKEY, I got a nickname that stuck. It took me a month to tell my then girlfriend because, as I predicted, it would make her mad, make her question my involvement in the violent game of hockey. She was a pacifist, in every way a true *girl*, which I suppose is why I liked spending so much time in the dark with her in the first place.

Anyway, I won a fight once. This is no deluded memory, I actually did. It took me until university to do it. (Actually, I won one in bantam, but I can't count it because the other guy didn't seem to know what I was doing and didn't fight back. And I sort of won one in midget, in a tournament in Quebec, but my single haymaker didn't connect with the fast little guy's head, and by then about ten other little guys had jumped me, and the rest of the fight resembled that scene in *Gulliver's Travels* when big Gulliver is pinned to the ground by all manner of little ropes and such.)

We were in Winnipeg, playing one of the universities there. I forget whether it was U of M or U of W. In any case, one of those institutions of higher learning offered up one of its student bodies for me to beat the shit out of. *Oh* yeah, that's what I did. I remember it well. I was being a good defenceman and had followed this guy, a bit smaller than me, around behind our net, and pinned him there. Maybe an elbow got a bit overactive. Escalation of hostilities commenced, a kind of arms race in microcosm, and before you know it this guy slugged me in the face, glove on. Now, in university hockey, a bare-fist fight will get you thrown out of the game, so some guys go at it without dropping the mitts. I always thought that looked a little pussy, a little too much like a slap-fight, so I dropped my gloves, ready to continue my career, well developed in junior, of tasting a bit of fist-flesh.

But the guy's glove-thumb caught my nose tip and it stung me, woke me up or something, because suddenly I'm wailing away. With both hands. *Windmilling* the guy. I guess I was mad. I don't know if many connected—lots of glancing ones. I bet his ears felt the shits for weeks, and I'm guessing he lost some temple-hair. He might even have been laughing—a sort of Holy-shit-what-the-hell-is-*this?*—such was the bizarre intensity of my onslaught. The prairie fool had likely never taken on a windmill before.

Anyway, long story short, I was kicked out and was all nice and showered as the rest of the boys came tromping in, and one of them—I remember it was Bobby MacAneely—looked at me in that sly way of his and said, happily and simply, "*Thrasher!*"

I had the name for the four years I played at UBC. The fourth year, when I lost a particularly ugly fight—ugly because I believe I turtled, though the guy was half my size—the name morphed for a while to Thrashed. But whenever I run into one of the guys, twenty-five-odd years later, it's still "Hey, Thrash!"

My girlfriend eventually came across and started calling me Thrasher, too—but, I like to think, for different reasons.

I'll get my other nicknames over with. My first was applied when, very early in my drinking career, I vomited in a friend's older sister's bedroom in the middle of the night. I opened a door in the dark, and assumed it was a bathroom and that therefore a toilet was right in front of me. So for a while I was Billy Boof-Boof. Then on hockey teams I was Gasser, which is the nickname I wish had stuck. In junior high, since my brother's nickname was Parrot, mine became Brother Parrot. Sometimes these days, at age fifty-two, I get called Willy.

There, that's me, I've exposed my soft underbelly. Now I can attack.

Oldtimer nicknames tend to be more witty than funny. Some of them can be nicely weird. Gone are the days—those corny old days, south of the border—when guys were Stretch, Fatty, Legs, Tiny, Dutch, Mack, or Bubba. I'm not talking about media nicknames, those pompous and awful things that somehow stick: The Great One, Mario the Magnificent, Mr. Hockey, the Golden Brett. Actually, those are not nicknames at all. They are royal titles, bestowed by a slavering press. Nicknames are what guys use in the room to get you to pass some tape. I mean, imagine the following, in the Team Canada dressing room:

"Why, hello there, The Golden Brett!"

"How are you doing, Mario the Magnificent? I did not know you were going to play for your country in this particular international tourney."

"Nor did I, The Golden. It was The Great One who finally persuaded me."

"Well, thank goodness he did. And is it true that The Russian Rocket purchased two plutonium knees on the black market and is making a comeback? I was—holy cow! Mario the

Magnificent, look at who has just come in the door: it's The Next One!"

See? It's all wrong. There's no way Bure's making a come-back. And there's no way Crosby's the next one.

Even in the big leagues, real nicknames tend towards the ironic and weird. I might be wrong, but from what I've heard, Don Cherry's "Grapes" didn't come about because a grape is a cherry-sized fruit. It's because Cherry had hemorrhoids way back when it was still fun to make fun of them. Ed Jovanovski, called Jovo Cop by the adoring press and TV commentators, is simply Jovo to his teammates. Apparently, though, because he makes so many iffy passes in his own end, more than a few call him Special Ed. Though likely not to his face. There are some good goofy ones, like Stumpy, Slats, and Mom. And you can't beat Punch as a nickname. And what would life be like if you were known as the Hammer? Finally, there are those downright clever goalie ones: the Bulin Wall. The Dominator. Some, like Olie the Goalie, just fall into a guy's lap.

Most NHL nicknames are boring, though. There are mil-lions, but to stick just to west-coast examples we have Nazzy (Naslund) and Bert (Bertuzzi) and Klooch (Cloutier) and Mo (Morrison). That's the usual pattern. Nice and buddy-buddy. Some guys, though, don't seem to generate nicknames. Or they're extremely subtle. Daniel Sedin's nickname is, I believe, "Daniel," while his brother Henrik's is the extremely dry "Henrik." (Though I believe that, as a pair, they are referred to as either the Porcelain Sisters, or Children of the Corn.)

Anyway, oldtimer names are better.

Lots of nicknames don't leave the room, and for good reason. On my brother Bub's team, as I have mentioned, there are no Cs or As on any of the jerseys, but rather an S, a B, an I B, and an L. The L stands for Lesbo, because of one guy's almost magical propensity for hitting on that particular kind of woman. The S is for Spanky (see "The Season So Far, February"). The B is for Blowjob, after a team poll was taken as to who still received them after all these years of marriage, and one guy was honoured with a sweater-letter because it turned out that he had enjoyed one just that day. The "I B" I'm still not telling you about.

Also on my brother's team there's the Deacon, a name he's had since bantam, because he's got moves like no one else. There's J Lo, because his real name is John Lord and, come to think of it, he acts a bit sultry.

A guy on our team we call Stent because of what was sewn into his heart to keep the blood flowing. Strangely, we too have a Spanky, but I have no idea where it came from. There's Moen, which is the brand name of a line of faucets, the nickname arising after a tournament when Moen poured a bottle of scotch into the hotel room's glass coffee pot, drank most of it, and later busted off the Moen bathtub faucet with, incredibly, his head.

I remember nicknames from back in junior. One guy with a tight little wave in his blond hair was Rughead. My friend Al, who's half Ojibwa, sometimes got called Red. There was Stud, a guy who was utterly loyal to one girlfriend for as long as any of us knew him. Our coach was the Hawk, because of his stare. One guy, because he was always injured, so much so that the trainer would just tell him to "tape an Aspirin on it," became Carter, after Carter's Little Liver Pills. Our captain and steady defenceman and all-round good guy was simply called by his number, Four. A less-liked guy, shy and not as good a defenceman, was Two, and it was somehow a little dismissive. Our slender goalie was Wire. I've played with two goalies called Target.

At UBC there was a guy who ate lots of fries and pop and nothing else, and he became Garbage Guts, quickly shortened to Garbage. I remember how odd it sounded—though later not at all—to hear in the parking lot while the bus idled, "Anybody seen Garbage?" And then, during the early days of the WHA, when Brian (his real name) got a tryout with the Winnipeg Jets and scored in a pre-season game, on a rebound from a Bobby Hull shot, our trainer came into our dressing room with the alliterative news, "Hey, Garbage got a goal!"

"Was it a good goal?"

"He said it was a garbage goal."

No one in the room, and maybe not even Garbage, was aware of the world-class punnery going on here.

Drop That Soap, Andy, or, Yes, We're All Gay in Here

C'MON BOYS, you know it's true. And if you don't know it, and get angry hearing it, well, according to the professionals, that just means it's doubly true. There, now that we're all comfortably out of the closet, we can talk about it openly, right?

Wrong. It seems that some teams are more gay than others.

I hate to pick on the Maritimes, but . . . well, actually it's fun to pick on the Maritimes. I only wish it was as much fun to pick on Toronto, but Toronto's such a boring barn door of a target. Anyway, the day I went on a scouting mission to Fredericton before moving out my family, I spent a gruelling hour strolling around nice neighbourhoods before I retired to an excellent pub called the Lunar Rogue. Sipping a pint, I watched the start of the CBC news up there on the big screen. It was on the big screen because Fredericton was tonight's lead story. I sat watching Peter Mansbridge report that Fredericton's newspaper, *The Daily Gleaner*, had run an editorial calling for the quarantine of anyone testing positive for HIV. In the report, Peter added a couple of other tidbits—one, that

Fredericton had banned a proposed Pride parade and, while they were at it, banned door-to-door canvassing by Greenpeace. I have to admit to pausing in my next sip, wondering what it might be like raising my family in a place that makes the national news for being so conservative.

Actually, Fredericton turned out to be a great place, for lots of good reasons, but you just don't get much gay humour in the Maritime dressing room. It's simply a more homophobic place than, say, Vancouver. Well, almost everywhere is more homophobic than Vancouver—here on the Island it certainly is—but you get my point, which is that in some dressing rooms you can yell at Ray that Donny's waiting in the shower with the special soap, and guys will chuckle, whereas in another dressing room it might get a little tense.

My brother's team in North Vancouver is a clutch of pretty sophisticated people for the most part. So when one of them, a slightly older guy we'll call Roy, decided he couldn't stand fags, well, the rest of the boys got a little merciless with him. Over the ensuing years, whenever he has betrayed some nervousness, he's been mockingly propositioned in the shower. Before tournaments, Roy is always threatened with having to room with an unknown ringer, who's huge and who people have heard rumours about. Once he was taped to a pole and threatened with buggery, and guys actually started lining up. Apparently some teams are confident enough in their straightness that they can take things to a bent edge.

Sometimes the edge gets a little blurred, I think. And some intellectual expert-types, especially female, will tell you that contact sports are homoerotic by their very nature. Even hockey violence, even fighting, *especially* fighting, they will say, is homoerotic behaviour. Well, I don't know about that, but sometimes I do wonder about some guys. I remember taking a shower at UBC, calmly sudsing up my hair, when one leg suddenly got weirdly warm. Yes, it was piss, and I shrieked and hollered. Most guys were sort of thrilled by this little prank, and it happened again to somebody else the following week, yielding another shriek of surprise. Nor was it the same guy pissing. Over the years I've reported on that event when guys start trading stories about pranks, and "pissing on guys in the shower" didn't happen only at UBC. Seems it's not rare, but since it isn't all that funny, if it happens more than twice it just sort of dies out. (If it becomes a nightly thing, and guys make saucy eye contact while doing it, my guess is that it's become something other than a prank.) So it's pretty harmless—by the time you're an oldtimer you've had most everything else on you at one time or another, so what's the big deal? Does this make me a recruit for the next pride parade? We'll see, but I doubt it.

But some people freak out about this sort of thing, and not just in the Maritimes. Once, in France, late one night, when we pulled over on the highway for a pee break, I happened to accidentally-on-purpose piss on a teammate's bumper and he went berserk. The weird thing is, it was raining at the time. It was the *thought* of it that got to him. And here in Victoria, in my very own dressing room, the anecdote of someone pissing on someone else in the shower came up, and one of our guys, who manages a junior B team, told us how, on the road after a first exhibition game, a rookie had pissed on another guy's leg in the shower and was sent home that night, in disgrace. They wouldn't even let him pack his gear and take it with him. In some respects, Vancouver Island is a bit like the Maritimes.

Unlike Vancouver. Again, on my brother's team, at the last Nanaimo tournament, we had a pick-up goalie who nobody knew all that well. A nice guy, kind of quiet. Shaved head. He made off-the-wall observations, and could be pretty off-the-wall himself. At one point during a game we were already losing, he joined a melee in the corner, bumping guys and winning the puck and stickhandling around with it—a goalie mocking the game of hockey. After another game, on the way from one bar to the next and finally to the hotel party room, he disappeared. When he showed up at the party a bit later, he told us all he'd been sidetracked at a gay bar. He looked serious, but his delivery was always dry. No one laughed, a few guys shrugged, the party continued. I think he was kidding, but clearly he didn't care who thought what about him (see "Men from a Distant Galaxy"). At one point he grabbed the communal guitar and launched into a brilliant, spontaneous hockey ditty he called "Po' Po' Canucks." The upshot of the whole bar-interlude thing is that no one on my brother's team cared one way or the other, except that they no longer call gay bars gay bars. Now they're goalie bars.

Ageist, Sexist, and Racist Jokes

IN AN OLDTIMER DRESSING ROOM, the first one of those is okay. And the closer you are to codgerhood, the more gallows humour gets directed your way. Sometimes age is remarked upon sadly, often in sombre comments from the bench along the lines of, "Jeez, Steve's lost a step, eh?" But it's exactly that sadness that kicks us into humour mode. I haven't yet heard of any team names that pun on adult diapers, heart stents, or defibrillators, but I expect to some day.

Sexism is also perfectly acceptable in the dressing room. Now, by sexism I don't mean the general stereotyping that's everywhere—billboards, TV ads, Britney Spears videos, etc. I'm talking about the loud kind that likes jokes ending with punchlines about her flat head you can rest your beer on while enjoying a blowjob. I'm talking about the kind of *jock*ularity that suggests a woman's only function is to be an eager receptacle. In other words, I'm talking about boyish, wishful-thinking sexism. I'd venture a guess that, while some guys still practise it at home, work, and play, in these more enlightened days most guys don't—except in the dressing room. The dressing room might well be the last bastion for loud, hearty, idiotic sexism. And it's quite possibly getting even louder, seeing as it's harder and harder for guys to practise it out there in the world. And I'm thinking it's okay. For one thing, it's so ludicrous that it obviously isn't meant to mean anything. For another, I'd opine that most women could sit there and get a kick out of it, and give it back in spades. It's basically dirty jokes. I'll also suggest that the guys who are loudest with it are also those who go home, take orders from the wife, do their share of dishes, and are for the most part gentle, doting husbands.

Racism is a different story. It's weird to see. I'm not talking about French jokes or Newfie jokes. Basically, these jokes get told only if there's a francophone or a Newf in the room. And if the guy doesn't like it, if he takes umbrage, the jokes increase and get louder and more insulting until he is beaten into submission and starts not only to enjoy them but begins to offer some of his own, and then the boys relax.

I'm talking about real racism. I have to say that the more rural and less educated the makeup of the guys in the room, the more you might hear some questionable stuff. Though not necessarily so. In white-collar sophisticated Fredericton we had a very vocal racist who was a business executive. He was also otherwise a generous and truly likable guy (see "Negative Capability"). He'd occasionally blame something on "the niggers" (oddly, I think there are about seven black people in all of New Brunswick), and more frequently on "fuckin' Indians." It got worse if he was drunk, and there was one pretty dicey time when he was downtown on a summer night in the crowded street and started yelling at some Natives in a car. They pulled over, there was shoving, cops arrived.

What's strange here is that this guy's best friend on the team, a big guy from Manitoba, happened to be part Cree—a half or a quarter, I can't recall. He'd smile ironically at his friend's racist barks, and then say, "Watch it, Whitey, I'm Cree," to which his friend would say, "Well, they're different."

Sports in general has played a sizable role in helping reduce racism, especially in the USA, where you have otherwise typical rednecks cheering their head off at a black guy making a tackle or stuffing a basketball. White kids everywhere try to act like Shaq and look like Iverson. In dressing rooms around the world, different races and cultures come together—they shower, they bullshit, they have a beer. NHL teams have become mini United Nations, and now a Canadian can insult a guy to his face about a "Russian shower"—deodorant sprayed over one's sweat after a game—instead of behind his back. It makes all the difference in the world.

Racism is weird, truly. We all know it's historical and global and has its roots in fear of the unknown invading your territory. It's also gotten more dangerous, especially when a bit of religious fervour and some weapons of mass destruction are added to the mix. But when racism pops up in oldtimer dressing rooms, it's one kind of nastiness that doesn't arouse much approval. In other words, most guys don't laugh at a racist funny. At the same time, it's a rare thing to hear anyone pipe up and say anything against it. On one of my teams, a teammate complained about the fucking dirty chink he'd just tussled with in the corner. Someone pointed out to him that the name on the back of the guy's sweater was actually Japanese—a subtle rebuke if ever there was one—but that's all that got said. People don't speak up. I include myself in that. It's almost as though you let it go because the guy's a teammate and otherwise a good shit. I'm not saying this silence of ours is a dangerous thing, but I'm not saying it's not a dangerous thing, either.

This Section Should Never End

SINCE THIS WHOLE SECTION is about oldtimer humour, I don't have a clue how to end it. The thing is, it never ends. It's one reason most of us keep playing: we get to have a laugh in the room. Entire books could be written about the goofy stuff that happens on any given team. If you've played hockey for a while, and you start thinking back, all sorts of good old stuff pops up.

When I think back, there's the time, in Anchorage, when a guy from the other team jumped into our bench and went toe to toe with our *coach*, who loved to fight, which is why we stood there watching while this little guy kicked the shit out of our coach, whose leather cowboy hat never did fall off his head. Thinking back, I remember the guy on the Hurry Kings who ate pucks, glass, and hockey sticks. He didn't eat the whole thing, but he definitely bit hunks off of those objects, chewed them up, and swallowed. He got famous enough that he was on the TV news for it, and once got invited to a Canucks practice where the team gathered round him while he ate part of the blade off Thomas Gradin's stick. I remember watching him eat some beer glass in a pub and there was blood dribbling down his chin, and when a waitress saw what was going on she kicked him out. He later worked at a strip bar, the guy in the booth who puts on records and shouts, *Heeeere's . . . the Lovely . . . Lola!*

There's the ex-NHLer who, playing in an oldtimers tournament in Alberta, decided to play goal for the very first time. Being a manly sort, he wanted to go maskless, but they made him wear a full-face shield, the clear kind. He'd had a few before the game (and during, given the number of pulls he took on his "water" bottle), and he got careless spitting his chewing tobacco—it spattered inside his mask. He decided to be happy with this and add to it— he spit and spit, and basically coated the inside of his mask with brown juice, which dribbled out the bottom and all over his sweater. He wasn't getting many shots, and after the game he expressed the opinion that playing goal was boring.

And there's the guy who, on the freeway on the way to a game, cut off a teammate. The teammate then gestured that he pull over to discuss something, so they both did, and the two of them went toe to toe there on the shoulder, witnessed by a third teammate on his way to the game as well, who said it was maybe the funniest thing he'd ever seen. And there was the team bocce tournament, seeing a guy cheating by nudging someone's wife's ball with his toe, and winning over seventy bucks in the process. And the team manager with the photo in his wallet of two enormous perfect breasts, one named Sally and the other Lisa. And how the guy on the team who scored the most goals was given Sally and Lisa—called "the team boobs"—to carry around in his wallet all summer. And I remember a truly sordid evening, a team party at a house that happened to be a palace, with an indoor pool. There was public nudity, and great food, and publicly burned underwear, and the party was an all-out success. Funny what a private indoor pool can do to grown men.

And there was the party on my brother Bub's team boat. This boat isn't really the team boat, but it's called that. (Bub's team has lots of team things. They have a team cooler, of course, but also team tape and team shampoo. There's talk of a team bus. My brother wrote a song, about converting lesbians, that's become the team anthem. At a Nanaimo strip club they refer to the team pole.) Anyway, the team boat is actually owned by a generous teammate, a dot-com fellow who diversified at just the right time and owns a fifty-footer with all the trimmings. The team boat party involved wonderful steaks, and crabs snatched right off the ocean floor, and great music, and nautical amounts of rum, plus hair-raising speed, seeing as this huge craft could go like stink. The team boat somehow made it back to its berth in Coal Harbour, and the punchline to this little story is that a few of the boys saw fit to pass out for the night in the team boat's elegant bow stateroom, and so full of oldtimer fun were they that none of them was nudged from sleep by the gangland execution, by machine gun, that took place during the night not fifty feet from their drunken heads.

But mostly this section is about you and a buddy sitting there in the room with a beer, too tired to consider a shower just yet, and you're watching a guy soaping up over there beside the spray. You're both disgusted by his body, which is patchy with hair like a sick Mexican dog, dominated by an immense, hard, barrel stomach, adorned with scars and a few unidentifiable stains, and it's having a difficult time showering with anything like coordination or grace. You both agree that neither of you will ever get that old or ugly. Your buddy suffers a sudden little spasm and he turns to you with wonder and says, *"That's our leading scorer,"* and you both laugh with an identical sense of horror.

THE RULES

As THE OLD SAYING GOES, it doesn't matter if you win or lose—it matters if *I* win or lose.

I don't mean the *rules*. Why discuss icing and delayed off-sides and obstruction whatever? That's all written down in some sort of "rule book" somewhere. (Though why do we assume such a book exists? Have you ever seen it? I haven't.) But we all know those rules. Even the occasional wife or girlfriend knows some. And the refs don't call them anyway. Unless there's an obstruction beheading. Or somebody falls down.

No, this is about the real rules. The unwritten ones. The team politics, the rites of respect and teamhood. The difference between top dog and bottom dog. Why certain guys get listened to in the room and others don't.

Do you remember hearing about that book called *The Rules*? It's a list of secrets a young woman must know in order to snare a man. Feminists sneered and hissed at it but it wouldn't go away, and lots of young women apparently bought it, and one has to assume they're using those rules right now. Such girl-rules are no doubt underhanded, disgusting, and nasty. Women on all sides of us are at this very moment reading it and learning such things as, probably, how to make their eyes go big when you tell them about the goal you nearly scored, when to stick their tongue out just a cute little bit, how to memorize everything petty we did two years ago, and how to point their breasts a little *away* from you. These rules are why all men remain helpless in all things. Anyway, this section is a bit like that book, only for old guys who want to succeed not in the board room, or the bed-room, but in the arena.

Intimidation

I HEARD A GOOD ONE the other day: old-time hockey was when a player didn't bother waiting to get hit, he just went ahead and *retaliated*.

But most of us aren't like that. Have you ever been lying in bed, unable to sleep after a game because adrenalin clings to you and keeps you awake? And that adrenalin is caused by that Number 10 guy, that little elbow he shot you, and then that look on his face as he stared you down and you did nothing? And now you spend restless pillowtime imagining ways you should have got Number 10 back? Admit it, you have lain awake with this stuff.

During the game—it might've been a game *years* ago, it doesn't matter—some guy stuck you, or slew-footed you, or told you to fuck yourself, or even *looked* at you a certain way. And now, lying in bed, magically you don't sheepishly skate away, which is what really happened. No, you give him back the same, only harder. And the guy retaliates. And now, though you don't want to, because last time you did your opponent was severely injured, you drop the gloves. You let him get a few shots in, and then, with an "I warned you" shrug, you cold-cock him with a sudden, single, Mike Tyson uppercut. His legs buckle like a shot stag's and he drops, his nose flattened, disfigured for life. You still can't get to sleep, so now one of his teammates steps in, a much bigger guy, their team's goon, in fact, and you have to destroy him as well, only it takes three disfiguring punches this time. You still can't sleep, so you search your humiliation banks for other times when you were intimidated but didn't respond like a real man, like a hero, like you should have. Like you *could* have. And now, in bed, you do. C'mon, admit it. I can admit that, in bed, I've kicked the living piss out of hundreds of guys, assholes all of them. And I'm also witty on my way to the penalty box, when the refs suck up to me and thank me for not ripping the guy's spine out this time.

It's what intimidation does to a fella.

Intimidation always has been and always will be. It's in the sandbox, the office, the bridge tournament, and the hockey rink. (It's even in other countries. In Russian there's a saying, "Throw one porcupine under me, I'll throw three porcupines under you." This is not only one of the weirdest expressions going, it's also a perfect portrait of exponential intimidation. And you have to wonder why the Russians don't actually use this tactic. If they had, the 1972 series might have been different. Not to mention even more fun to watch, though they'd have had to interrupt the game while the gals in fur coats skated out to sweep up all the broken quills.) Philly won a couple of Stanley Cups with it, and up until recently Canada has been able to win a few international games with it, too. And isn't it odd that it still works in oldtimers? In non-contact hockey? How is intimidation even possible in non-contact hockey?

It's the constant *threat* of violence. And anyone who plays the game feels it everywhere. Even in nooners, or pick-up, or hacking around. There are certain guys you just don't want to check too hard, or check at all, simply because you know their stick is going to come back harder than yours did. Then it's your choice to escalate, or lay off. It's plain to see that lots of hockey players are hard-wired to hit back harder than they were just hit. It's called "being aggressive," and it's called "not backing down," and it's the honourable Canadian way. It's why

we all nod our heads in understanding when we hear that
Punch Imlach told his players that he'd fine anyone who won
the Lady Byng.

I'm not saying violence is good or bad, I'm just reporting on
it. Some of you might enjoy it from time to time. I admit that
on occasion I've enjoyed being a bit of a bully myself, though
I've far more often been on the receiving end. Still, over the
years I've had the honour of playing with and against some
world-class intimidators, and everybody involved has lived to
enjoy another day. Playing beer league here on the coast, for
instance, I sometimes had the pleasure of playing the Portland
Buckaroos and the notorious Connie Madigan (who had a
cameo in *Slap Shot*, giving the finger to all the fans), who was
thrilling to watch, even while he sliced up my brother Bub
from stem to gudgeon.

But by the time we hit oldtimers, most of us manage to
simply skate through it. We manage to pretty much avoid it
and yet maintain our honour and dignity, and not remotely
resemble a wimp. It's like, a stick might come up a bit, and
you eye him and he eyes you, and in that shared look you
both agree that you *could* do damage to each other if you
wanted to, but you are agreeing to keep it civil. It's just not
necessary to buy into needless violence to maintain your honour as a hockey player.

Which is why, especially in beer league and oldtimers,
where we're all paying money to have some simple fun, violence and intimidation get me riled. In fact they keep me up
late at night beating the shit out of guys.

Maybe my worst taste of intimidation's vile fruit happened
when I played for a North Van beer-league team called
Pharaohs Retreat (sponsored by a nightclub of the same name),
during the playoffs against the dreaded Burnaby Lakers. The

Lakers had a history of being both really good and really tough. Like a few other teams of that era and area, the Shmyr Flyers and our own North Shore Hurry Kings, it was so tough a team that even the smaller skill guys could act chippy as shit and survive. Anyway, we were quite openly afraid of them. We had Wade, who had fists the size of cantaloupes and was the toughest guy in the league, maybe the world, but he was injured. So we had two or three tough guys against their eight or nine tough guys, and their tough guys liked to hurt people more than our tough guys liked to hurt people. In terms of brawls and nastiness, it was a truly bad league, and mood. In fact, during game two, when we had the injured Wade sit in the stands behind their bench, they protested on the grounds that they might be attacked from behind. The ref actually made Wade move.

It was so bad a series that after the first game, three of our guys quit. Quit hockey. They weren't getting paid to play, they had day jobs to go to in the morning, and this was no fun. The rest of us gamely stuck it out, suffering that odd fear of the soldier who is less afraid of being killed than he is of being seen as a coward. But we demanded of the refs that they call every damn thing or we were packing our gear, and they did try to do that. And because of this, we found ourselves in a catch-22. We secretly wanted to be beaten in four (though nobody in the room would dare say this, of course). Yet because The Lakers couldn't help gooning us and, because the refs called penalties on them, we were often on the power play, we scored some goals, won some games, and prolonged the series. (Which, ouch, is exactly what the Lakers liked. It actually went to game seven, whereupon the Lakers played smart, took few penalties, played real hockey, and beat us anyway.)

I say all this because there was one incident in the series against the Lakers that I think made me quit playing beer league, enter the Great Abyss, and not skate again until I was thirty-seven. I'm pretty sure it was this particular straw that broke this camel's back.

They had a D-man I'll call Lance. He was their best guy and also one of their dirtiest, and a punishing fighter too. Since we both played defence we rarely came in contact, which was fine by me. But on this one occasion, I found myself joining the rush. I was the second man on a two-on-two. I was bearing down on Lance. Lance was looking me in the eye as I got closer. He was actually smiling a little. The thing is, we knew each other, from junior, when he played for Kelowna. We'd even played together for part of a season, when I joined a team for the playoffs. So he knew me, he was smiling, and when I got close enough he brought his stick up near my chest, with the blade pointed down. And he gave me the dirtiest little stab, right above the solar plexus, on the breast bone. It was all wrist, a perfectly hidden hack, not enough to make the ref put his arm up. It was a thing of beauty, really, a perfect bit of cruelty. I couldn't believe how much it hurt. It didn't take me down, but it did take me out of the play. In the morning I had a black bruise the size of a plum, with just a little cut where the point had dug in. I wouldn't have been surprised to learn that Lance had filed it sharper.

The reason it threw me so much, and made me really *tired* of the game, was that this was now the exact opposite of fun. Lance knew me, he knowingly hurt me, and he was smiling when he did it. He knew exactly what he was doing. We both knew he would beat the shit out of me if I dropped them, and I didn't drop them.

But I've dropped them in bed. *Oh* yeah, I've gone back in time and dropped them and hurt Lance a hundred different ways. Sometimes I toy with him, sometimes it's one fast punch, and I'm never smiling.

The Cage

I DON'T KNOW ABOUT YOU, but whenever I check out an opposing team during warmup and see that most of them are wearing full-face shields or cages, I know we're in for a long night. Here's the formula I've come up with: guys who tend to wear cages didn't play much serious hockey growing up, and guys like that tend to try harder now. They get more excited in general, and are more likely to be in shape. Now, I know that any visor generalizations make me sound a bit like Don Cherry here, and I know that my formula is often proven wrong, but more often than not it fits.

I'll go out on a limb and narrow the formula down even more: if the guy you're lining up against wears no visor at all, chances are he's a wily old vet who makes some good passes and might stick you in the corner. If he's wearing a cage, more often than not he can skate like hell but otherwise isn't that good. He probably also has a fresh, folded towel in his hockey bag, which likely also has wheels.

Okay, okay, I know I've painted myself into a dinosaur red-neck corner. And while I'm at it I'll admit I'm full of shit. I'm exposing my underbelly here because my formula also tells me that a high proportion of readers of this book—that is, hockey players who *can* read—are the same cage-wearers I'm so vigorously denigrating. (And I'm *really* hoping nobody is actually wearing their cage as they read this—but if you are wearing your cage right now, I apologize profusely, I like you very much, and please don't come after me at home, where I live, in Corner Brook, Newfoundland.)

The thing is, I wear a visor myself. A half-visor, all scratched up and covered in dried spit and shampoo and bar soap and whatever I've used to try to keep it from fogging over once I get a sweat up. I've worn a visor ever since I started playing oldtimers, the main reason being that I also wear glasses. I didn't used to. In my earlier days I wore contacts. And during my beer-league days, when I didn't pay too much attention to things like cleanliness, when I just popped my contacts into my hockey bag and put my specs back on, the contacts absorbed lots of salt from my sweat. I somehow always forgot to clean them, and forgot again, and again, and a whole season's worth of salt lodged in there and stayed, and one September I stuck them in my eyes and they burned liked hell. Of course I kept wearing them, all season, and they never stopped burning. Had I cleaned them, even then, the problem might have been solved, but once the cooler's lip opened with its coy little squeal, I always instantly forgot, and into my bag they went.

So it was funny, getting ready to play oldtimers. I found my old contacts—*still in my bag a dozen years later*—and when I opened the case and saw them, innocently pale blue, pretending not to be loaded with salt, my eyes instantly started to tear up! Just *looking* at them made me cry like an infant. So I thought to myself, Oldtimers? Non-contact! Hell, I'll just wear glasses!

One of my first games wearing glasses, I was zooming (well, in a manner of speaking) down the left side, went wide on the D-man, and was cranking things up for a rocket-like snap shot, when—*tink*—the errant stick of said beaten D-man came up and *hit me right in the eye*. Well, not in the eye, but rather on the right lens of my glasses, which were glass, not plastic, and which shattered in a neat spiderwebby design but otherwise stayed intact. I had a tiny cut on the brow as well and later, in the room, I discovered that the lens had been pushed in against my eyeball and there was the tiniest slice on my eyeball skin. (Weirdly, the ref didn't even call a penalty. I got the shot off, then skated right to him, screaming at the non-call. When I showed him the blood on my brow, and my shattered glasses, he said, "I didn't see it." I asked him what he'd been looking at, since I was carrying the puck at the time. I guess I swore a bit as well, and otherwise made a bit of a scene, and he had no choice but to give me ten. Hockey has some wonderful ironies, doesn't it? Ten minutes for nearly losing an eye?)

Anyway, it was visor time, and it still is. Would I wear one if I didn't wear glasses? I seriously don't know. Actually, I'd love to locate some vintage Al Arbour glasses — thick and ugly as can be, the frames weirdly flattened to your face and held on with big honking straps. And I'd forget I was wearing them, and get drunk wearing them in the room, and then drive home with them on, and scare the roadblock cops, and then my wife. You could *sleep* with Al Arbour glasses on and not even know it.

Ice Time, or, Why We Need a Higher Power

IF YOU PLAY on a beer-league or oldtimers team and your best guys go on when the other team gets a penalty (what's normally called a power play), somebody on your team is taking it far too seriously. Basically, when guys pay to play, the rule should be that everybody takes an equal turn out there. Well, maybe if it's a tournament, and you're down one goal with five minutes to go . . .

I loved it in Fredericton, where on the Stinkhorns we insisted that our seventy-one-year-old, Norm, take a regular shift, even if it happened to be on a power play. Norm used to be good, was better than any of *us* would be at seventy-one, but time had caught up with him and he was, well, a bit slow. Norm wasn't too bad defensively, because he followed his wing all the way in, clinging to him like a giant old leech, but in the last couple of decades he hadn't been popping very many goals. But so what? We took pride in making sure Norm never got short-changed. This attitude did a few things for us. One, it put the game in perspective: winning didn't *really* matter and, look, everyone, we're proving it by playing Norm in any situation. Two, it gave us a great excuse when we lost. Three, it made it feel even better when we won.

Ice time can be problematic, can't it? Is your team free of problems in this area? Are all your lines careful to take no more than their equal share? Has the second line ever thought the first line stayed out there too long, so they stay out there longer, and then the third line says, hey, and stays out longer, too, and then the first line, who didn't think they were out there too long, stays out even longer, and then so do the other lines, until the shifts are seven minutes long, no one's even pretending to backcheck, and a few guys no longer even bother to move?

And is everyone on your team happy to be on the line they're on? No? And should you "balance the lines," meaning you mix your best players on a line with your shittiest, or should you "stack" them, meaning you put guys with the same speed and talent together?

And who should decide this stuff?

Hopefully, the right people. While I'm sure we can all agree that the vast majority of guys who play hockey are good shits all around, let's face it, there *are* a few jerks who wear skates. And, just like out in the real world, where it's often the jerks who want power, and take power, so it can happen in the dressing room. We've all seen it, where the wrong guys run the show. Sometimes it's a case of a guy "owning" the team, in that he's been organizing it since it began, and continues to, and guys can like it or leave. Sometimes it's easy to spot this "owner" the minute you walk in the room, because he's talking loud and he's boring but he's acting like he isn't, because he can. He'll cut guys and decide who goes to tournaments. On the bench he'll coach guys, and his advice will be all the stuff he can't do himself, and it'll be sour and awful. Anyway, teams like his often have lots of turnover. As W.C. Fields once so wisely said, "If I want to play with a prick, I'll play with my own."

But running a team can be as difficult and chaotic as the game played on the ice. We're into heavy politics here. Even an oldtimer team is nothing less than global politics in microcosm, and it needs a political system. Communism would be great, in that "everybody share everything and be happy" way that Marx intended and has never happened. But since communism appears doomed in the dressing room, too, we're forced to use one of two basic systems: democracy or dictatorship.

I prefer dictatorship. Democracy is messy, and too often the guys with the loudest voices end up deciding things, and it's them who end up playing with Bruce, your star centre, the only guy capable of—as Pierre Maguire puts it—excellent puck distribution.

Real hockey uses the dictatorship system, of course, except the guy in charge is called a "coach," a word with less historical baggage than "dictator." In the NHL, a coach is actually a puppet dictator, because you can be sure that if the GM (i.e., the Great Mind) wants Krutov to play with Lukkonen, then Krutov will definitely be playing with Lukkonen, and the puppet dictator will pretend it was his idea, even though every guy on the team knows it's a ridiculous move and the coach could never be that stupid.

When oldtimer teams use the dictator system, often it's the best guy, or longest-playing guy, or the organizer/ice-time owner, who acts as coach. Anytime there is an actual coach, though, even if his job is just to decide the lines, the system instantly breaks down into a "royal court" situation, wherein the dictator, who's usually a nice enough guy, gets surrounded, or "courted," by those who want to "curry favour." That is, later in the bar, Ernie, who wants to play left wing on the first line with Bruce, huddles up with the coach, buys him beers, laughs louder at his jokes, and spreads nasty rumours about Bruce's current left-winger, Nick. He'll suggest that Nick not only can't seem to handle Bruce's nice bullet passes, but that Nick only dropped a five into the beer jar last game, but he definitely guzzled twice that. In fact, Nick's been guzzling pretty hardcore lately, hasn't he, Coach?

Basically the one hope is that your coach is both compassionate and wise, sort of like the Philosopher King that Plato went on and on about. But since not too many philosophers or kings play oldtimers, outside of Europe, I'd propose that in order for a team to run smoothly we'd need no less than God behind the bench. Who else could know best? Who else could *settle* all this stuff? Failing that, if we can't enlist God, we need someone who can at least channel Him, someone who, when asked who should play left wing with Bruce, would slowly rise to his feet, eyes rolling back into his head, and point to the right person and announce in a voice like calm thunder, "YOU."

Otherwise it's just muddle. My brother Bub's team has a decent enough system, if only because they take turns being dictator. One guy does it for a whole year. Most guys report hating the job, mostly because of the constant lobbying they have to suffer through, the pouting and wheedling and sucking up and strategizing over who gets to play with whom. Though the free beers are nice.

Why Everyone Listens to Bruce

LEO TOLSTOY SAID, "Amazing how complete is the delusion that beauty is goodness."

If you're asking, "Wasn't Tolstoy both a count *and* a commie, so should he be trusted?" I can't help you. But if you're asking, "How can that awkward quote have anything to do with hockey?" just change "beauty" to "talent," and you'll see that hockey is what he's talking about. More exactly, he's talking about status and power in the dressing room.

It's no different than a gang of seven-year-olds who ignore a certain kid, Nigel. But one day Nigel brings to the playground an X-Green TurboMurder Cube, the kind advertised relentlessly during Saturday-morning cartoons. It's the toy no kid has been able to find anywhere in North America because they're all sold out. Nigel's dad just paid five hundred bucks for it on eBay, and suddenly Nigel is the most popular kid in the neighbourhood. For the first time in his life, Nigel talks and others listen. In fact, they are hanging on every word he says. Change "beauty" to "X-Green TurboMurder Cube," and we see that Count Tolstoy is still right.

Anyway, notice how a brand-new guy gets treated after his first game. Beers get popped, guys are starting to joke around. The new guy, Zack, was the best guy on the ice, netting two goals plus setting up two nice ones, and you won 5–3. Clearly he's played some hockey. In the room now, everyone's alert to what he says. If he cracks jokes, they're probably funny. If he's a wacky loudmouth who won't shut up, guys are grinning at his wacky energy. If he just sits there quietly, it's sort of, well, *noble*. If Zack offers up an opinion about your team and what it needs, guys listen. Same if he says something about how cold our fucking winter's been, or Iran's problematic trade deficit. Now, if the new guy's Ernie, and his game didn't go so well, if he was a clumsy slug and the worst guy out there, failing to pass to wide-open guys and causing a few goals in his own end, things are different. If he's funny, sure, guys still laugh, but not quite like they do at Zack's jokes. If he's a wacky loudmouth who won't shut up, guys will be looking at each other, not grinning. If he's sitting there quietly, guys won't notice his nobility—they won't notice him at all.

In the room, talent is status. It's not the *only* status—guys can be "good in the room" no matter what they're like on the ice. And after playing with guys awhile, you naturally make closer friends with some than with others, nothing to do with anyone's ability. But, like beauty, talent gives a person a big social leg up. Somehow, talent looks like personality. Bruce, your leading scorer, can say something like, "C'mon fellas, we gotta dig down and give a hundred and ten and leave it all on the ice and most of all let's go have some fun," and not get told to fuck off or have water bottles thrown at his face full force, which is what might happen to Ernie if he said that during his first, and last, bad game with you.

So to return to Tolstoy's quote, it's true: being a really good hockey player is identical to being a beautiful woman. Guys are nicer to you, maybe even a little nervous around you. They listen to your most boring little story, and they agree with your opinion on politics, or philosophy. They might buy you things and offer you rides. They want to be in the same room with you while you put on, and take off, clothes. Most of all, they want to watch you move, and see you do that little thing you do.

Memory #7: La Ligue du Sud

I HAVE MUCH FONDNESS for my time in La Garde, playing for Toulon, in *La Ligue du Sud*.

I had a decent little studio apartment, meaning the foldout couch became my bed each night. It was on the ground floor, and it had french doors (!) that opened out onto a patio, and beyond that, a vast artichoke farm. Across the lane was a graveyard, but I couldn't see it from any window, and I think that's why it didn't bother me. That and the fact that its ghosts didn't speak my language, or have family feuds they wanted to settle.

But in some sense I *had* returned to my family, my roots—you know, my last name, "Gaston." I don't know when it was that my distant ancestors left the mother land, though I've been told we're Huguenot stock and that we got turfed for religious reasons in the seventeenth century. Apparently, so the story goes, in an attempt to avoid being burnt at the stake, my Huguenot ancestors tried throwing away their last name, and using their middle name—Gaston—in its place. And now, having escaped the flames, I had returned.

The first game I played, they announced the starting lineup over the P.A., and I was *"Numero quatre, Gaston Beel!"* Gaston was a first name over here, and the French had changed it back for me! The other thing about the name Gaston: as a first name, it's goofy and old-fashioned. I was told that, in English, "Bartholomew" or "Cecil" would be in the same league as Gaston. Sometimes when I was introduced as Gaston, people would actually smile and look down at their feet.

But here, for a year, I was Gaston Beel.

Things went well, once I figured out how I got paid. Again, I'd arrived flat broke, so I eagerly awaited my first paycheque. I waited and waited. Lacking a ticket home, and knowing this was the last team in France that needed a playing-coach, I didn't want to ruffle any feathers. I waited some more. I actually lost weight. Lacking even bus fare into Toulon, I walked there and back, maybe five miles each way, in order to wire my parents for money so I could eat. Eventually I did ask someone about when I was getting paid. I thought Monsieur Roquebrun (Mr. Brownrock) was the team president, but he wasn't. It turned out there was no president, but a weird circle of men who constituted the organizational committee. I won't try to describe French political procedure here, except to say that it's only a little less chaotic than Italian. What I learned from M.

Roquebrun was that "It was M. Papillon's turn to pay you," and with that he picked up the phone to yell at someone I gathered was Mr. Butterfly. I learned that this circle of committee members had agreed to take turns paying me, and that they paid me out of their own pockets. It seems that the year before they voted to hire a playing coach for the first time in their history, the aim being to make the playoffs for the first time in their history, too. All the other *Ligue du Sud* teams except for Marseilles had playing coaches.

Anyway, I got into a routine of asking M. Roquebrun whose turn it was to pay me this month. The man whose turn it was never once came forward to pay me on time. A few times I took a taxi to the man's address and asked for my money there on the porch. I would knock and a child would answer and see me and run into the house, yelling, *"Gaston Beel est arrivé!"* One man looked suitably shamed in front of his family as I asked for my money and he dug into his pockets. I knew some French by now, and the phrase *"en retard"* served me well for the first time since grade school.

It was all part of French hockey, which was weird every which way.

I spent a lot of time in my little apartment. I went to the market each day, watching and learning from the women who also shopped there daily. I learned what meat was fresh, and I learned the words to use. I soon had the accent of a La Garde housewife. I cooked nice meals for myself, spending a good amount of time preparing them, always with decent table wine. Sometimes I even lit a candle. I experimented with a few foods, the outer limit being a can of lark. Yes, a can, identical to a can of beans you'd find here, except it was filled with little chunks and slivers of cooked lark meat, all held together in a fine mesh netting. It tasted like any canned meat—tough and tasteless. I got way more adventurous when I went out to eat. Some things I didn't like—some of the goat-dump-aroma cheeses in particular. But I did quite enjoy sheep brains (mild taste, oyster texture, served on toast) and pig testicles (which I ate at the La Garde arena's glassed-in bar while I watched some excellent figure skating).

I also wrote a novel in that apartment. I wrote it freehand in a series of scrapbooks. (When I got back to Canada I tried reading it and it was so awful it wasn't hard at all to simply toss it in the garbage.) I played lots of guitar. The apartment had no TV, so I read lots of books. My brother Bub sent me compilation tapes of stuff he was currently listening to, and now I think of France whenever I hear Roxy Music's third album, or Supertramp's first, or any John Cale at all. Also, that year a group named Abba won the Eurovision song contest, with a ditty named "Waterloo." All the French bars started playing that song, whenever they weren't playing "Popcorn." The Rubettes' "Sugar Baby Love" was also big in Europe that year.

So I had a lot of time to kill there in La Garde. I had but one game on the weekend and one practice midweek. The practice wasn't with my team, almost all of whom were still suspiciously out at sea in that submarine. The practice was with the teenage team—roughly midget age, if not ability—which was the only team I had to coach after that first-day practice fiasco. They'd found a translator for me, Chris, a guy from Richmond Hill who was here doing some teaching. (He was a nice guy, but a little strange, and I suspect still that he was a NATO spy of some sort. He drove one of those goofy Deux Cheveaux tin cars with cartoon duck decals all over it, as a sort of cover. Chris, were you a spy?) So, with Chris on board, coaching got easy. I could say to Chris, with a bit of a yell, "Tell NayNay to backcheck for once, and maybe go into a fucking corner. And tell him he's a greasy coward." Chris would give me a tired look before explaining to NayNay that Gaston Beel had requested that he put more energy into his defensive technique.

The game, on the other hand, was with my team, the sub-mariners—some of whom, come to think of it, were NATO spies for certain. How else did the submarine manage to be in port every weekend? In they'd troop before the game, some of them actually sporting those thinly ribbed Jacques Cousteau tuques. They'd get dressed, cocky, joshing each other, brag-ging about what they were going to do tonight. They barely noticed me. Some I don't think spoke to me or looked me in the eye all season.

Here is what I think was going on. The first fact is, all south-ern French males are fundamentally psychotic. The second is that every one of these guys was *convinced* that he was by far the best guy on the team, owning all sorts of highly intelligent rationalizations as to how this was possible while still being, say, the team's tenth-place scorer. While I was no Bobby Orr, I was far better than any of them in every way, so I stood as a threat to everyone's status as best player. My mere existence in the dress-ing room was a challenge to their continued delusions, of which they were quite fond. So they had to pretend—no, they had to *believe*—I wasn't really there.

I remember making the mistake of trying to coach some of them. I suggested a basic play, where the first forechecker takes the man and pins him on the boards while the next one in picks up the loose puck. I remember them looking at each other, and then down at their feet. They mumbled something lengthy to Chris, who in turn told me softly and more briefly that they'd played together since childhood and knew what to do.

I won't go into any more detail about my failure as a coach. But I will try to sum up my team for you. Here's one detail that might help: some of these submariners played with no under-shirts under their team jersey, and before each game they would put Band-Aids over both nipples. Do I need to say more? I will. I saw more than one guy take a puck off the shin pad, crumple into a heap, and not moan but *shout*, "Non! Non!" in an agony that made European soccer players look like Bobby Baun. As far as their playing style, well. A lot of them had good wheels but no hockey sense at all. Basically, teamwork consisted of one guy picking up the puck, and his two linemates standing there cheering him on as he tried to go through the other team. It was chaos. I actually saw two of our guys, while slowly "backcheck-ing," discussing tactics, conversing about what had just gone wrong on their latest assault on the opposing net. One of our guys actually had one glove off and was flapping and pointing his bare hand to punctuate his points.

Playing in *La Ligue du Sud* had its colourful moments, too.

The rink in Nice, for instance, was its own can of larks. Nice is quite the place. Any Canadian seeing it for the first time would announce, "There's no way hockey has ever been played here." It has an azure ocean and miles of beach, and palm trees. The rink is outdoors (the ice plant must be chugging away pretty good, because even in winter it's 60, 65 degrees Fahrenheit), and ringed with said palm trees. It's primarily a figure-skating rink, so much so that there are no blue or red lines.

Before each game, a tubby, moustachioed old gent in white shirt, tuxedo pants, and suspenders (he might have been wearing spats, too, but that might be me wishing he was) appeared with some paint, blue and red, in tins the size of bean, or lark, cans. Leaning over with a brush, walking back-wards with bum in the air, he would brush on the lines. Even with big tuxedo bum in the air, this old guy exuded a great deal of pomposity.

Lines done, the ref blew the whistle and the game was set to go. Now, any Canadian witnessing this would have immediately announced, "But jeez, they haven't even flooded over the lines, eh?"

I think it was poster paint, and the lines were vague smudges within minutes. French refs were pretty iffy on offsides to begin with, and I guess maybe this gave them more leeway.

Every game against Nice was a bit of a war, which Nice usually won. They were the wealthiest team, and I suspected that they paid some French players to relocate. Our team hated them, in any case. I think it may have been a class thing—us Navy guys from Toulon, a working port, against the rich bastards from Nice, a chi-chi tourist bordello.

Another completely wacky rink was Briançon, which lies over towards Spain. France, along with much of Europe, was very conscious of energy even in those days, particularly electricity, which was very expensive. You'd see room lights on timers, and lots of dim, low-wattage public buildings. Briançon was apparently quite poor, as a town. I recall being told that their civic government was *communiste*. And one cost-cutting measure involved their ice rink. I'm not making this up.

During a hockey game the rink was pitch-black inside, except for two spotlights, which were manually aimed to follow the play. I think they were aimed by chimps. Or maybe the wrinkly grandfather elephant from Babar. In any case, picture this: the puck is in Toulon's end of the rink, and Gaston Beel, frustrated, shoots it down the ice. Two spotlights wobble off in search of the puck, which curls around the end boards and is now on its way back. The spotlights continue their search. Gaston, squinting, has correctly sussed the puck's trajectory and intercepts it on its way back to him, at mid-ice. He picks it up and skates with it. Under his feet it's dark, then suddenly bright white. He almost stumbles.

It's dark again. Now it's bright as the sun. Now it's. . . . It was the only game I played in Briançon, and I learned that, as much as possible, they scheduled games during the day—the arena had nice banks of windows along the sides.

Another highlight, and strange rink, was the last league game of that *Ligue du Sud* season, in Gap, a town up in the southern edge of the French Alps. Gap's rink was also outdoors, but it was outdoors in every way that Nice's wasn't. In Winnipeg I didn't play indoors until I was twelve and had a championship game in the old Winnipeg Arena. So when I stepped on that Gap ice, took a stride, and heard that first *crunch*, my heart was instantly in my throat. I also realized my ears were cold. And there was a cold breeze. And *there*: that feeling of the insides of my nostrils freezing when I breathe. *I'm playing outside!*

Actually, I'd say that the sound of the blade on outdoor ice is more like a *croak* than a *crunch*.

It was wonderful to be playing outside. It was a night game, and even the slightly weak lighting resembled the Winakwa Park rink in St. Boniface. Gap was a hockey town, and the stands were jammed and loud. It was a Saturday night, and this was the best thing in town. Dark, so you couldn't see the mountains, it could have been any town on the Canadian prairies.

Maybe for these reasons I was inspired to have a great game. It was also a game we had to win to make it out of our league and into the national playoffs. In any case, it was the only game I played in France that I remember truly going for it, passionate, bursting into corners without a doubt in my mind that I was coming out with the puck and going with it up the ice.

I was flying. Al was at the game, having driven down from his home in Megève, a bit deeper in the Alps. Between periods he came up and told me I'd be an idiot to pass it anymore, all game, that our best chance lay in me trying to go end to end. I knew he was right, but I was still burdened with that bad Canadian habit of passing to teammates. The funny thing was, if I started ridiculously hogging the puck, my teammates would find no fault with me. Quite the opposite. They'd probably watch me, nodding their heads. They'd remove a glove to gesture and punctuate the discussion about this new, desirable *cochon* tactic of mine.

But I did take Al's advice, and it worked. I had about a dozen quality chances, scored two goals (I was still a defenceman, after all), and we led, 2–1. With about five minutes to go, I found myself on a clear-cut breakaway. I was flying in. The puck was up on its edge—damn this snowy outdoor rink—and it sort of got into my feet a bit and BOOM.

When I came to I was on all fours, staring down into a pool of my blood, a stream of drips adding to it. I'd been banged a good one on the brow. I was helped up, and got over to the bench, where Al waited for me.

"Fuh happen?" I asked him weakly.

"You sort of lost it in your feet."

"Wha' hi' me?"

"Goalie cold-cocked you, man."

"Goalie?"

"Yeah."

"How?"

"With his stick."

"Did I run into him?"

"He sort of came out and got you."

"Why?"

"Well, you had a breakaway."

"Ah, right, right."

I was in France and it made perfect sense—it was more of that French genius for innovation, for doing what had to be done. I'd been peppering the goalie all night, so *of course* if I had another breakaway he was going to use the next tactic available to him, which was to leave his net and club me on the head with his goal stick.

Someone taped a wad of rags to my forehead and, being Canadian, I tried another shift, but almost passed out. Off I was taken to the house of a doctor, who came to the door miffed and in his pyjamas. He sat me down in his living room and laid out his tools. I saw him filling a needle, so I told him, "*Pas de novocaine.*"

"*Pas de novocaine?*"

"*Je n'ai pas de besoin de novocaine.*" It was February or March by now and I knew how to tell him I had no need of novocaine. I think I may also have added, "I am Canadian!" anticipating the TV commercial by about twenty years.

I had gone without novocaine once before, in junior. We were playing the Cougars, in Victoria. I'd butt-ended—but softly, as a warning or an experiment or something, I'm not sure—their best player and captain, a short guy, Ted (you still live in Victoria, Ted?), and, skating back up the ice side by side, as an answer to my soft, exploratory butt-end, he brought his stick up lightning fast, and I was on my knees with a neat little gash over my eye. I didn't fight him, both because I deserved it and because I would have lost the fight. In any case, the Victoria Cougars' doctor stitched me up in our dressing room using no novocaine, never offering me any, and I think he enjoyed that much more than me. Each time the needle and thread stabbed in, it hurt way more than the injury itself. But I did feel kind of macho. Anyway, here I was in the French Alps, demanding no novocaine. Maybe I wanted to spread some Canadian culture to a tired doctor, offering him the only thing I could think of, besides hockey, that we could maybe beat his country at.

The doctor sighed. Each time he stabbed me with needle and thread, he whispered softly, "*Gaston. J'ai preek.*"

One last thing. We won that game against Gap, 2–1. We were in the national playoffs, for the first time in team history. It meant a road trip to play St-Etienne, in central France, in two weeks.

And two weeks later I arrived at the arena early in the morning. It was crisp and sunny, the artichoke fields beginning to show some weird grey-green. Monsieur Rocquebrun and Monsieur Papillon had secured vans for the trip. I was excited. Even a little proud. Toulon had never made the playoffs before, and now we were going to play a team from central France, and maybe I had helped. I loved playoffs. I still do.

One guy showed up, then another. We waited. M. Rocquebrun was whistling, I noticed, nervously. But, hey, it was the playoffs. Only amateurs aren't nervous. Another guy showed up. Then two players from the teenage team arrived, with their gear. I asked M. Rocquebrun why. He explained that he expected we would be short players, so he'd asked some of the stronger young players along. I asked him if the sub was out at sea, and he shook his head. *Non*, that was not the problem. We waited and waited some more, and there were maybe six or seven players all told, including the youngsters. I asked M. Rocquebrun what *was* the problem.

"The players, they are afraid. I am surprised there are this many, Gaston Beel."

"Afraid? What's happened?"

"Gaston? The players they are afraid of St-Etienne!"

In my faltering French I asked him why they would be afraid of a town. I was getting a little nervous myself.

"It is not the town. It is the *team*. St-Etienne. *They are animals*."

"Animals?"

M. Rocquebrun's face scrunched up and he was sweating. Even he was afraid of them. He explained, "Their tactic is to fall on their backs at full speed and come at you with their skates held high. *Comme ça, Gaston Beel!*" In his suit and tie, M. Rocquebrun fell to his back and shook his feet at me, and squinted his eyes to demonstrate St-Etienne hockey anger.

This looked serious. Yes, I thought, French hockey was so strange that maybe one of the teams had developed a new tactic, extreme intimidation the likes of which even Philadelphia didn't dare use. Maybe St-Etienne's tactic was so magnificent that they never even had to *play* anymore, because every team on St-Etienne's schedule forfeited the game—like we ended up doing that day, ruining our first and only chance in the playoffs. Maybe I didn't want to play these St-Etienne guys either.

But my trusty translator Chris explained it to me later. He knew the nature of French ambition. Napoleon had been a freak of French nature. Generally speaking, the French wanted to conquer their apartment, or perhaps their local bistro or even their street, but not the world. My Toulon team was happy to have made the playoffs, and quite content to leave it at that. Travel to central France and probably lose? That would be a backward step, and what point would it prove?

This logic reminds me of plenty of oldtimers teams at tournaments. You know, it's the third game, and if you win it you have to play on Sunday? No one even has to say anything. Your team scores to tie it up in the third, and the cheers aren't that loud. Buddy roofs it late in the game to win it and you're no longer that fond of Buddy. In the bar later, you'll stare at your beer before quaffing from it, knowing exactly how much this one's going to hurt you during warmups in the morning.

Memory #8: The Hired Guns of Marseilles

ONE THING I REMEMBER about playing in Europe: it was fun, but the most fun was when a couple of Canadians got together.

It could be lonely, being the playing coach on a team that didn't speak your language. It could be even lonelier if almost all the guys—potential friends—spent all week out at sea on a submarine. (Or maybe, come to think of it, it was all an elaborate French hoax. Maybe it was a kind of, "Sure, of course, Gaston Beel, we'd love to come and visit you and be your friend but, you see, we all, um, we all spend all of our time on a—yes, that's it, on a *submarine*. Way out there on the ocean. Yes, whenever we are not playing hockey, we are on our *submarine*.")

Anyway, if the other team's playing coach was Canadian or American, we'd link up after the game and have a beer and swap stories. First we'd talk about our hockey histories, where we'd played, and how we would have been drafted if only rumours about that time in that Lethbridge motel hadn't leaked to some scouts. We'd see if we had friends or enemies in common. We'd share our homesickness, which was sometimes profound. And then we'd get into swapping anecdotes about how frikking weird the hockey was here in France.

You make best friends in an evening like that. One time, the Canadian was Québécois, and he "didn't have much English." The thing is, his French was so Canadian, and their French was so weirdly southern (it's called Midi, and Parisians consider it a sub-literate ape language) that they didn't understand each other very well. I'd been in France about six months now, and somehow I ended up having to translate some words for them, because my Midi was better than his, and my Québécois was better than theirs. Somehow, I knew that "to bar the chariot" meant, in Montreal, to lock the car door.

Another time, Montpellier came to play in Toulon, and their playing coach—Mike, a guy from Saskatchewan—came to my place later to have a beer and spend the night. Now, I'd been extra lonely that month. Hadn't really talked to anyone at all. In actual fact I had cabin fever. Anyway, poor Mike. When I remember that night, I wince.

I recall how we demolished the beers I had lying around, and guzzled a bit from the huge Cinzano jug the apartment's owner had stashed under the sink. We ate whatever food I had on hand too. We traded life stories. He was a nice guy, I think, though I didn't really give him much time to talk. I was classically bushed—I was the mad trapper who hadn't seen another human in years. I had stories to tell, and my mouth wouldn't stop flapping. What's worse, a Toulon hockey mother had given me a Christmas hamper that contained three bottles of fine red wine, the kind you needed a corkscrew for—which in France, where twist-top plastic jugs of good wine abounded, meant it was fine wine indeed.

To make a long story short, we killed the wine too, of course, and I remember that, sometime near dawn, Mike opened his eyes in amazement. He'd fallen asleep in his chair, and now he was opening his eyes and looking at me, registering what it was he was seeing.

"Jesus Christ," he whispered, "you're still talking."

Yes, I was. And I believe I kept going.

AL AND I HOOKED UP for a long spell at Christmas, when hockey leagues in France took a break. I went up to visit him in Anmasse, which is right across the Swiss border from Geneva, and which is where his girlfriend lived. He told me to bring my skates.

I hated crossing borders with Al. My hair was long enough, about Mike Ricci length, which was standard for the day. But

Al's was ass-length, and he was, again, half Ojibwa, and to the Swiss border guards he looked like not only a carrier of hashish but the *inventor* of hashish. I'll just say that I hate strip-searches and leave it at that. That Al had hockey gear in the car didn't matter at all. It just gave them more stuff to throw out all over the ground.

When I arrived in Anmasse, Al informed me that we were playing in a Swiss tournament, for money. It turned out that, during league play, teams were restricted to the players on their roster. For tournaments, though, teams could use any players they could afford to pay. During Christmas-break tournaments, Al had been hiring himself out to the highest bidder for years.

We played two games for a Swiss team—Davos, I think—in the Geneva tournament. It was fun, mostly because I got to play forward on a line with Al, who sent me perfect saucer passes that, even with my defenceman's hands, I tapped in from the edge of the crease. I didn't mind that I was getting paid about half what Al was getting. He was famous in the area, and I was in the French *Ligue du Sud*.

I wasn't too wild about what I looked like, though. He had the same gear for me that he'd scrounged for the tryout in Dijon: the little Jofa helmet, giant shoulder pads, ridiculously tiny pants that showed some bare thigh skin. Al took one look at me and called me Bobo. In fact, he had them list me on the official scoresheet as *Gaston Bobo*. I tapped in a few of Al's passes during those two games and I should have been amused to hear "Gaston Bobo" announced in that big Geneva arena, except that, being with Al during Christmas break, I was always quite hungover. So hearing "Gaston Bobo" over the loudspeaker had more the effect of making me spasm and shut my eyes.

I must have looked truly idiotic. But also fearsome. I remember that my hangover also made me a little, well, impatient. If I put forth the effort of going into a corner, nobody was going to interfere with my getting the puck. I nailed a few guys, bashing them with my big Bobo shoulders. I recall one little guy in particular who just abandoned the puck and fled when I went to Bobo him. He whimpered, in what I could swear was a Bronx accent, "C'mon, *lay off!*" after I lunged and missed. I had no idea what that guy was doing playing for a team in Switzerland. He looked like a pudgy little seminary student, which might have been what he was. He probably had some hockey stories weirder than mine.

AL SAID *au revoir* to his girlfriend and before heading south to a tournament in Marseilles we drove to the rich ski resort of Megève for a single game—a bunch of us ragtag Canadians against the French national team. It was great meeting these other guys, and apparently they loved getting together so much they'd made it an annual thing. Some guys came down from Holland, Denmark, or Sweden for the game. I met one older guy, an anglophone named Pete LaLiberte, who was maybe the first ever Canadian to play in France, had lived here for maybe twenty years, and had a line of French skates bearing his name.

I mention this game mostly because it was against this same French national team I had already played during my humiliating tryout with Dijon that fall. The guy who was now playing in Dijon in my stead—I'll call him Lester—was also suiting up for this all-Canadian game. Now, of course I was aware that it wasn't Lester's fault that he had made Dijon and I hadn't. I was also aware that it was somewhat spiritually challenged of me to want Lester to fall on his face. But that's what I wanted. Who wouldn't? And that's exactly what happened—Lester was hardly noticeable against such stiff competition, and I scored four goals in a 6–4 victory. That my goals were slam-ins on nice passes from Al is beside the point. After the game I wanted to rent a loudspeaker truck and have it drive through the streets of Dijon, trumpeting my scoring prowess and mocking Lester with nasal French laughter. I wanted to phone the Dijon owners right now, I wanted to set the record straight, I wanted an apology. I was aware that Lester likely would have scored six goals had he played on a line with Al, but that didn't matter. It still doesn't. I still want an apology from Dijon. I will continue not buying their mustard until I got one.

Next, Marseilles, first aiming for Toulon to pick up my gear so that I could quit being Bobo and once more become Beel. A lovely drive south, warmer and sunnier with every mile, a bottle of wine passed leisurely, a bit of hashish to keep things at an angle. I think we played a game of chess during the drive, too. The French roads were pretty casual back then. You could tuck in behind a farm tractor and nobody would bat an eye.

I loved Marseilles. It had a cobbled, narrow-streeted old part of town that made Toulon's *Cheecago* look like a Disney World theme ride by comparison. I'd seen *The French Connection*, and knew that here in these dark streets all the Asian opium was made into heroin and then shipped, from this port, to North America. Apparently at night there were swarms of rats, kept in check by swarms of feral cats, kept in check by packs of wild dogs, which also killed humans who were stupid enough to walk these streets alone. The whole place smelled of industry and European piss. Marseilles was home to the French Foreign Legion—that pack of jilted French lovers who joined up in order to die forlorn in lands they'd never heard of. Marseilles was one dirty, *uber*-tough pocket of French-underground genius. When the Germans invaded France and tried to run everything, I doubt Marseilles even noticed.

Al had one reason he wanted to play in this Marseilles tournament: he wanted to play for the Marseilles team. Al had two

reasons for wanting to play for the Mars
had never won a game and, two, they had

I'd already noticed her, of course, beca
La Ligue du Sud and she was hard not
bench. She was maybe thirty-five, blor
pretty. Lots of makeup, in the sophisticated Parisian manner,
and smartly dressed. She was too young to be any player's
mother, which would have been the obvious explanation for her
being the coach. I remember right off the bat asking a teammate
on the bench what she was doing there.

"She is the coach," he told me.

"Yes, but why do they have a woman for a coach? Especially
a woman like that?"

"She has excellent tactics."

Further prodding earned me the French shrug, that tired
one that said, "Gaston Beel, we find it tiring that you are puzzled by a beautiful, fashion-model coach."

Anyway, Al and I rode into town and parked at the
Marseilles arena, and Al wrangled from someone the beautiful
coach's phone number. I stood at his side while he spoke to her,
offering our services and negotiating the terms. I was getting
pretty good at the language by now, and I could understand Al's
flat Ojibwa-French.

"Yes, both of us. Both myself and my friend Gaston Beel."

". . . ."

"But you have never won a game, isn't that correct?"

". . . ."

"You've seen Gaston Beel play. He can score against you at
will, and he has injured several of your players. Between the two
of us, we can—"

". . . ."

"You have no money at all?"

". . ."

"Okay, we'll play for room and board. A hotel room and meals. And some wine. Six bottles of wine."

". . . ."

"Okay, a room only. But we need two beds."

". . . ."

"Well, ask your cousin for a mattress then. For the floor. One bed, and one mattress for the floor. But no way the hallway. We won't play if we have to sleep out in the hallway. That's in a bad part of town."

". . . ."

"Great. So what time's the first game?"

". . . ."

"Fantastic. And, tell me, will your husband be at the game?"

Al took the phone away from his ear and shook it—something had apparently malfunctioned.

Anyway, I pointed out to Al that in this tournament there were other teams, rich teams, who might pay us more than a bed, a mattress, and some wine.

"She didn't go for the wine," Al said. "She doesn't like her players drinking." He added, nodding, as if he'd always been of this opinion, "It can hurt their performance."

"So we're playing with Marseilles?"

At this, Al looked at me, and then he shrugged an "of course," almost like a Frenchman. "They've never won a game."

When we walked into the Marseilles dressing room the players gave us a mixed welcome. I think some considered us a threat to the purity of their losing record. Also, they'd never had foreigners, let alone paid foreigners, playing on their team and they didn't want to start now. Some didn't want to play with a hated rival, a *Toulonaise*—me. One guy, whose collarbone I had apparently broken, wouldn't look up from his skates. But others seemed excited. I was a good player, yes, but Al was famous, his reputation having reached all the way down to the bottom-sucking team in *La Ligue du Sud*.

As for this tournament, I won't say much about the hockey itself, because the more interesting part involves us getting thrown in a Marseilles jail later that Saturday night. Suffice to say we won the first two games, against mediocre opponents. It was a cheap tournament all around, with few fans, in a dark arena in a city that hockey had absolutely no business being played in. Hardly any other teams had foreigners or ringers, so Al and I had a pretty easy time of it when we hustled and worked the give-and-go, sometimes all the way up the ice. So we were in the final, tomorrow, against Nice, who not only had their good Canadian, but also, so the rumour went, had hired on a bunch of good French players from first-division teams.

If Al had any intentions of wooing our pretty coach, they were dashed right off. She introduced herself as Madame (which means married) Grandcourt (which means wealthy snob). She was never not Madame. Even the players, some of whom weren't that much younger, called her Madame. I didn't bother asking any of them why she was coach, because I sensed that any answer I got would just make it weirder. She had no tactics that I could determine. She told us who was playing with whom, and was canny enough to stick Al and me on a line together, but that was it.

After the two victories, the first in their team's history, the Marseilles players showed a remarkable lack of celebratory spirit and simply went home to their homes. Al and I got our hotel address from *la Madame*, along with the instruction that its doors closed at eleven o'clock, which was common with *pensions* of a certain kind, often in rough parts of town. And then we wandered off to eat, drink, and be merry, which we were both pretty good at. And Marseilles didn't disappoint, if I can recall. We found a little restaurant by the docks that served something called "fisherman's stew," which was heavy with garlic mayonnaise, and rich with butter and saffron that turned the tomato base a glorious orange. Full of clams and white fish and tentacles and a lobster tail. Baskets of heavenly bread, and of course endless robust red wine. (You wine guys out there might sit up straight and ask incredulously, "*Red* wine with *seafood?*" All I'll say is, in France, where I believe they invented both food and wine, I never saw anyone drink any white wine anywhere, except maybe if you count that five-year-old girl one time.)

Al and I proceeded to celebrate into the evening. We found a dark basement bar with a trio of old American black guys playing jazz. We continued a steady sipping of plonk. As eleven approached, I reminded Al that our hotel shut its doors soon. He didn't bother looking at me and shrugged. At about ten to eleven I reminded him again. He said something like, "We'll get in. Check out how the fat one goes cross-eyed when he hits the high notes."

I sat back and sighed. Why would I question Al, who'd been in France for years and knew the ins and outs? Well, I questioned him because he always did this kind of thing and it always got us in trouble. For example, taking trains with him was awful. In the French system, you bought your ticket, got on, and somewhere down the line, maybe two hours later, a conductor would come through and punch your ticket for you. Sometimes your town came and you got off without having your ticket punched at all, so you *could* have ridden free. Well, Al always refused to buy a ticket, and when I wanted to buy one, he gave me that look and said that he knew this route, and the conductor wouldn't come through before we got off. Well, guess what? *Every* time I rode a train with Al, we *never* bought a ticket, and we *always* got fucking thrown off. Al was always mad getting off, kicking gravel and feeling hard done by. And we would then have to wait, maybe hours, for another train — which, unbelievably, Al wouldn't buy a ticket for, because he knew they wouldn't be checking this time.

So he *knew* we could get in after eleven. We listened to jazz, we got turned down by a few women, we found another bar or two. We had an important game tomorrow, so we decided to call it a night around, I think, three.

We found the *pension* on a street that looked more alley than street. Walking through the dim gloom, passing all manner of professional villains, I was glad we both had broad shoulders, and visible facial scars, and that cockiness Canadian junior hockey gives you. I was glad Al looked like the person who had invented hashish. In any case, as predicted, the door was locked. Not only that, it had a mesh sort of cage over it, so that when Al yelled and kicked it with all his might, it just sort of rattled. Al yelled some more. We looked up at its brick wall, and its windows, which were also covered with metal mesh, hoping the light would come on in one of them and the proprietor would come down and let us in. No such luck.

In the process of cursing and booting random trash barrels and boxes around, Al found a lost *boule*. A *boule* is basically a small cannon ball, and is from the French version of bocce, the game where you bowl big coloured balls, trying to get closest to the little white ball. It's like curling without ice, curling rocks, winter, or Canadians. In any case, a *boule* is solid iron and, when thrown, it dents metal mesh enough to break the window behind it. And after Al had succeeded in breaking two windows, a light did come on and a proprietor did poke his head out his window. He held up a finger and said, "*Un moment, s'il vous plaît!*" Awfully polite, I thought, until *un moment* later the little navy blue police car came roaring up the alley to nab us.

I lied a bit about the Marseilles jail. We didn't actually get thrown into a cell. Thank God, because judging from the look of the fellas *not* in jail, I winced to think about being closeted with any of the meaner and stupid-enough-to-get-caught breed. But they "took us downtown," and treated us a little harshly, and Al came perilously close to getting into a shoving match with a police clerk, who kept implying that Al was from Algeria because he looked "*noir.*" In the end, after many explanations about *hockey sur glace* and the tournament, etc., it turned out that Madame Grandcourt also had a cousin on the force, and we were driven back—and, incredibly, let into the *pension* whose curfew we had violated, not to mention its windows. The proprietor-cousin was more sleepy than angry as he led us up to our room. Well, hallway—our one mattress and single blanket in the dark hallway by the bathroom. I was too tired to complain, and Al was too tired to kick anything.

The first thing we saw the next morning was La Madame's pretty face. She was standing not a foot away and tsking down at us, unable to hide her ironic little smile. Taking us both in, she said, in English, "Cute." I was still fully clothed but, crammed beside me, Al was naked. We'd been asleep maybe three hours. I can only imagine what we looked and smelled like. La Madame now smiled at Al, and Al, naked, smiled coyly back. I couldn't believe it: he still had designs on her. In fact, staring at her, he pinched his blanket at his chest and drew it down a coy inch. His eyebrows went up. Our coach snorted and turned on her heel. I really wanted to be back at my little apartment in La Garde. I wanted nothing but to sit out on the stone patio and watch my favourite field of artichokes grow.

Now, as some of you likely know all too well, a wine hangover is unlike a good old healthy Canadian beer hangover. No matter how many beers we're talking about, last night's damage can be nursed by going out and painting a fence or, if it's really bad, by eating a can of Campbell's vegetable soup while watching some basketball on TV. A wine hangover isn't like that. It isn't very Canadian at all. It tends to make you testy and introspective. It gives you a headache that makes you wonder about existence, and suicide. It gives you dark and publishable ideas about life and makes you lash out ironically at people who happen to be standing too close by. In short, it makes you French.

So, that morning of the big game against Nice, I was feeling a little too French. And in case I haven't already made this apparent, Al liked attention. He was a Leo, a hockey hero, an intellectual who loved Rimbaud and Lévi-Strauss and chess, and he knew that playing hockey in France, especially the south of France, was completely absurd. So he often used hockey as a kind of stage. Sometimes, for instance, he would find the ugliest, weirdest helmets imaginable—remember those three-piece leather things?—and wear them for effect. Once, he wore a football helmet, and before my French was up to snuff I believe one fellow tried to explain to me that Al had once worn some sort of turban. More than once I saw him arrange his long hair in braids positioned to stick out the top slits of his helmet so his head looked like a ridiculous five-legged spider. Anyway, that sort of thing. And I say all this so that you might believe me when I swear I haven't made this next one up.

Getting dressed for the last game—which, if we won, meant *Marseilles would win the tournament*—Al complained of stomach pains and said he was going to rest for a while, so we should start without him. I knew he was, simply, as hungover as me, and as I strode unsteadily out onto the ice to take on Nice all by my Canadian self, I wrote him off as a bit of a puss.

Nice's playing coach was Canadian, a guy from Sudbury, and also a defenceman, but I didn't like him much. After a league game we'd had a beer together, but only one. He never smiled, or looked you in the eye. He was clean-cut, and I got the sense that he didn't like me or my long hair—which, to put things in perspective, wasn't really much longer than, say, Reggie Leach's or lots of those guys. But he seemed the type who wouldn't have many friends on any team he played for. Anyway, he was maybe the one Canadian I didn't instantly bond with over there.

So I didn't mind going head to head against this guy. But, playing forward, I wanted to get on the ice when he wasn't, and I suggested this to La Madame, and she saw the logic. And about ten minutes in, I'd managed to club in a rebound and we were down only 2–1. Then, with maybe five minutes left in the period, the guy on the bench next to me shot me an elbow and pointed across the rink, saying under his breath, "Ooo la la."

Al was lying balanced full-length on the top edge of the boards, and then he slowly let himself fall onto the ice, heavily, letting his gear take the blow. He lay there quite a few seconds before struggling up, all floppy, as if drunk. Then, skating on his ankles, he started flailing around, blind. He was blind because he had pulled the neck-hole of his sweater up over his helmet and tied it with a skate lace. Out of the little hole a tall, stiff sprout of Ojibwa-black hair looked as kooky and impossible as something from Dr. Seuss. Play was still going on. The ref had seen the headless maniac by now but just stood there staring. Now Al was blindly ramming into the boards and slapping his gloves against the glass, as if trapped, resembling Frankenstein's monster impersonating Marcel Marceau.

The whistle eventually blew and Al was led to the bench. Smiling knowingly, the beautiful coach untied his skate lace for him, and when Al's face appeared, he smiled at her shyly and softly said, "Thank you, Madame." Meantime the ref was consulting the tournament manager, and someone wearing what looked like a mayor's outfit—with a big, red band angled across his chest—about what sort of penalty to assess. It was decided that Al must sit in the penalty box for the rest of the first period.

Between periods—we were now down 3–1—I didn't feel like talking to Al. I was tired of being a hired gun with him. I was tired of Al clowning around. I was tired of drinking wine and getting no sleep. I was tired of French hockey. But, the thing is, for some reason, I wanted to win this game. I don't know why, I just did. So I wasn't in the mood for Al anymore. I guess Al knew this, because when I said to him, "Let's just do it," he said only, "Okay."

We went out for the second period. Now, over the course of not just this tournament but also the others we'd been playing in, Al and I had worked up this silly play. He'd get the puck to me somewhere mid-ice and I'd go wide, a big rearguard with a head of steam. I'd keep going, into the corner, behind their net, and out the other side. I'd hit Al with a pass as he came in behind the play, lazily striding over the blue line. Most of Nice would be chasing me, and Al only had to beat maybe one guy and he'd be in on net alone. Or he'd just let a shot go—Al had one of the most accurate slapshots I ever saw. It wasn't the hardest, but he could hit the corner about six inches off the ice every time.

We used this same play again and again, and with ten minutes to go the game was tied 5–5. Nice did eventually catch on, and instead of chasing me into the corner, they all turned away and went for Al, so twice I just came out of said corner, went to the net, and smashed my third or fourth rebound in. We might have been ahead by now, except that at one point the jerk from Sudbury took a premeditated run at Al, clearly not liking this French hockey hero, this Leo Ojibwa hippy who made fun of the game, this ambassador from a version of Canada he didn't want to recognize. Well, it was a joyous time of my life watching Al get up off the ice, suddenly all business, and go toe to toe with the bigger, stronger defenceman and tag him with some good ones. Now, it could be a dangerous thing to fight in France, because not only did the officials not know when to step in, but they weren't aware that they were supposed to step in at all. So in this case I took it upon myself to help Al out a bit. I was worried because the Sudbury guy was a bulldog, one of those never-give-up fighters who can take lots of punches and then emerge during a lull to do some surprise damage. I knew how hungover Al was and that he had to be really tired by about punch number four, so I came off the bench, slid behind the Sudbury guy, and got my arm around his neck for some boa constrictoring. In any case, no one got hurt—let's say the Sudbury guy had two black eyes and Al had only one.

Nor am I making up this bottom-of-the-ninth, full-count ending. It was tied 5–5 with maybe a minute left. Al and Mr Sudbury were out of the box by now and there was time for one last go at ultimate victory. Al carried the biscuit out of our end. He hit me with a pass along the boards. I went wide, then into the corner, then behind the net. We were doing our play again—everyone knew it. Mr Sudbury certainly knew it. I could see him coming at me, his big face all fat and red and full of hate. I could see he didn't give a shit about losing the game now, he just wanted to hurt me, paste me against the boards, and that is exactly what he did. I barely got the pass off to Al, and didn't see him score or hear the cheers or anything at all, because the Canadian redneck asshole took me in, both elbows at nose level, leaving his feet at just the right time to inflict the most damage, and as me and my hangover made contact with the glass and his 220 pounds kept coming and the bright yellow light came on in my head, pushing out all else—in a sense, blasting me back to Canada—I was reminded of what I liked least about our national sport. "Ah, right—*this!*" said a faint voice from the bright yellow light. "Remember? *This* is perhaps why you did not pursue hockey as a career? Gaston Beel?"

FEBRUARY IS THE CRUELLEST MONTH in this northern land of ours, but I did achieve my main goal in what's probably my last hockey season: once again I made it to the Nanaimo tournament with my brother Bub's team, the North Shore Old Goats.

It was the best of times and the worst of times. First, my brother came close to suffering the best and worst old injury ever witnessed. In a bar after the Friday games, sipping a rum and Coke, he forgot that his drink had a short, stiff straw in it. I think he also forgot it wasn't beer. In a fit of thirst he banged it back, the straw got him in the eye, and he yelped—it was great. It nicked the eyeball skin a bit and hurt, but not enough to keep him from seeing further action, both in-bar and on-ice.

The tournament is put on by the Nanaimo Tubbers, which is what I'd term a "clever" team name (see "Team Names"). "Tubbers" refers, first of all, to the annual Nanaimo Bathtub Race, where maniacs in wetsuits climb into modified, motorized bathtubs and race thirty miles across Georgia Strait, to Vancouver. "Tubbers" also has the pun on "overweight" going for it, which is a bit cute for my taste. I suppose it's better than a name based on the other thing Nanaimo's famous for, which would be "Dessert Bars So Rich Only Big Excited Women Eat Them"—a clumsy team name at best. Though even that's better than another possible Nanaimo name, "The Highest Heroin Addiction in Canada Per Capita Capitals."

More importantly, the tournament went well. It went great, actually, though maybe not the hockey part. For the second year in a row, the Goats didn't win any of their three games, and failed to make the final. And this is a tournament they've historically won, or at least made the final, going back fifteen, twenty years to when they were the Senators.

I would have liked to have helped more than I did. That is, I would've loved to have risen to the status of "ringer," as opposed to what I actually was, "Bub's brother, who lives on the Island anyway so, sure, we can find a spot for him, he's a pretty good party guy, though he keeps Bub up too late." I *could* have been a ringer. I have taken my shitty, pudgy body and forced it to play eight league games thus far, plus the Pacific Cup tournament, where it got lots of exercise pivoting its head watching Murray, the true ringer, blast past. So I figured I might have a bit of jump by now. I might enjoy some non-rust. I might be able to go hard for more than seven seconds, plus have some timing and intelligence and what is often called grace.

Instead, humiliation. I'm only now getting over it. What happened was, in the first game, they started me on the best line, centring these two new good guys from Friends of Jesus my brother had told me about. A couple of shifts later, the lines were "adjusted," and I was demoted to the third line, stuck with two wingers more my speed, my brother Bub being one of them, and another decent partier, Owen, being the other. Like me and Bub, Owen used to be good. But more on our line later. My point here is, damn, I could have been a contender.

———

WHAT WAS REALLY GOOD about the weekend, what was a true success, has to do with tradition. Actually, with *spanking*.

Now, one problem with this semi-humorous writing style of mine is that, on the occasion when I do tell the truth, why would a reader believe it? So I face a dilemma, because this next bit is one of those occasions where I do tell nothing but the truth. And it's literally stranger, or at least better, than fiction. So although it's quite unbelievable, I swear it's true. I know I've said that before—but in this case you can phone anyone on the North Shore Old Goats and ask.

A little background. Again, the Goats have been going to the Nanaimo tournament every February for years, dating back to when the core group was the Senators. For years they have spent the Saturday evening eating at a French restaurant which I will leave nameless, for reasons that will soon be clear.

This restaurant is a fair drive north of town and requires a convoy of taxis, but it's worth it. Up a narrow flight of stairs, in what was maybe once an attic, is a wonderful private room with a long table that seats a dozen guys perfectly. There's a private sound system, and a little bell you can ring for service—which gets disconnected for the Goats because it gets abused. To the side is a big bench built into the wall—a little cave that has seen some peculiar Goat action. It's a high-end establishment, especially for the Island: each guy drops between fifty and a hundred bucks for the meal, depending on how much wine gets guzzled. It's *haute cuisine*, which I believe translates as "tiny portion centring big plate, with balanced herb sprig smirking at you." It's one of those eateries that hires certain waitresses, those well-groomed, upright, twenty-something beauties who cause middle-aged men to yearn from their animal core and become instantly pathetic and foolish.

A main attraction is the chef/owner's sister, who works as the hostess, and let's call her Lola. Lola's gorgeous in that saucy, pert, and minky way some women have. She's maybe forty-two, but she could gently place a finger just under the chin of any old-timer in Canada, whisper, "Would you mind jumping in front of that cute little truck for me?" and within seconds there would be another dead oldtimer to clean up. Lola also has a sense of humour and mocks herself for being so naughty, which of course makes her sexier still. It's also strangely sexy that her owner/chef brother is just down through those floorboards, working fever-ishly and professionally with a whole array of sharp knives. And the main thing is, over the years, upstairs in that private room, Lola has let herself be draped over the lap of a lucky Old Goat or two, and be gently and deliciously spanked. And then she might gently and deliciously spank him. The Goat with the S on his jersey where the C would normally be? His nickname is Spanky, and he was Lola's first.

That's the background. The Goat tradition is that on the Saturday evening the team gathers there to eat fine food, get drunk, and howl during ritual spankings. Sometimes a younger waitress or two will look on with some concern. It's all joyously juvenile and innocent as can be. It's wonderful because of the contradictions: it takes place in an elegant restaurant, Lola is so beautiful and we are so not, and her dark brother is down there with the knives. And tomorrow morning we face playing a hungover championship game, and the day after that we are back at work.

This year it was different. We learned the restaurant had been sold. It was now something called "World Fusion," and more expensive. No Lola, no gorgeous young waitresses, no spanking.

When Wayne announced in the room that the place had been sold, but he'd made reservations at the new place anyway, guys moaned, shrugged, and in general chalked it up to yet another of life's pleasures going down the tube. But we decided to go for tradition's sake. Also, the private room was likely still there and it was one place you could get a little Henry VIII-ish without bothering other patrons.

After seating us upstairs, where nothing much had changed except the colour of the tablecloth, our new hostess somewhat pompously explained that the chef had just previously worked at a certain establishment in Calgary. Some of the more sophisticated Goat eyebrows went up. Apparently the restaurant ranks in the international Michelin guide. One Goat's casual question, "So why the fuck he get traded to Nanaimo?" didn't get a response from her, but it was good that he said it, because now she could see what she was dealing with here. She added that this was their very first night, so we applauded, a little too loudly. Departing with our spectacularly lengthy drink order, she cast a look over her shoulder and asked, "You guys are a hockey team, right?"

I'm going to cut to the chase at this point. The food was indeed excellent. I had a bison, wasabi and wild rice creation that, according to the lengthy description, was "made drunk in a reduction of gin and bog cranberry," which needless to say, was the reason I ordered it. Bub and I said what the hell and splurged on several bottles of decent wine. One of the waitresses was worth yearning secretly and pathetically for. We were getting expensively pissed, and full, and they didn't disconnect the signal bell until well into the meal, after it kept getting pulled because some guys wanted to see one good-looking waitress in particular "work up a sheen of sweat." The noise level rose. Wine got polished off. Bread got dipped in world-class sauce. Sambuca shooters got lit and coffee beans crunched. We were happy enough that we had come back to this place. And at this point the captain, Wayne, asked a waitress if she would please summon the hostess.

The hostess arrived and Wayne spoke. Now, Wayne is one of those guys who would never get elected to office, but he could be a soft-spoken presidential adviser anywhere he chose. His aura is one of intelligence and trustworthiness. He began his little speech by asking our hostess, Lilly, if she believed in tradition. He continued by outlining the Goats' history here, in this very room, and how much fun we'd had over the years and how we valued it. He started describing the previous hostess and how much we liked her, because "she understood our sense of fun."

It was clear Wayne was going to try to get some spanking going. We were now squirming, giggling. Some of us were embarrassed. I found the speech downright creepy. Wayne sounded bureaucratic as a librarian. I downed what was left in my wine goblet. What were the odds of this woman—who was by now smiling crookedly—doing anything but spinning on her heel in disgust?

" . . . and so we were wondering if you could please help us out? Here, stand up, John, and show Lilly your spanking shorts."

At this point John—Spanky—rose and pulled his pants down to reveal his American flag boxers.

Wayne continued, "See, we always have a theme—" (not true) "—and John, being American—" (also not true) "—isn't happy about what his government is up to down there and he wants his government, you know, severely punished. So, we were wondering if you'd graciously keep our tradition alive, and help John out with his problem—" (John not only kept his pants down but had begun to position himself at the spanking bench) "—or maybe ask one of your staff if she might. You want my belt, or John's there?"

We were all silent as Lilly stood in the doorway. Her crooked smile had gotten crookeder. Her eyes suggested she was reviewing where she had hoped to be at this point in her life. She stopped looking at Wayne, and John, and gave us all a quick scan. Then she said, "I think Jane might want to see this," and fled downstairs.

We hooted and hollered in her wake because it did seem like, incredibly, some spanking might be on the agenda tonight, here, in this fancy restaurant, with the Michelin-Calgary-chef, on their opening night. What were the odds?

Lilly reappeared with not only Jane but another beautiful waitress, both of whom wore dubious expressions. From the bed, John lay on his stomach. He offered up his belt, which Lilly took. And Lilly proceeded to give that American flag a few little whacks with it. The team howled like a dozen chimps and hyenas. Finished, Lilly held the belt out to one of the waitresses, who was a bit eager with it, so much so that John had to tell her to please ease off. I think she wanted to use the buckle. What was with these Nanaimo gals? Were they anti-American? Anti-oldtimer? Hardcore S&M felines? And now this waitress let herself be bent over a lap and lightly hand-smacked, though she leapt up when that hand tried to linger. Meanwhile, Lilly had disappeared downstairs again, and back she came with the chef, who wore a gigantic chef's hat—as if there might be any doubt—and an older, rotund woman, maybe sixty, who turned out to be Lilly's mother. We learned now from this mother that she herself was part-owner of this restaurant, and that, yes please, she wanted to do some spanking too. And so, with the world-class chef looking on in wonder, his matronly employer wailed away on Ol' Glory, the fat on her upper arms jiggling lustily. It was one of the best things I've seen in my life. There was no reason to any of it.

I'll just ask again: what were the odds of that Old Goat tradition continuing? What were the odds of a spanking? At a virgin, first-night, high-end restaurant? And a *staff* spanking! A *family* spanking!

The only explanation I can arrive at is that the Goats are somehow blessed.

ANYWAY, AGAIN, hockey-wise we had a mixed weekend. The Friday-afternoon game saw us come back from a 5–1 deficit to tie in the last three seconds, which had us pumped and yelling, a celebration which I'm afraid probably satisfied us for the weekend. It's as if we had had our rush of success and it was enough, now where's the booze? In our next game, later that Friday night (guys our age playing two games in an evening? Is some demented Tubber bureaucrat secretly *hoping* for heart attacks?), we played a truly crummy team and managed only a 1–1 tie. But since we tied these first two, if we won the third game, Saturday afternoon, we'd be in the Sunday championship. So the Saturday situation was "win-win"—if we won, we got to play on Sunday, and if we lost, we didn't have to play on Sunday.

Personally, because I wanted to make Bub proud of his little brother, and because I wanted to qualify as a ringer, I was stinging from that demotion to the third line after only two shifts on the big line. On my second shift I'd actually gotten an assist. True, it was the kind of assist any klutz could get—I just lobbed it up to the streaking winger—but it was an assist. I mean, I hadn't screwed something up, I hadn't fanned on a shot and fallen on my head in the process. So the demotion stung.

The sweet part, though, was that in that 5–5 comeback tie, I had four points. Two goals and two assists. Okay, both assists were random passes that happened to lead to goals, and, true, one goal went in off a leg during a goalmouth scramble, and the other went five-hole even though I was aiming for the short side, but who besides me knew that? So it was a four-point night, which as far as I was concerned was ringer territory. I was a bit miffed that no one came up and confided that in their opinion I *was* a ringer and *should* be back on the first line, but that's the essential nature of oldtimers—no one but you sees how great you really are.

I got a goal the next game too, stuffing in a nice pass from Owen. Not that I kept count, but over the course of the tournament, our fat-guy line scored precisely two more than the slim, fast, good-guy line. Not that I counted, but my three goals were exactly three more than the slim, fast, good-guy centreman they promoted to take my place.

So, individually, from a personal point of view, from that selfish place, that hot little nugget of babyish ego that we all pretend not to have, the weekend was sweet. I made sure Bub knew exactly how many points I had amassed, reminding him long into the night, my pronunciation of the word "assists" getting a little slurry in the wee hours.

Those wee hours were fun. But there weren't enough of them and soon it was morning.

I'll just say that the Saturday game, which we had to win to make the finals, was horrible in all ways. It confirmed my status as a non-ringer. The enemy team was comprised of A-1 bastards, mostly because they lived in Nanaimo and cruelly lacked hangovers. They lined up for face-offs as eager and jumpy as men our age can get. Anyway, my first shift, I had the puck and Bub was breaking. I don't know how or even why, but he was. Maybe it was because he had had even less sleep that me—that is, none—and so his body was less confused, less torn between sleeping and waking, than mine. In any case, if I got the puck to him, he likely had a breakaway. He was only about ten feet from me, breaking. There was no one near me, hounding me, so all I had to do was feed him the puck. The word is "headman," and

I think it was the fault of that word itself for getting in and occupying my head and clouding my vision. I don't know how else I could put a puck twelve feet behind a guy who's only ten feet away. I mean, Bub just isn't that fast anymore.

It went downhill from there. My line was still "a good fit," because we had all deteriorated several notches in unison. Watching Owen struggle to keep the puck on his stick made me recall him in the biker bar the night before, hauling around and drinking from his private jug. Owen bought Bub and me, his linemates, our own private jugs as well, but at least Bub and I had the decency to share.

As the game drew to a close and it was clear we were going to lose, and not make the final for the second straight year, I understand that on the bench a few of our team's less party-inclined guys grumbled amongst themselves about the value of ferrying over to the Tubbers tournament if half the team was going to get so bombed on the first night that we had no chance of success. At the same time, the party guys were feeling *very* successful, because losing meant that tonight we could do last night all over again, without fear of having to play tomorrow.

DRIVING HOME from Nanaimo, passing the airport and heading towards Ladysmith (which was named after a British general who conducted a successful massacre in South Africa), I realized that every time I left this tournament and drove this stretch of road I had the identical feeling I was having right now. It's an odd one. Bub's team heads to the ferry to catch the boat to Vancouver. A few non-drivers have a beer in hand as they circulate in the lineup amongst the cars, the party continuing. But I'm alone and my party is over. I head south along the Island highway towards my real life. I am hollowed out, exhausted plus hungover, and I am well into making myself a list of guilty promises—work harder, be a better husband and father, learn to see hockey and beer as separate things. Today, on this same stretch of road, I recall these same promises and the number of years in a row I've made them.

I remind myself that the Nanaimo tournament, with Bub, was all I really wanted out of hockey this year. And it happened. We had some laughs. We talked about nothing remotely real, nothing about this game of life, this goalmouth scramble we are all engaged in, one that, here in middle age, we are learning how to relax with.

Zooming down Vancouver Island to its southernmost tip, I find myself fighting sleep. It's one in the afternoon. I snap on the radio and learn that it's Chinese New Year, and it's the Year of the Cock. Actually it's the Wood Rooster, but if people want to declare a Year of the Cock, I'm for it. Maybe we need a Year of the Cock. Some might say the cock has been celebrated enough, but others might beg to differ and suggest it's taken a hit in the last few decades. I smile at my own bad joking and wake up a bit, but I'm tired. I picture my skates, heavy and wet, in the trunk. The thought of strapping them on again any time soon makes me more tired still. How long will I persist in playing this game? When will I decide to relax completely?

But I goofed around with my brother and some decent guys this weekend. And I popped a few goals. Hey.

MEN FROM A DISTANT GALAXY

TO SAY THAT GOALIES ARE DIFFERENT is a cliché, but it's a fine cliché and worth exploring further. For instance, there's the chicken-and-egg question to wrestle with. That is, are goalies nutbars *before* they start playing, or does playing goal damage them and turn them into nutbars somewhere along the way? In other words, do certain kids possess that necessary intergalactic quality that causes them to *choose* being a target? Or do all those pucks to the skull jostle the pudding?

Let's imagine a typical goalie experience. The other team is breaking in on you and you go into your crouch. Your heart starts beating, your breath shortens and hisses through your mask as you try to pick up the puck beyond the hulking stupid D-man screening you. Suddenly a puck thuds shockingly off your chest. It drops too far out in front to grab, and anyway a crush of bodies is all around you, you're smacked in the neck, another shot goes off your elbow and then the post, and an asshole little centreman lands on you accidentally-on-purpose, and your stupid D-man clubs you while clearing the guy off, then another puck pinches your ear and hits the glass, bouncing right back out in front of the net, and someone's stick, you don't know whose, pokes you behind the knee, and finally the stupid D-man golfs it out to centre and everyone chases it, leaving you—suddenly—very much alone.

Call me a goalie myself, but I'm thinking that the cause of a netminder's oddity isn't so much the deluge of pucks, or the huge responsibility of being the last line of defence. I'm think-ing it's all this solitude. This *sudden* solitude. All that wild, pounding, scrambling, crowded chaos, and then, boom — noth-ing. Everyone's gone, you're all alone, and whatever fans are in the building are looking away from you, as are the two benches of players, the refs, everyone. If you could find it in all that gear, you could pull out your unit and waggle it and not a soul would notice. You're completely alone.

What's it like for a goalie to be alone? All you can hear is your own breath. There's absolutely nothing to do. A glob of salt sweat stings your eye. You're behind a mask, which is a further separation from the rest of humanity, maybe even reality. So naturally you start to talk to yourself. You congratulate yourself on that last save. You ask yourself if that clicking in the knee is cartilage or something worse. You start humming a little TV commercial, the one you hate. You start whistling tunelessly. Then, suddenly, it's those voices again, those weird ones . . .

There's a goalie in our league who looks completely nuts, but he actually might be the sanest netminder around. What he does is, as soon as the puck leaves his zone, he drops and gives himself twenty. Then he leaps up and skates behind his net and practises his bank-shot-off-the-glass motions. Then he does stretches, then practises angles. In other words, he doesn't give himself a second to be alone or hear those voices. And he's a fan-tastic goalie, for an oldtimer. Rumour has it he has abs.

WE ALL HAVE OUR FAVOURITE GOALIES, and our favourite goalie stories. While it's true to say that all goalies are insane, it's false to say that they are all insane in the same way. I think we have goalies to thank for showing us that insanity has remarkable range. It's these different forms of weirdness that are fun to explore.

It's no accident that one of the best and most singular nicknames in pro sport, Gump, was conferred upon a goalie. He wasn't pretty, he probably looked in the mirror every morning and said, "mask, shmask," and I'm guessing that he was the only rich, famous athlete in history who couldn't have gotten laid even if he paid for it. But he has my vote for best goalie who ever lived.

One famous goalie oddity was, of course, that Glenn Hall barfed before each game. The casual fan might think this a sane reaction to having to go out, maskless, and have pucks slapped at your head, but they don't know that Hall also puked before taking out the garbage, or walking his dog. No, seriously, what made Glenn Hall's puking so wonderfully quirky, so supremely goalie-like, was that he did not look like a puker. Or a goalie. Glenn Hall looked like the vice president of an insurance corporation. Not a guy who put on a colourful uniform and then knelt to puke.

Who else? Well, there's Jacques Plante, who knitted, and who, next to the Rocket, had the most intense and nutty Gallic stare in the game. And there's Ken Dryden, who in his between-period interviews sounded like he'd been boning up on writs and torts since he was nine and conjugated Latin verbs while leaning on that long-tall stick of his. Then Terry Sawchuk, who has my vote for second-best 'minder of all time, and who died one of the weirdest deaths, impaled on a barbecue. There's Patrick Roy, who has my vote as most overrated netminder, and who was spectacular mostly for his arrogance. If he'd played for, say, Columbus, we would have seen a fairly ordinary goalie, who would have ended an unspectacular career far earlier than he did, and would now be playing somewhere extremely rural. He was ordinary except for his bizarre passing skills. I don't know why he thought he could handle the puck, and his Colorado coaches were too afraid of him to tell him to stop, but I once counted five passes in a row that were picked off by board-pinching opponents, who couldn't wipe the smiles off their faces.

But the famously insane goalies aren't as colourful as their amateur brothers. Here are a few I've known and loved.

A guy nicknamed Wire, who weighed maybe a hundred and one pounds but loved to fight. He had a hard time finding opponents because, after sticking or hacking an opposing forward, the forward would hesitate before attacking Wire, both because he was a goalie and because he was so small. And then a D-man, sometimes me, would jump in to Wire's "rescue," because that was the job. More than once I saw Wire pull his D-man off a guy and jump in himself. He was kind of frightening to watch, kind of like a ferret killing one of those turkeys that are too fat to walk.

Then there's Donny, our just-retired netminder here in Victoria. Donny just might have been the best guy I've ever seen at playing angles. Guys flying in off the wings, or in alone on breakaways, or even from the high slot—Donny would stand there, perfectly positioned for the shot, unbeatable. Puck after puck just bounced off him. The thing is, Donny was also one of the, well, *portliest* netminders around, and if the puck actually got passed to another guy, well, Donny was still way over there playing that first angle, and the new shooter had, as they say, a yawning cage in which to deposit the puck. Same if Donny was called upon to go down. If that happened, just don't call on him to get up again. More often than not, if Donny saw the need to go down, he would just stay down, lying on his side, covering the low half of the net extremely well. He would stay down and follow the puck with his gaze as it went behind the net or into a corner, and if he had to he'd shoot an arm up or maybe even a great big leg. But he'd more or less just wait there for that next whistle, or for the puck to get across the centre red line, before beginning the long process of climbing back up onto his feet. More than once, his style generated discussion on the bench about how a small winch-and-pulley system might be installed in the net.

Chris, our other goalie, can be spectacular in all ways. We can be thoroughly outplayed, and outshot 40–11, and win 1–0. Other times, Chris is known for going behind the net to stop the puck on a shoot-in, and somehow the puck hits something on him, flies up over the net, and lands right on the stick of one of their guys. It's so perfect a setup that Chris looks like nothing more than a paid saboteur, but I don't think he is.

There was another goalie, in New Brunswick, who filled in for Dana, our regular 'minder. This new guy, Ernie, a real estate agent from down near Saint John, had the best gear anyone had ever seen. Everything was new, bright, expensive. He also had the most impressive dressing-room warmups we'd ever seen—all sorts of yoga postures and such, and I think in one of them he actually levitated. Before and after games, his wife—who brought him to the dressing-room door and always waited outside for him after—pulled out various tonics and oils and rubbed him down in an impressively professional manner—arms, legs, shoulders, head, cooing words of praise in his ears as she did so. Anyway, the first time Ernie showed up on the scene, pulled out that gear of his, and told us some stories of his goaling exploits (his talk was as expensive and professional as his gear), we were pretty darned excited to finally have an exceptional netminder on the team, Dana being exceptional in, well, other ways. The thing is, and you may already have guessed it, Ernie was ridiculous in goal. If he'd ever played before, even one game, in all his life, it wasn't apparent. What was apparent was that he had never been, and would never be, good. Not even remotely. He could not move a foot to stop a puck that had been lobbed from centre. I will say without exaggeration that every six-year-old boy or girl in New Brunswick could kick his ass in net, while simultaneously eating cereal and watching Saturday-morning cartoons. I would not be so mean to him here if he hadn't talked himself up so much, and let us all down. He was fabulously insane, even for a goalie.

I don't know what it is that makes a goalie. It's not intelligence. In midget, our goalie couldn't read, but he had the reflexes of a hungry weasel, and maybe the best natural glove hand I've ever seen. I bet if you told him to grab that passing hummingbird by the left wing, he could. He might eat it, though, and smile benignly while awaiting your next instruction, but there you go.

Nor is it bravery that makes a good 'minder. In Fredericton we had a D-man, Arden, whose eyes and nostrils widened with desire whenever Dana was a no-show. Arden loved being called on to play goal. He even used his regular skates, and would make kick saves with his unpadded instep without complaint (I believe he used the one-beer-per-instep-bruise method to ease his considerable pain). But we liked it when Arden played, too. We liked to sit back, put the skates up, and watch. You know Dominik Hasek's style? The way he twists and flops on his back, then a leg shoots up impossibly to make a last-ditch save? Well, Arden looked like that, except a ridiculous version of it—a drunken, crazed Hasek, whose leg would shoot out impossibly, yes, but at the wrong time and for no reason at all. Arden made more saves with his head-bone than with his leg pads. He'd be as likely to catch a puck with his blocker fingers as his trapper. Bravery? He would put his neck in the way of a howitzer in the last seconds of a 13–1 loss, and he'd be snorting and fire-eyed as he did it. Remember the Tasmanian Devil on Bugs Bunny? How he spun like that? Arden Doak played similarly, only picture the Devil fallen over on his side, spinning slower and grunting, smelling of rum, a leg pad flapping randomly around, and a puck nowhere near him.

But that leaves, finally, Dana himself, whose insanity is so complete and pure that he has gained some kind of threshold and is likely the most sane man I've had the pleasure to meet. He was our Fredericton Stinkhorn goalie and I've already mentioned him on occasion. For one, he's such a gentle man, with such innocent demeanour, that I seriously think he might be a saint. For another, he was one of the guys I wouldn't sit beside for three years because I knew I wouldn't understand him. For yet another, he's in some sense the perfect oldtimer: he could be either thirty or sixty, depending on how the light strikes his face. He has formidable muscle, but it's hidden under a formidabler layer of lard. And, finally, one year he turned yellow because he enjoyed himself too much. Otherwise, I don't know if the English language has words for this particular tender of the nets. First, picture a face that blends Gump Worsley and Jimmy Stewart in a specially sad and hopeful moment. Add eighty pounds. That's him.

He strikes one as an innocent child, until you see his forearms and you realize he could kill you without breaking a sweat. Yet those forearms are hairless, like a baby's—he's that kind of conundrum. Sometimes underemployed, but in that respectable Maritime fashion that might involve creative solutions to feeding your family, Dana might have been drawn to the position of goalie mostly because, on our team, goalies didn't pay. Our goalies tended to get hit with a lot of pucks.

Which made Dana's gear all the more marvellous. I don't know where it came from—I suspect it was given to him as a practical joke, with no further gear forthcoming. I'm also guessing it came from various yard sales, or perhaps the Sally Ann. And I'm speaking only of the gear you could *recognize* as gear. He did have a helmet, and skates. But I think his trapper was a first-baseman's glove. His chest pad, or whatever it's called, was nothing but a thick layer of dirty, stained felt that shredded and fell apart a bit more each game, and didn't even begin to cover his impressive belly. His arm padding was comprised of two felt tubes, full of holes (for some reason, the biceps had been cut out altogether), which was tied by shoelaces to his shoulder pads, which were ancient and built for a child, the plastic shoulder cups once red, but now faded pink. His helmet had a cage of sorts dangling from it, also attached with shoelaces, and various kinds of glues and tape held bars and chunks of mesh in place, for a while. If he waved his trapper at you it wobbled and flapped limply like cooked pasta, and was about as protective as one layer of lasagna noodle. I could go on. Also, all of it stank like bad meat, especially, for some reason, the helmet. In any case, in tournaments, or whenever we encountered a new ref, the game was often delayed while the ref prodded Dana's gear in disbelief, and more often than not—usually because of that damned useless helmet—made us madly scour the arena for something more protective, and more resembling actual hockey equipment.

Needless to say, because of that gear, and the amount of pucks he stopped nightly, Dana had a colourful body. The spring he turned sort of yellow, his bruises stood out beautifully. He looked like Homer Simpson painted in leopard.

It wasn't Dana's fault he turned yellow. It was probably the rum's fault. Or perhaps it was the Maritimes' fault, for treating rum as, well, an ordinary thirst-quencher. I never did get the hang of that one, and tended to pass the rum bottle to the next guy when it circled the room after the game as we sat there still puffing, our skates not even off yet. But Dana was a rum drinker, and aside from turning him yellow it was actually good for him.

During most games he was an average goalie, with certain strengths and weaknesses. A strength was breakaways—he was almost unbeatable, if he tried. A weakness was angles—sometimes he'd float out and think he was diligently guarding the cage when in fact the net was way over there somewhere. Also, if Dana went down, that was where he'd stay for a while.

But for tournaments the team brought an extra-large bottle of rum. It was an added expense no one questioned. Quite simply, when Dana had a pull of rum, he was spectacular. When he nipped at it all weekend, he was miraculous. His wobbling trapper snared everything that came near it; on bullet drives labelled for the low corner, he did lightning-fast splits like a twelve-year-old Romanian gymnast. And he sprang up after all of this. It was the rum, and too bad it turned him yellow and he thought best to quit.

But after those tournament shutouts, where we won tournaments against far better teams, all on the strength of Dana's performances, he'd sit in the room like always, his shredded-meat gear hanging off him by threads, and he'd smile as innocently and sweetly as always, his gentle voice hard to hear. I realize now that I never once heard the man raise his voice, or yell. He'd shake when he'd laugh, and you couldn't hear him.

Memory #9: Hockey Night in China

LONG, LONG AGO, When Earth was still cooling, I played with the University of BC Thunderbirds, and we went to China—Red China, as it was called then. It was December of 1973, China and Russia were glaring at each other, and the Cultural Revolution had cut its blood-red swath. No white folks had been in China for about twenty years, except a few diplomats, and an Aussie volleyball team that went in a month before us and had reportedly been sent home in disgrace "because one of them grabbed a woman's buttocks." We were on what was called the Friendship Tour, a kind of probe sent out to see what might happen to us, much like a worm thrown into a pond full of koi. Before the trip we were briefed by the Department of External Affairs, which told us never to touch a Chinese person, not even to offer a hand to be shaken, because it would be overly familiar and insulting. We were given some fancy-assed parkas—thin blue felt, with orange embroideries of polar bears and other everyday Canadian stuff.

It will surprise no one to hear that our government got it wrong. Once in China, we froze in our cute felt parkas. The Chinese laughed sympathetically and supplied us with heavily quilted coats, thick enough for a Winnipeg winter, which is exactly what a northern China winter is like. And the Chinese guys, from players to translators to mayors, in every region of the country, were hand-shaking fools. They often liked to walk along the sidewalk with an arm around you.

First, in Peking, which is what Beijing was still called, we played the Chinese national team and, even though we were all lagged and disoriented, beat them badly. We suffered not just standard culture shock but hockey culture shock: we played in front of twenty-five thousand fans, what looked to be an equal number of men and women, who were all dressed the same. It was a new arena that smelled of fresh cement, but between periods its ice got swept with twig brooms. The crowd sat silently as the game began, which felt odd. Picture a "moment of silence" that goes on and on indefinitely. But then a player tripped and *fell down*, whereupon everyone in the crowd *laughed*. Twenty-five thousand people laughing sounded like a deep rolling, like a weird thunder. With a Chinese accent. And they were all wearing quilted black parkas. Now they all held their breath, waiting for the next funny thing to happen, a hilarious slapshot, for instance. That's what it was like.

The Chinese did want to win. At a banquet the night before the second game we were seated at huge, round tables — Canadian, Chinese, Canadian, Chinese — and the Chinese team was under obvious instructions to try to get us drunk. The conversations were very basic. You'd point at your glass of beer and say, "Beer," and they'd point at the same glass and say, *"Pijou,"* and then you'd both laugh nervously, and then you'd take a big gulp of beer and they wouldn't. They were really bad actors in their style of urging us to drink up, but they didn't meet a lot of resistance, because the basic Canadian instinct had already kicked in, the one that goes, "If you're at a party or something, and there's, like, free booze, you drink as much as you can, eh?"

The beer was excellent, very European. The wine was the shits. It was usually plum, and sweet, and almost as bad as '70s Ontario wine. The national beverage, pronounced *mowtie*, was clear and overproof and served in little porcelain thimbles. If you didn't drink one of these whenever somebody shouted *"Gumbye!"* it was apparently an insult, akin to saying, "Your Revolution Is Inglorious and Your Mama Wears Red Army Boots." So we drank lots of those. For some reason, the Chinese players weren't allowed to. (It didn't matter. The next day, though a little wobbly and irritable, we beat them even worse.)

One of our guys, Ned, had played pro and quit to come back to school after only a half year, but he had picked up some professional moves. One involved climbing onto a banquet table, putting a friendly arm around the carved-vegetable peacock sculpture, and smoking a giant stogie with his belly button. Ned was singing something, too, but I can't remember what. His bucking gut produced an impressive amount of smoke, and I can still see his head sitting majestically above it, like a mountain peak above the clouds.

Apparently we ate dog, in one of those hot-pot fondue affairs where you chopstick up your choice of several kinds of raw meat and stick it in some bubbling sauce to cook. I don't think the Chinese were being sneaky. After we learned of it a few days later, some of us wondered aloud if that is where our word "chow" comes from.

Up north, we got a sense of hockey politics. We were touring with their national team and playing exhibitions against them, and in each city a local line would be added to their roster. We saw that these local guys were typically better than the regular national team players. The three locals would be six foot one or two, and strong, and decent hockey players. In the north, it's very Canadian—colder than hell, and people eat bread and stew, and grow big. They claim that hockey is indigenous there, and that they in fact invented it, or some form of it—but what country with a winter and frozen ponds doesn't make that claim? In any case, the players were good. But we still beat them by scores of 8–1 and the like.

Because of the imbalance we decided to have some fun. Any forward who wanted to play defence, and any defenceman who wanted to play forward, did. I jumped at the chance, and was suddenly a centre. And a damn fine one. What defenceman, who spends his life sending his forwards beautiful passes only to see them blow it time after time, doesn't think—doesn't *know*—that he could do it better if only given the chance? Well, here was my chance. And for my first game as a forward we were playing at an outdoor rink (which seated thousands), and I felt like a kid in Winnipeg. The ice made that deep crunching sound when you dug in. The clacking of stick on puck was thin and echoed off into the night. As for my new career as a forward, I had to admit I was a tad rusty around their net, and roofing it wasn't as simple as it looked, and maybe I hurried things, and didn't really know what to do coming out of our end, and backchecking was so hard that I decided not to include it in my style of play—but otherwise I was excellent. I scored a goal. It wasn't credited to me, but to my linemate who was in the goal-mouth with me whacking away, but I know it was me and that's all that counts in life. No one else noticed quite how great I was at centre, because as soon as we played in Japan I was stuck back on the blue line. But *I* knew. And the day I started playing old-timers? I was once again a sleek and excellent centreman.

When travelling, a hockey player's chief concern, next to the availability of beer, is the food. And I have to say that the food in China was incredibly good. Though I also must report that some of our guys were, to put it tactfully, your basic small-town redneck jocks who missed their fries and ketchup and got loud about having to eat all this fuckin *Chinese* food all the time. But for my brother Bub and me, who lived within walking of some good Chinese restaurants and ate at them a few times a week, and whose idea of the perfect hangover cure early on a Sunday afternoon was to smoke a joint and go gain eight pounds on all-you-can-eat dim sum, this place was heaven. I mean, this was where Chinese food *came* from. So we tucked in. Sure, the chicken-feet appies and gelatinous sea slugs were a bit sketchy, but everything else was glorious shovel food. I think we freaked out a few of our teammates. The boiled dumplings, pronounced *jowtzu* — or just "jowzers," which was simpler to say — treated the back of your throat to a gorgeous spurt of spicy hot grease when you bit into one. Sometimes the grease squirted out the side of your jowzer, so the boys tended to slide their chairs away from my brother and me if dumplings were on the menu, and they were disgusted when we gazed longingly at their plates and asked softly, "So you gonna eat those jowzers?"

Speaking of rednecks, we saw a colourful display during one game. Now, I like rednecks, but only the kind who don't really mean it, who are just being funny and living up to their reputation. The other kind, who truly do hate strangers, especially strangers of different races, I think we can agree that they are best not encouraged. One game, one of our D-men just, well, snapped. He started gooning guys, hacking and high-sticking them in the chops for no reason. Neither the Chinese players nor the refs knew how to respond to him. They tried penalties, but that didn't slow him down, and then they asked if he'd please sit on the bench and not play anymore. Our coach obliged. In the room between periods (where they always had nice long tables set up, with white tablecloths, bowls of quartered oranges, and hot jasmine tea) he went nuts, screaming about "all these fucking chinks." He punched walls and yelled and laughed and looked on the verge of crying. Clearly, it had nothing to do with the Chinese and everything to do with him being submarined by all this strangeness, and being so far from home. Also, he was one of these guys who, back home, wasn't at all violent around violent opponents, but was happy to rough up anyone he knew wouldn't hit back. Anyway, the team doctor calmed him down with some contentedness pills, and he was fine for the rest of the trip, and actually over-the-top buddy-

buddy with his Chinese foes, making amends. (Isn't that the truth, that rednecks aren't really mad, just sad? Or maybe it just takes the right drug to make them see the light.)

In Beijing we were in this huge old hotel built by the long-gone Russians, and it was the only hotel in the entire city. It was olde colonialist European-style, meaning the wooden furniture is uncomfortable, the mouldings ornate, and instead of closets they have wardrobes, which smell like Humphrey Bogart's suits. The ceilings are so high you can hardly see up, way up, through the hazy blue of Bogey's cigarette smoke, to what looks like a fan turning slowly. The room is five or six storeys up, which is very high for Beijing, and lets you see off over the city and on to the distant plains. It's night now, though, and you can't see anything out there. In the corner of the room is a huge, ancient radio, a floor model with beautiful rounded wood. It has three immense ivory dials to turn, and several needles that travel over incomprehensible graphs of numbers and bandwidths. It's the middle of the night, you can't sleep, and you're standing there naked with your blue felt parka on. The city of six million is silent, because they all work at six in the morning and in any case there's nothing to do. But the radio is anything but silent. You spin a dial and pick up all sorts of languages. You recognize Italian, and French. You spin through all sorts of Asian languages you can't distinguish from each other. You turn a bit more and hear the barking dog of Russian. You spin a whole bunch and you hear English—the London kind. You're standing in this hotel room and you realize you can get the entire planet on the radio. You adjust the dial back a bit and you hear, "This is Radio Free Europe." You spin to an American Armed Forces broadcast from Germany. You spin a whole bunch more and it's a San Francisco station, a Grateful Dead song that goes on and on. You have an odd moment of feeling certain that you aren't far from home, but right at the Earth's centre, and that your home has just gotten way bigger. You can see over oceans and mountains and prairies in all directions at once. You're twenty-one—a hockey player, but maybe not that into it anymore. You don't have a girlfriend back home waiting for you. You have no clue, not a one, what the future holds. The Vietnam War is winding down, back home Greenpeace is driving Zodiacs at whaling ships, you're in university but don't know why, and right now you're in a Russian-built room in China, tired from playing a hockey game today, listening to the Grateful Dead, who you've never really liked. The whole world feels strange yet utterly familiar, and here in the middle of the night, in the middle of the planet, you feel hollow with loneliness, yet completely full to bursting. Anything is possible.

MAYBE BECAUSE WINNING was too easy in China, we started to search out amusements other than hockey. For instance, one day three of us outwitted the secret police. Rich, Spike, and I were walking along a crowded market street on a clear, crisp day, when Spike suddenly lost his mind. We were always being followed by our invisible "hosts," who were always making sure we "didn't get lost." These were secret police, of course, and they made sure that we didn't see factory workers who weren't smiling, or that we didn't talk to anyone who might say he didn't love the Chairman, or the government, more than life itself. Anyway, Spike, a Saskatchewan guy who was not normally given to acting up, suddenly began walking really fast, muttering, "Let's lose these bastards." He tore across the street. Rich yelled, "Let's meet by that flat building," and took off through a gap in a fence. I looked back. Three men were in a sudden huddle, discussing us in loud voices, gesturing at each other angrily, keeping us in view. I started running. I flew down an alley, dodging a donkey cart. It was great, like being ten in

Winnipeg after raiding a garden for carrots.

We met up by the flat building, then ducked through a gate into a courtyard. The courtyard was full of kids of all ages, who stopped what they were doing. It was a schoolyard and these kids each had a chore. Some cleaned the school's walls, some swept the dirt with twig brooms, some supervised the littlest kids in calisthenics. Everyone stopped and stared. Then some came up and started talking to us, a mile a minute. They touched our clothes and grabbed our hands. One did something that looked like dancing the twist. Most stayed back and stared, while a few looked frightened.

An older woman approached. She, too, talked to us a mile a minute. She kept looking back over her shoulder and also out into the street. Then two more teachers came, and finally "the eenreesh teechah," who spoke English maybe a little better than we spoke Chinese. She told us that we were her most friends and that it was a true, organized day and everything was being successful. She explained some more, her smile never quavering. Then some children took us by the hand and led us through a door, down a hall, and into an auditorium, where kids and teachers alike were in a panic of preparation, setting up chairs, donning costumes. Eventually we were seated in the front row of chairs. An ancient record player was wheeled out. The English teacher, flipping through a worn dictionary, informed us that we were about to experience something called "enjoy children pageant."

It was delightful. As tightly choreographed as any show on Broadway, groups of kids took the stage to sing and dance. Their voices were a bit like Alvin and the Chipmunks, and the backing music was that reedy Chinese violin, but it was a splendour. The talent was remarkable. I think I saw flashes of genius, I really do. The dancing in particular was breathtaking—I saw where all the Cirque du Soleil conscripts would later come from. It was both cute and creepy to see seven-year-olds end each dance in a tight, multiperson sculpture of raised fists and severe scowls, the posture of soldier-workers ready to kick ass for the State. In their faces shone true belief, though I wondered how deep the belief went. I'm of the opinion that even kids "know what's going on." Standing in strategic positions in the auditorium and sitting scattered throughout the crowd were children of various ages who were wearing a red band on one arm. These were Red Guards. I'd read about them. They were the creepiest of creeps. They were like the class suck, but the class suck from hell, because they would turn in their best friend, teacher, and even parent if they suspected them of slacking off a little bit in their loyalty to the State. I would've loved to have slew-footed one of them as they goose-stepped by, but to tell the truth I was afraid of them myself—especially the smallest ones, the six-year-olds, who were, well, *six*, and could have you hurt. I had the feeling that if I tripped a six-year-old Red Guard I would somehow be dead in seconds.

Anyway, it was fun to be in the audience for a change and watch someone else put on their uniforms and play their game.

Eventually we noticed some newcomers entering the auditorium at the back. I could tell from the fierce whispers and bobbing heads that teachers were being congratulated for putting on this show and keeping us here while they were summoned. When the show ended we were surrounded by these officials, including our three duped secret police, all of whom were smiling broadly in the way any foreign culture does when totally pissed off. One guy introduced himself as the Mayor of Peking, though I don't know if he was using the right word. On the outskirts of this huddle, being led away, children of all ages were smiling and waving to us. And so were some of the teachers—

especially the English teacher, who I could see would've loved to practise on us long into the night. They were all being herded by the tiny, insane Red Guards, who weren't smiling at all, not one bit, because they had important work to do.

WE ALSO SAW some politics mixed dangerously with hockey. Harbin was a city of a couple million at the time, and it sits just north of North Korea. The rink was truly a beaut—it was outdoor, but seated twelve thousand. Strings of lights dangled over the ice—a bigger, brighter version of what I recall lit the Winakwa Park rink of my youth, in Winnipeg, where I played shinny every night of the week if I could.

Between the first and second periods, as we sat resting in our huge dressing room, each in a private wooden chair, sipping hot jasmine tea and sucking quartered blood oranges, we heard thunderous noise outside. It was deep and booming and came in waves. It grew louder, and then the building itself started to shudder. Our room was windowless, and a trainer went to check things out. The noise continued, and grew, and the trainer came back puzzled, saying that no one would tell him anything, but that he had seen through a window that there were huge crowds of people outside the building.

"I think it's, like, a *mob* or something," is what he said. He looked pale.

The noise grew, and the shuddering of the building had a kind of ebb and flow to it. The between-periods break went on much longer than it should have. Then, just when the roaring noise grew even louder, it suddenly stopped. In the gap we could hear a stuttering rattle, which only later did we understand might have been a machine gun. Then the roar picked up again, but it faded and faded as, we determined, the crowd withdrew. We never did learn if anyone died out there, but we did learn the reason for the riot. It seems we were in a highly militarized region, and all tickets for the game had been given to high-ranking soldiers. Yes: the peasantry had rioted because they wanted *to see us play hockey* and couldn't. As amazing as that might sound, foreign entertainment wasn't at all common in those parts, at that time. They probably would have rioted had they been denied the chance to see the latest new colour of shirt. But I believe the real reason was that these common citizens, seeing class favours being handed out in a supposedly classless society, decided to tell the government to put its money where its mouth was—in this dictatorship of the proletariat, we're gonna do us some dictatin'. And good for them, I say. I never did like those Mao statues everywhere. He talked team spirit non-stop, but he was one of the biggest puck hogs in history.

MOST OF US HAD BROUGHT along some extra gear to China, in case something broke or wore out. And then, to a man, we left it all behind, accidentally-on-purpose. You should have seen the equipment some of their guys were using, especially the local pick-up line that joined the national team each game. Eaton's catalogues would have been a step up. The gloves looked like those cartoon renderings from the Dit Clapper era, drawn by artists who had never played. Sticks were glued back together. But we had to leave a note with the left-behind gear, otherwise, guaranteed, it would've been shipped back to us. The thing is, early in the trip a teammate had lost his wristwatch down south in Canton. He didn't have a clue where he'd left it, and didn't care that much anyway, and didn't even report it lost, but the wristwatch somehow found its way back to him—more than a week, several cities, and two thousand miles later, up north in Harbin.

Memory #10: A Beautiful Girl Giving Me Roses over the Boards

PICTURE THIS. After a game, I'm skating off the ice, tired and sweaty, and a beautiful girl I don't know is shouting my name and holding out a dozen red roses for me. Maybe this happens a lot to some of you, but for me it was just the once.

It was in Japan. I was there with the UBC Thunderbirds after our tour of China, which, being so cold and communist and Third World, made Japan look like one big decadent explosion of neon. The Tokyo skyscrapers were tall and glass, the billboards had movies of half-naked gorgeous white blond people on them, the smog smelled expensive, everyone was loud and drunk, and no car in the constant traffic jam was more than twenty minutes out of a car wash or more than six months old. It looked as though Japan was trying to outdo the US of A in the materialism department, and there was no question it was winning.

The glitz started as soon as we got off the plane in Tokyo. In the airport, Kagey and Yoshio, two Japanese exchange students who had played the season with us, were swarmed by TV cameras and reporters. Flashbulbs popped. Yoshio, who was a good player and apparently a star in Japan, looked rather bored—he was used to it. Now, the rest of us were a bunch of over-the-hill juniors, meaning we were a typical Canadian university team, and not even a top-flight one, and back home if we beat the University of Alberta we were lucky if the *Vancouver Sun* even printed the score. That was about the extent of our media coverage. TV cameras?

The Japanese businessman who sponsored our visit owned the Seibu team, their country's perennial champion. He also owned hotels, the national railway, and maybe a small island nation or two. We were told he was the world's second-richest man. We stayed in one of his hotels, were given free everything (including a hugely expensive watch; he also owned Seiko), and at a banquet of lobster and Kobe beef, we formed a line to shake the rich man's hand. After China, with its steamy radiators, dark streets, and uniform smiles on all the uniformed people, we were all very tired, and strangely suspicious of all the Japanese glitz and wealth. I was particularly disgusted with Japanese TV—all the talk shows that used "educational panel discussions" as a pretext to show naked breasts. I didn't mind the breasts, I just hated the sleazy way it was done. Incredibly, on *The Mother-Daughter Show* a naked mother stood there with her naked daughter while a guy in a lab coat holding a pointer pointed out what age and gravity do to genetically similar female breasts. Both women, who may or may not have been related, were dyed blondes who struck typical models' poses.

A pleasant kind of sleaziness marked the typical bar there. Even a hole in the wall swarmed with "bar girls," all about twenty, all beautiful. They would come over and tell you "how handsome and interesting" you were, and ask politely if they could sit on your lap. Once on your lap, they asked very sweetly if you would buy them a drink. Once the drink arrived, they would toss it back and ask for another. These drinks, I learned, were basically coloured water. The girls would stay on your lap, all sweet as could be, as long as you kept the coloured water flowing. I recall buying only the one water for my bar girl, and it almost emptied my college-student wallet.

But it turns out Japan isn't all commerce, because after closing time my bar girl came back to my hotel with me. (My brother wasn't so lucky with his, even though he had her convinced that he was Mick Jagger's cousin.) She told me her name was Gail, and her sweetness continued. I tried explaining hockey to her, and she nodded, a very serious expression on her face, but

I could tell she was having trouble with the concept of a dozen people playing a violent game on a sheet of ice. We got to my room and I knocked first, because of the hour. My roommate, the Japanese player Kagey, might be up to something himself, or asleep. He came to the peephole, sounding asleep, and in hushed tones I asked very politely if he could go grab a bed somewhere else because I had a female companion with me.

"Japanese girl?" His voice was rather clipped.

"Uh, yeah."

"No."

I stood there for a moment, asked him, "Say, what?" or something, and he repeated that he wouldn't budge. I whined for a while, to no avail, and then got angry, and eventually Kagey stomped out, looking at neither of us. I didn't feel too bad about it because, well, in my world it was a given that you'd do this sort of thing for a teammate.

Gail and I went in and got comfy, and though one thing led to another I could tell it wasn't going to lead to anything too memorable because, lo and behold, it seemed that Gail was a typical, well-bred eighteen-year-old, the kind I was used to in Canada — that is, a girl who wouldn't give it away on a first date. Which was fair enough. So we were getting comfy with that, and having some middle-of-the-road fun anyway, when the phone rang. It was security. The security man asked in a very sugary voice if I had a visitor. I told him no, and asked him not to wake me up again. With no loss of sugar, the voice told me that a gentleman had reported to him that I indeed had a visitor with me, a Japanese guest. I asked him if this was against the law, that I had "a guest."

I could see that Gail had in the meantime risen to get dressed. She didn't seem surprised. Blowing me kisses, she pantomimed that it was time for her to go. I hung up the phone and asked her why. She told me, simply, that any Japanese man who knew we were together would be very, very mad, because I wasn't Japanese. In fact, Gail told me, she was expecting some very angry lectures in the lobby, so she was going to try to sneak down some stairs. No, she didn't want me to come with her. No, please, especially because you look angry now too.

In any case, Gail left, I didn't follow or argue, and I had just discovered Japanese racism, which allowed a hotel employee to give a paying customer grief for doing something perfectly legal and none of his business. As for Kagey, the next day I was cool to him, and he wouldn't look at me. Sure, he'd been turfed from bed, but I was a tad miffed that a guy I'd played with all year, a guy I'd feathered a few passes to and then taken the hit, considered me less than worthy to be smooching one of his country-women. Now, I suppose it's a good lesson for every one of us to experience the shitty end of racism at some point in our lives, but not at the cost of some nooky. Thank God I hadn't been in the middle of getting lucky, or Kagey might have been on the wrong end of some old-fashioned Canadian trouble come next practice.

Speaking of which, we did play a few games in Japan. I think we won two and lost one. It was another case of a bunch of speedy guys wanting to beat the Canadians at their own sport, but after a month in China we didn't care, we just wanted to be home. Then, at the end of the third game, skating off, I heard someone shouting my name. It was a piping little voice, and it was calling my name, except that my name sounded like, "Beer! Oh Beer!" And there she was, a young beauty, her face beaming, blushing, shy and proud and afraid, and she was holding out a bouquet of roses. I stopped, a couple of dull-headed and tired teammates thudding up against me. And I took the roses. A teammate or two said something like, "Jesus holy shit, look at *Gaston.*" I'll never forget the moment, or Yuria's eyes. When I took her roses, she actually thanked me—she was honoured that I'd taken the time to stop and take her roses from her. I knew even in that moment that I would never again come so close to knowing what it was like to be an international heartthrob movie-star king of the world.

I didn't know why she singled me out. I was no Brad Pitt, and we had a Brad Pitt–type guy on the team—but now I saw that he was getting roses from someone else. So maybe I was Yuria's second pick. Later, she said she had picked me because she liked the "forceful" way I played, and because—she giggled here—I had a cute but very big nose. In fact, she said, I had "the biggest nose of everyone."

It was all strange and getting stranger. She asked me my room number—she already knew what hotel we were staying at—and asked shyly if she could come and see me. I said, "Well, uh," and then, as deftly as a brick hitting dirt, asked how old she was. As I'd guessed, she was fourteen. In response to the horror on my face, she laughed and told me that it would be all right, she would be with a friend.

When she did call later that day I told her I'd come down and meet her in the lobby. She was with several friends, all of them smiling and giggling. Yuria gave me the gift of an eight-by-ten glossy photo of herself, in an innocent and respectable pose, but with a coy frosting of sexuality. She asked if we could shake hands, and we did, and there were more giggles.

It was extremely odd to have experienced bigotry the night before and now a kind of worship. It was only remotely sexual—it was more the kind of social silliness that pop musicians suffer with adoring teenyboppers. But, what the hell, why me? Did these girls have no understanding that I wasn't deserving? That I was an average player on a team that was lucky to get a linescore written up in our local paper? That my bank account had seventeen dollars in it? That during certain off-seasons I had reportedly been seen living at my parents'?

I decided it was all a labyrinthine psychological carry-over from Yuria's father having lost a war against people who looked like me. I did take Yuria's proffered pen and jot my Vancouver address down in her special pink book. A week after I returned home, I received a letter. I wrote her a single short one back, saying I was glad to have helped her practise her English. She sent another letter, and another, and tons that followed. I stopped opening them. It was too weird. It felt hollow being adored—not for me but for some kind of concept. And my nose isn't *that* big.

Though I did enjoy being called "Beer." Who wouldn't? But I feel sorry for the likes of Wayne Gretzky, guys who have to stand and sign autographs while fans wait and drool a couple of feet away, having no idea what sort of guy Wayne is, or even who he is, but they drool anyway.

I'm a bit hesitant to reveal the happy ending to this story, but I will. Yuria phoned me ten years later, when she was a flight attendant for Japan Air Lines.

That wonderful soft voice over the receiver, asking shyly, "Beer?"

She was in Vancouver for the night. She was recently divorced from her husband, an American who'd been teaching English in Tokyo. She'd looked me up in the phone book, and what was I doing later? Knowing now that I was just another North American with a nose and that that was apparently all that mattered to her, I said, "Nothing," and drove downtown. But that's another story, more of a lecherous oldtimer sort of tale, one involving room service at the Hotel Vancouver, and more than one instance of me thinking she was calling desperately for more beer. But you won't hear the rest of the story outside of a dressing room.

THIS SEASON SO FAR

March

I TAKE IT ALL BACK. All my whining about oldtimers, all my questioning of this our beloved sport of hockey. Because it's a wonderful game, it really is. It's more than that: it's a means and end in itself. It's a reason for living and it's the meaning of life.

The thing is, I've started having some fun again. It appears that the assorted games I've played, plus those walks I've taken the dog on, plus those two intense tournaments almost back to back have added up to something. I found some jump! I have some *jump!* There are only seven games left in our season but they're going to be great ones, because suddenly I can skate by guys. I can dig in the corner and come out with the puck and still have a bit left. I can dish to a guy and then take off for the give-and-go instead of just watching. I could even backcheck, a little, if I had to.

In the room I crack a beer and talk a mile a minute, rehashing plays, mocking guys and getting mocked, laughing. I've popped some goals, set some up. We've won a few. I had a blast being restrained while screaming at the ref one game, because he said I put my hand on the puck in our goal crease even though I didn't, and the resultant penalty shot cost us the game, but it was great fun. Even the bitchiness on the bench seems like good ol' fun. Most of all, though, the muscles working like this feels just like what a body is created to do, which is to exert itself with grace. In the chugging moment, in the zone, wind on the face and a six-inch gap to shoot for, it feels not just like life intensified, but life fulfilled.

This isn't my last season! I want to play until I'm eighty! Why the hell not? Give me one good reason.

FINE. A reason was delivered, last night. Thanks, God, or Whoever's rotten job it is to dole out the reality checks. (Whoever He is, I hope He feels guilty.) But last night I got a reality check, and my one good reason.

Here's what happened. We were playing the Sabres, a bunch of guys who live up near the airport. There's an airplane on their jersey. Like almost every team in our league, they're better than us, mostly because they have a few more younger guys, and at the start of the third period we're down 4–2. But I'm having fun—fun with my bit of jump. I've got a goal, I'm hustling, I'm a bit of a threat out there. I set up Dave, my fave winger, so I also feel generous. I've even begun to consider the possibility of backchecking, and it might indeed happen, especially if we tie it up. In any case, there I am, cruising out around the red line, waiting for a pass from someone doing all the work—when, lo and behold, my left winger, Big Mike (the guy on our team who's usually the most pregnant) chips the puck up the boards past a pinching blueliner.

I have a breakaway. Horny as hell, I take my first digging step towards that beautiful and naked puck and, *GUNK*, something big in my inner thigh *goes*. I'll call it my groin, but it's more mid-leg, halfway between my unit and my inside knee. I've had scads of groin pulls and this is nothing like that. It's as if a big muscle just decided to give up, then and there, and detach itself from bone. "That's *it*," it said, almost with a sigh, "I'm not playing anymore. The rest of you muscles play. I'm just going to fall apart." It didn't even hurt that much.

What did I do? Most of my brain knew that what had just happened in my leg was bad, especially for an old body that no longer heals, and that it might be the last injury of my career, and *the last shift of my life*. So what did I do? Go to the bench and bow out gracefully? No. Fall into a heap? No. No, a loose breakaway puck turns anyone into a bug-eyed seven-year-old, even a guy whose leg no longer works. So of course I kept going. I wanted that puck, I wanted that breakaway, I wanted to score. Knowing that this was maybe my last shift probably added to my desire to score.

It was a clear-cut breakaway. I basically went in with one leg, standing and gliding on my bad one and pushing with my good one. My skating style probably looked a little uglier than usual, but in I went. I came curling in from the face-off circle. Since I'm a lifelong defenceman and still learning the subtleties of scoring, especially scoring on a breakaway, I did the wrong thing. What I did was *plan*. I planned, in advance, to cruise across the front of the crease, get the goalie to go down, and then tuck it upstairs with my expert backhand. Not a bad plan, except that a real forward, a real scorer, would have waited to see what the goalie did. A real scorer has no plan. He waits and looks and acts appropriately. He sees a hole open up, he puts the puck in the hole. A defenceman on a breakaway makes a plan based on a preconceived hole, a hole which might turn into a blocker or a giant padded stomach.

My plan could've been good. In my one-legged cruise across the face of the net, the goalie did go down. Maybe because I knew this was my last-ever shift, I had a kind of Spidey sense and everything was in clear slow motion. I began to shift the puck onto my backhand, to pull it into my feet, away from the evil goalie. He was down, he was my helpless bitch. But the bitch shifted his blocker for a sudden different grip on his stick, and with my Spidey sense I could see he was going for the poke check. A real scorer could have adjusted to this and reverted instantly to his forehand and put it top-shelf, but being a defenceman I was locked into my plan, I was a dinosaur whose hard-wiring won't let him adapt and eat the new, unknown foliage after the meteor-winter kills all its usual food. It was exactly like that.

So, he Johnny Bowers me. Last shift in my life, last chance at a goal, and the fucker Johnny Bowers me.

The puck went wherever. I turned back up ice on one leg and floated to the bench, calling for the key, my voice wooden, the manner of one who has just failed the last shift in his life. I caught the key and continued across the ice to the gate, even though the game was still on. Someone probably jumped on for me, I don't know. Point is, I made it to the gate, let myself out, closed it behind me, and the play never did stop. I glanced back through the glass and took in the spectacle. Nothing had changed. It was a hockey game in progress. Such was the impact that my life's last shift had on the game. It just kept rolling, guys on the bench catching their breath, watching the guy with the puck, moaning at a close call, shouting a bit of encouragement, waiting for their next shift. I didn't need Spidey sense to tell me that this is exactly how it is when you die. Life goes on. Exactly as it should. Maybe in the bar later someone would buy me a shot of bourbon to go with my beer, but other than that nobody would commemorate my passing. They were too busy playing the game themselves.

IT IS A WEIRD INJURY INDEED. This morning, I check myself out. It really doesn't hurt that much. I can walk with hardly a limp. But if I try to "push off"—yikes, it hurts a lot. Strangely, it feels like there's something missing in there. And there's all this purple on my inner thigh, midway between unit and knee. The only explanation, according to my amateur diagnosis, is that it's a tear, somewhere deep. The weirdest thing of all is that the surface of my kneecap also really hurts, for no apparent reason. The surface of my kneecap? What the hell kind of muscle is connected to the surface of my kneecap?

I ponder the deep-purple colour of my thigh and give it tentative, ignorant pokes. No puck hit it, no stick. Something in there just sort of burst apart on me, it seems, and now there's a big mess of dead blood sitting in there. I wonder if I am about to develop flesh-eating disease, or if that's what I already have. Or some kind of instant cancer. I wonder if I should go to the local clinic. In the end I figure that, since I can walk okay, except on stairs, there's no need.

I decide my break from hockey will be pure and absolute. My wife, the suspicious FeeFee, finds me limping around in an oddly cheerful mood. I've told her several times, wearing this odd smile, "I'm done!" I tell her I'm thinking of buying some seeds—beans and tomatoes—and getting an early start on the garden. She reminds me that I don't have a garden, and I tell her that that's an even better reason to start one. Or maybe I could take up Tai Chi. I've heard that Tai Chi is great because not only do you get enlightened, you also sort of get in shape. And you don't need gear. Lots of beer after Tai Chi might be a contradiction, but we can cross that bridge when we come to it.

THIS AFTERNOON I caught four crabs off a local dock. Not only are they great to eat, but I seem to enjoy crabbing, and so does Lilli. We love hauling up on the yellow polypropylene rope, and then the trap comes into view and we squint to see if there's anything in there, and who's won the bet. And are they male, female? Will they be big enough to keep? Dungeness or Red Rock? Sometimes giant sea stars come up in the trap too, and occasionally a dogfish, which I sometimes keep, making sure I skin it fast so the urea in the skin—basically, piss— doesn't soak into the meat, which then tastes of ammonia. The bright white flesh resembles that of ling cod but it's actually even better, and more delicate than that of a bigger shark.

I like to kill the crabs with an axe before I cook them, because I'm thinking that instant death is a little less cruel than being boiled alive, in a shell. Trouble is, Lilli likes to watch, up close, when I smash them with the axe. I find that a bit unnerving, because it's a violent smash of shell and guts. Lilli's six, and she always insists. But it would feel weirder to not let her witness the honest butchering of her food.

So this is what I'll do. Instead of oldtimers, I'll crab twice a week. Instead of last-minute tape-buying and skate-sharpening, I'll rush off for salmon heads and chicken backs. Beer goes extremely well with crabs, and you don't have to wait till after. Thing is, there's gout, which is the main injury oldtimers face when playing with seafood plus booze. I did come down with gout a few years back, and I believe the combination of crabs and beer had something to do with it. An older and larger writer friend of mine, hearing about my gout, explained that he too got gout once, "after eating a deer," and that he'd since found a cure, which was to go ahead and drink your beer and eat your crabs, or your deer, but afterwards drink so much water that your stomach hurts. You wait for the pain to go away, then drink water until your stomach hurts again, and no gout will follow.

I'm done. Life without hockey will be busy and rich and fulfilling.

THE STATE OF OUR GAME

WHERE DO I, or any oldtimer like me, come off thinking that he has the right to spout off about the state of our national game? Simple:

Oldtimers Are the True Connoisseurs

IF YOU'VE PLAYED HOCKEY for any length of time, you've had this experience. You're sitting there watching a game on TV, and let's say a Leafs D-man floats a shot in from the point, Tucker gets a stick on it, and in it goes past the befuddled goalie. Somebody—probably your wife, but even a guy, even your best friend—says how awful the goalie just looked on that play, and you wonder if you are watching the same game. They didn't see that deflection—or the back pass, or the slew-foot, or that the goal was obviously kicked in. Missed it entirely. Sometimes even the commentator missed it. So while you saw, during live action, that Tucker got his stick on it, and it was his goal, it takes the commentators two video replays before they figure it out, before Pierre Maguire sees it and then tells us to watch how Tucker "utilizes," rather than uses, his stick. Your wife or friend sits there nodding, seeing nothing, taking in whatever the commentator spews. (Sure, they're sitting way up high, plus they have to talk while watching, plus not spill their coffee-double-bourbon, but still.)

I recall the first time the glamorous FeeFee forced me to go to the ballet with her. I dutifully sat and watched. The dancers were all a bit skinny for my taste, but those outfits—flesh-coloured, and showing all the curves and fissures—were worth the price of admission. Meanwhile, while the dancers did their elaborate jumping around, at my side the appreciative FeeFee gasped and shook her head and even laughed—at stuff that was a complete mystery to me. It was like she was watching an altogether different performance. Which, of course, she was.

I have since learned that the highest ballet jump isn't necessarily the best ballet jump, and I have even learned the names of some of the jumps. I know now that dancers go through scads of those stiff toeshoes each year, and that they make your feet bleed, sometimes soaking right through—sort of like Curt Schilling during the World Series, except ballerinas bleed every week. I now know that Barishnikov was a freak of nature and was likely an alien and, most importantly, was heterosexual enough to exhaust himself, what with unlimited access to all those curves and fissures. But I still don't know the *little things*, the things that make a ballet expert gasp. Because it's the littlest things that make us experts gasp, isn't it?

I say "us" because it's no different with hockey. If you play, you know how hard it is to be falling yet still make that little pass—through a guy's legs, no less. If you play, you know that the way the D-man just angled that guy off into the boards is actually modest perfection, something he'll never get an award for. We who know the game see endless little things, which is why we watch to begin with. Friends will sometimes notice that guys who play hockey will generally not be quite as fanatical about home teams. We'll grunt and exclaim and shake our heads and laugh, but we'll tend to go with the underdog, or with the team that has the most quality guys—and what we mean by "quality" might be a bit of a mystery to people who don't know the game.

So I'll just go ahead in all modesty and say that hockey is an art, and that we who play the game are the art experts. The thing is, like all art critics, we too have our disputes, because we see different things. Some of us see better than others, and some see only what they want to see. It's funny, sitting on the bench, and there's a close play at the blue line, and three guys stand and yell about the offside call, while you sit there knowing that the whistle was a good one. It was clear as day. And then, five minutes later, it's you who's yelling, while the guy beside you calmly says to you, "No, good call." Eventually you come to see that certain guys on your team just aren't that good at seeing; they'll laugh about Billy Bob's point shot hitting Ray in the ass when clearly it hit him in the kidney, and they'll make similar mistakes time and time again.

I know that generalizations are dangerous and often wrong, but I'll make one and claim that the better hockey players are also the better hockey critics. That is, the best players, whether sitting on the bench or in front of the tube, also have the best eyes. It's sort of simple logic: those eyes are part of what helped them be the best players. Think about your own experience, your own team, and tell me if I'm wrong.

Anyway, hockey players are a weird and reluctant kind of connoisseur. Because if I were to say any of the following in the dressing room, the boys would get quickly uncomfortable, or bored, but I'll just declare that, while wearing steel blades on our feet, helmets on our heads, plumes of breath pumping out of our faces, we sit on the bench, in a row, all our eyes fixed on the game as we truly appreciate—like no one else—the male body as it works its art. We love to watch it do what it can do. We watch with intense interest as the guy with the puck chooses to do something and then tries to do it. We nod internally if we agree with his choice. We flash a bit of judgment if he does the wrong thing, or makes the same mistake we've seen him make a bunch of times before. But our breath might catch when he does something surprising, supple, fast, or powerful—or maybe all four. It can be quite beautiful, largely because we know where to look for the beauty. And, sitting there on the bench, none of us thinks it's weird to be watching so keenly like that. Sitting in front of the tube, our wife or best friend might joke about our silence, or our intense stare, but we can hardly hear them.

Wayne Gretzky and the Battle of the TV Spines

THAT LAST SECTION made me remember a show I once happened to catch. Every hockey player out there will be interested in this one. In fact, you'll want to keep a copy of this handy in your pocket for the next time a certain wifely person gives you those narrowed eyes on your way out to sacrifice yourself to the game you love.

Did you know that a hockey player is the most advanced form of life on the planet? It's true. I use as my source none other than the scientist Dr. David Suzuki. (You know, *The Nature of Things*? Don't watch that show? It's on the same channel as *Hockey Night in Canada*. You know, the Coach's Corner channel? Anyway, *The Nature of Things* is an actual show, and Suzuki is an actual scientist. In fact, you might say that David Suzuki is sort of the Don Cherry of science. He dresses a bit more normally, but just like Cherry he has loud opinions about things.)

Why did Dr. Suzuki say hockey players are the most advanced form of life on the planet? First of all, as I've already mentioned, before we met, the bodacious FeeFee was a professional ballet dancer. She had a good career going, but she left the profession in her early twenties. I had nothing to do with this.

In any case, when we were first married, and living in Toronto, sitting in our first little house watching TV, *The Nature of Things* came on. We didn't have cable, or a remote, otherwise

I likely would have changed channels—but I'm glad I didn't. We sat through Dr. Suzuki telling us about the evolution of the nervous system, beginning with the pre-vertebral critters in the oceans, basically blobs of jelly. He traced the origins and development of the spinal cord, and the advent of a smart little bulb growing on the top end of it—namely, a brain. Basically, the nervous system developed as a way to enable a critter to both catch food and escape danger. The winning combination was an intelligence involving speed and agility and strength—possessed by whatever critter was best at hiding and popping up and grabbing something to eat. It all had to do with the spine and brain. Humans, of course, became the best. (In fact, said Dr. Suzuki in his Cherry-esque way, humans got too fucking good at it, and now look at this planet of ours.)

Near the end of the program, Dr. Suzuki reckoned that two human activities were arguably the most heightened physical expression of humanity's success as a species: the hockey player and the ballet dancer. I swear this is true! And here we are, me and the languid FeeFee, retired hockey guy and retired ballerina, watching him say this. He went on to say that, after the commercial, we would learn which human activity—hockey or ballet—represented the highest form of human development. It was great—the smug FeeFee and I made a bet—ten bucks I think it was. She was confident, sitting there all regal and diva-like, barely cracking a smile. Me, I expressed my confidence and excitement by performing a top-notch string of armpit farts and running off for a beer.

The rest of the show compared ballet dancers and hockey players. Ballet dancers had achieved the pinnacle of physical *control*—grace, power, beauty. The hockey player was deemed more developed than athletes in any other sport, football or basketball or whatever, because he wears extensions on his feet, skates on unnatural ground, and uses a second extension, the stick, to control the puck. All of this takes place at unnatural speed. Not only that, but he performs in an environment of chaos and hostility. So, lugging the puck at top speed, looking to make that pass, surrounded by bad guys trying to smash him, adapting to constant change instantaneously—all of this made the hockey player the most highly developed form of human being on the planet. Better, in any case, than the silly ballerina, who may have an incredible body, sure, but who performs only what's choreographed, what she has already practised, learned, and remembered. Not only that, but no goon's going to blind-side her at any second, and though she's up there running on impossible tiptoes, while doing so she doesn't have to stickhandle through danger to stuff the biscuit where granny keeps the vanilla bottles.

At one point Suzuki interviewed Wayne himself, trying to sound like one of the boys and asking him something like, "So, whaddya think of all this spinal development stuff, eh, Wayne? And what's with this famous Gretzky peripheral vision I keep hearing about?" Wayne looked around, a *really* flat expression on his face, and said something like, "Geez, hockey players don't think about stuff like *that*." In other words, Wayne didn't come off as the most fully developed human on the planet. But I didn't care, I was now rolling around on the floor, laughing and pointing at the haughty FeeFee, who stared daggers at both the scientist and perfect-brained Wayne. Her neck, nearly as long as a swan's, looked a little stiff. Being her superior, I stopped rubbing it in after a few minutes. Though I still bring it up from time to time, don't I, FeeFee?

Oldtimers Who Happen to Be Women

THIS IS A DIFFICULT SECTION TO WRITE, because there really isn't much to say. But that's not my fault. Plus, I'm going to do my best to rectify it.

There might be some guys around who still think a woman's place is in the kitchen and the bedroom, not the rink. Some guys might even say a woman's place is also in the boardroom—but still not the rink. And, because they think this way, these guys might think themselves to be the true oldtimers, but I think they're wrong.

First, let me say that when I use the word "women" coupled with the word "oldtimers," I'm reminded of a horrible twenty seconds I suffered fifteen years ago. I was almost forty, and had played on my Fredericton team a few years. Because of travel and such, I hadn't yet attended the annual spring barbecue, but that year I did. I pulled up to Arden's place and got out and went in to join the guys and their wives. (The snooty FeeFee had declined, citing her abhorrence of both beer and hockey players as sufficient reason.)

So I knocked and walked in. And there were all my teammates. But they were *sitting with a bunch of old ladies*.

Now, over the years I'd been to countless hockey parties. Parties with, you know, real women along. But I guess that was years and years ago, when the women were *chicks*. They were girlfriends, they were young wives. So Arden's party was a shock. I was one of the younger guys on the team, and that was part of the problem. Many of these women were pushing fifty. Another part of the problem was that, no matter what your age, when you're in a dressing room with a bunch of guys, joking around and showering, you tend to see yourselves as a bunch of eighteen-year-old friends. I don't know why I entered Arden's expecting a bunch of young chicks, but I sort of did, and it was a jolt to find myself in a room with (sorry, ladies) these paunchy and dyed-headed dowagers who all looked like Liberace, minus the jewellery, nice clothes, or piano. It was like seeing myself in a hellish mirror—it was basic and inarguable proof that I had gotten old. These were my friends and these were their women. It felt like I'd gotten old when I was looking the other way.

BUT THIS SECTION is supposed to be about women old-timer *players*. Oldtimer hockey, female version. What's the state of it in Canada?

I didn't have a clue. Now, the main principle I've followed while researching this book is that I wouldn't *do* any research at all. This book would simply be a discussion of hockey stuff that I, and a bunch of other Canadians, know about. Why show off by divulging lots of arcane and fancy detail, pretending to know stuff no one else does?

Well, I did know *some* stuff. I know there's coed nooners, where women can play, because I've seen them on rec centre schedules. In Fredericton, I noticed a women-only pick-up slot, one hour a week, but the following year it was cancelled, I don't know why. When we first moved to Victoria seven years ago, the twentyish daughter of a friend was playing in a league here. In Ontario, a fellow I know who's well placed in the publishing industry met his wife while the two of them were playing hockey. (I wonder how many times they've heard the lame "two minutes for holding" joke?) Anyway, I suspect there are smallish women's rec leagues scattered across the land. And women's competitive hockey is booming, of course—there's a solid NCAA league in the States, and a strong, though smaller, university league here in Canada. And, of course, our national team rules.

But, getting curious about the state of women's oldtimers, I've decided to break my no-research pledge. One reason is, I want to know where all these young competitive players are going to play later. The current crop of elite female players is going to turn thirty-five and need some oldtimer teams to play on. And, for the rest of the athletically inclined women in the suburbs of our nation, Pilates is going to get boring.

So. I've just consulted that know-it-all Google and found . . . nothing. No women's oldtimers league. I found all sorts of websites and statistics about women's hockey, though. It's flourishing. For instance, in 2002, which is the most recent stat, more than fifty-five thousand females registered to play within the Hockey Canada system. That doesn't count the many casual pick-up players. There are development camps and tournaments galore. There are the usual bantam and midget divisions, but the oldest league is called "Open," which is where you play if you're over twenty. So I'm thinking that women's oldtimers is inevitable. Simply, there are soon going to be scads of forty-year-olds getting really bitchy about all those twenty-year-olds constantly blowing by them.

And I'd love to see women's oldtimers. For one thing, a burgeoning female oldtimers system would be proof that we fellas have long been onto a great thing. Women playing oldtimers will be tantamount to admitting that we were right all along—in other words that we are, in fact, superior.

BUT OF COURSE there are women playing oldtimers. Most of us have seen them. One plays in our league on the team her husband plays for. What's maybe significant here is that I played against her for two years before I knew that that slick, smallish defenceman wearing the cage was actually a she. My teammates had been playing against her for years and were used to her, and the "two minutes for holding" jokes had stopped. When informed that she was a woman, I took note of her graceful, almost effortless style, plus her ease at getting up close and pesky in front of the net, and how her physical effectiveness owed more to judo than karate. She saw the ice well, and laid down the nice pass to a teammate hitting the hole. She was exactly the kind of guy I liked to play with.

I've never asked the guys what that team's arrangement is with respect to showering and such. Most likely she throws on her duds all sweaty and goes out to wait for her husband. Or maybe he comes along all sweaty, too. Either way, she misses out on beers with the guys, and all the gossip, good times, and bullshit strategy that goes with it. Unless, of course, they've all reached a noble level of maturity, and can be naked and shower and hang around together, males and females both, with no one getting uncomfortable and no one making obnoxious or harassing jokes.

Nope, can't see it.

It all has to do with our basic natural difference, which no amount of pretending can do away with. Our basic natural difference is, of course, this: all men, all their lives, find all farts at least mildly amusing, while all women lose this quality at about age nine.

Watching Our Kids Play

MANY OF US HAVE WATCHED our kids play hockey. It's fantastic, isn't it?

I have four. In Fredericton I watched my oldest, Lise, play ringette exactly twice. She liked it "okay, but, well, it's okay." She moved on to volleyball, and track. I watched my second son, Vaughn, attend two hockey practices before he quit. For some reason, in two attempts he couldn't master stickhandling while skating at full speed. Now it's basketball, rugby, and break-dancing. My youngest, Lilli, likes to skate, but on the several times I've mentioned hockey or ringette to her, she's declined.

But back in Fredericton I had the experience of being a hockey dad with my oldest son, Connor. He started playing at six, and I was the typical hockey dad, grumbling over his gear and my coffee as I got him dressed in the living room. It's not yet quite light out, a snowstorm, it's 50–50 whether the car will start, and we're not entirely sure where his game is. But somehow we get there on time, and I watch, and of course there's no place I'd rather be.

Watching your child play a game should be a relaxing, pleasant experience, right? Shouldn't it? He's entertained, he needs no looking after, it's a break for you, and it's "a game." So why do we hockey parents watch like fierce birds of prey, never blinking? We're watching for signs of progress, that's why. We're watching for that sudden blinding speed, or that great move, that cool delay, those hands that can go top-shelf. In other words, we're looking for some evidence that our kid might be a star.

As parents, we wait and wait, and while some parents do have kids who do become stars, for most that isn't the case. And for some it's hard to accept that their kid is ordinary, or even less than ordinary. I recall one Fredericton mother who, whenever her little Igor touched the puck, which wasn't often, would start screaming and stand up, pounding her fists on her thighs. Most of her barking was unintelligible, but there was lots of "*Do it like Bobby. Like Bobby! Do it like Bobby!*" Bobby was the star of the team, and poor Igor could hardly skate. It was clear to everyone else in the rink that Igor would never "do it like Bobby." It was probably clearest of all to Igor.

So for some parents it's agony. We've all seen them. (Unless, of course, they are us.) And we shake our heads at the worst cases, those who confront the coach because their kid isn't on the first line, or he's playing defence when it should be obvious that he's a born sniper. Of course, there are worse parents than those, and they're the ones we read about in the paper. And there are others, maybe even worse, who we don't read about—they're the ones yelling at little Igor in the car on the way home.

But enough of that. Most of us are decent kid-watchers, and we have a fine though intense time watching our kids fall down, get up, score the odd goal and cause the odd goal, and sometimes learn from his mistakes, and mostly not. But it's terrific watching him get better and better, isn't it? Doesn't it feel nothing short of miraculous to see our own flesh and blood skating at all? Learning how to do a parallel stop and send up a modest snitch of snow? Or making a pass? Or high-fiving with a teammate, acting cool, after someone scores? God, it seems like only yesterday they were learning to walk. How can he do all that stuff? His muscles are all, well, *geniuses*.

Then it's another year, the skates don't fit, we go out and get some bigger and probably better ones, and maybe we spend a bit more on some better sticks as well. And the kids' skating has improved quite a bit, and they can see the ice better now too, and some guys on the team actually pass the puck this year, and sometimes your kid is one of them, and the whole concept of "team" starts to kick in. As does the concept of linemates, and who plays better with whom, and now your kid has an opinion of the coach, too. Before you know it, there in the car going to and from games you are actually talking a bit of hockey—talking about a thing you love, with a person you love. And it doesn't get much better than that. Even *Hockey Night in Canada* takes on a new shine. Now, watching together (though he only stays interested for a period or so), you can trade little comments like, "Wow, through the legs," or, "How'd he *see* that guy?" You ask, "Did that go five-hole?" and he says, "Yup. Five-hole," and the replay confirms his good eyes. And sometimes you're watching and something small but great happens and you both spontaneously mumble "nice," and that's it, and it's enough, because you both know you saw the same thing, and it was a thing so small that you and he are the only ones in the world who could have seen it.

Watching Our Kids Quit

YES, IT'S GREAT watching our kids compete. But unless they're physical freaks of nature, crazily ambitious, and lucky as a leprechaun, they won't make it a profession. And at some point in their lives—usually when they're still kids, in fact—they drop the sport. Which can be hard. I'm thinking it's *way* harder for the parent who's watching. Because when the kid drops a sport, it means he's no longer excited by it. No way it's as exciting as the new *Hades Doom Passion of Xorr* expansion disc he's burned at a buddy's house.

My brother Bub's kids are older than mine, so before I had my own I watched him watch them play some sports. And I watched him watch them drop them, one by one. When his daughter Sammy kept playing fastball, Bub thought he'd maybe encourage things further by coaching the team. Now, coaching your kid's team has its own set of horrors you have to tiptoe through, but it was largely a good experience. He saw his main job as coach as to instill a will to win—no, simply to *try* harder—because on this team, and in this league, nine out of ten girls were more interested in getting their pants to hang exactly five inches up their calf. That, and not perspiring excessively. And coming up with wittier insult-songs to sing at the opposing team, who would then quickly sing a sassy rebuttal from their own dugout. They had a pretty good time, and Bub managed to instill a will to compete in a few of them, his logic being that you have even more fun if you grit your teeth and enter a fantasy world and behave as if winning this game *means* something. (Which is, of course, the illusion that we nurture in oldtimers hockey.) But the following year Sammy shrugged, dropping fastball to pursue interests in makeup, literature, and old films.

Bub's an enlightened, inward-seeing kind of dad, and knows the warning signs that suggest he might be "living his life through his children," but I could see his disappointment nonetheless. When his son Max quit hockey it was especially hard on him. It's not at all a case of him loving his son more than his daughter, not at all. But Bub's a guy, and hockey's his game. So when your little guy rejects your sport, well, you feel it in your gut. In fact, some very main part of your gut looks up at you and asks, heartbroken, "How can this be?" But Max is a true west-coast lad, and soccer was his first and only real game. So he shrugged off hockey, and Bub's posture slumped a bit.

Now that it's too late to ask, I sometimes wonder about how my dad felt about all this. He was a basketball player, a centre with both Washington State and Gonzaga. I remember as a kid sitting with him watching what's now called "March Madness," and hearing him describe how excited he was to play in it, and travel to New York, and play ball in Madison Square Garden in front of all those people. I can't recall if he was in the final eight or the final four, and it didn't impress me much anyway, my thinking being that, if you played basketball, well of course you went to Madison Square Garden to play. I remember him telling me that no one used jumpshots then, and that half the guys, him included, threw foul shots underhand, like Wilt the Stilt. And on the way to that final eight, or four, he had his front tooth knocked out with an elbow—he'd grimace at me, showing it off, a big front tooth framed in gold, plus the scar under the lower lip where it went through.

So I don't know how disappointed he was when, now living in Canada, he watched his two young Canadian sons take a look at a basketball and not even bother shrugging. Our driveways always had nice hoops, and basketballs were always rolling around and getting wedged under car bumpers, but they hardly lost their sheen. The thing is, we were in Winnipeg and our heroes were Norm Ullman and George Armstrong. Strike two was our height—though my dad was six foot five, for some reason I topped out at six feet and Bub at five ten. I suppose us being shitty at it was strike three. I did play pumpkin ball through junior high in Toronto, but my main asset remained my hip check. That and my jump ball, where I would accidentally-on-purpose fall into the other guy, who was invariably skinnier and taller than me.

Nor do I know my dad's disappointment when his two sons began to drift away from serious hockey. He probably felt proud, and a little lucky, that we both played on the same junior team, and he watched all our home games religiously, sitting up there in the crowd with my mother, who watched the play only when neither of us was on the ice. When we were she'd look away and tear paper coffee cups into little pieces. (It's odd when I think of it now, that during the game I couldn't see their faces in the crowd and I had no idea if they were there or not. Only when I next saw them and heard their reaction to the game did I learn they were there. They always were.) But when Bub and I started to drift away from serious ambition, we never included Dad in the conversation. When I quit junior to play at university instead, Dad was not consulted. When Bub finished junior and flew across the pond for some fooling-around hockey in Denmark and Sweden, who knows what Dad thought?

Well, I have tried and tried to never actually come out and say to my kids, "Gee, guys, I sure do hope you keep playing and

playing, and getting better, so I can live my life through you."
Though that's how I feel. And I'm sure they can sense exactly
that in the way I always ask, "So, when's your next game?" I'm
generally more eager than they are, I think.

Now, just last night I watched my oldest son, Connor, play
in the South Island finals against their arch-nemesis Oak Bay.
That all sounds fine and healthy, I know, but I have two disturbing revelations. One, my son is a goalie. Two, his sport is soccer.

I was infuriated when Connor stopped playing hockey. Before
you think I'm the "Do it like Bobby" woman, let me explain. Of
all my kids, Connor was the only one to take a shine to hockey. He
was developing exactly in my own image, which of course is how
it should be: he was a little beefy, not the best skater, a natural D-
man. Most of all, he loved the game. Once, as I was kneeling at
his feet in pools of meltwater, untying his skates, I remember him
asking me when his next game was. He could hardly wait.

We followed a full-time job and its dental plan west, to
Beautiful B.C. We weren't out here long before I was looking to
get both myself and Connor on hockey teams, because it was
my understanding that it was played in some form or other out
here on this verdant island. The Courtnall brothers, Mel
Bridgman, Grant Fuhr—a bunch of guys had learned their
skills on Victoria ice. But, phoning around, I was told that the
waiting list for kids his age was 190 kids long. I called other areas
with rinks—Sooke, Duncan, Mill Bay, Sidney—and there was
nothing. Not even any pick-up hockey available, just general
skating. So Connor didn't shrug and quit hockey, he was forced
out and was pissed off. But maybe not as much as me.

Watching *Hockey Night in Canada* together, we can still
grunt in unison at nice plays because Connor still knows the
game. He sometimes wonders aloud about how good he might
have gotten. But he plays soccer now, a goalie for Gordon Head,

a suburb mostly famous for Steve Nash, another local kid who opted for a non-hockey sport. So, soccer: some of his buddies yell when they're tripped, and roll around like Europeans, but it's fun to watch. Last week, Connor gooned an Oak Bay guy during a corner kick. But he gooned him in honourable Canadian fashion, by taking the man, not the puck. Or, sure, "ball." Anyway, the guy stayed down, not moving much, and had to leave the game. Now, I'm no bully, and I'm no advocate of violence in any sport, but I know when I'm proud. The thing is: Connor never did quit hockey. He was just forced to play it on grass, without pads.

I hope my pride in watching my kids play their various brands of hockey doesn't spell trouble ahead. I can take their occasional shrug and dropped sport in stride, and it's not as if I'll go buy a gun and go postal if all my kids drop all their sports en masse. But if that day does come, it will likely see me having a reflective beer out on the patio. I'll be in my extreme old age by then, of course, and by then I'll probably be living the solid fantasy that all four are actually playing in the NHL, and I'm their coach. *Playing* coach. At eighty-three, I'm leading the league in scoring. Come to think of it, dream-life on the patio might turn out to be not so bad.

The State of Oldtimers

PICTURE THIS: a rink full of guys chasing a puck around. One goalie's in a crouch, and at the other end the other goalie looks bored. There are no spectators. The hollowness of the arena booms, chirps, and clacks with the classic sounds of hockey. No one is getting paid to play, and no one's being made to play. Winning is not that big a deal, but for some reason everyone is trying pretty hard. There's laughter on the bench. On the ice there's a smatter of ill will and a bit of minor violence, but in the corners guys sometimes laugh and share a funny word, and if someone falls badly or gets hurt, everyone stops and wants the guy to be okay.

It's oldtimers in the twenty-first century, and it's in good shape. If growth is any indicator, it's in great shape. And it's sort of going global. You can travel to tournaments in foreign lands, strap on your gear, skate out onto the ice, and see a bunch of old farts like yourself, only they're all Japanese. And though they're decent enough guys you do come to hate it when they apologize and make that little bow as they blow by you.

Maybe there are reasons oldtimers is in good shape. One might be that all the players there *want* to be there. There's no other possible motive. Another reason could be that, though it's organized, the major decisions are made by the people playing it—not parents, not paid officials, not the corporate marketplace. And there's a fair amount of choice. As an old-timer, especially if you live near even a moderately sized town, you can choose pretty much any level of competition you want. You can play league, coed, or lunchtime pick-up. You can play with your kids, if they're old enough, and if they let you. You can switch teams if things get too competitive or the team has too many coaches. (Notice that these reasons why oldtimers is in good shape are inverse to why some other kinds of hockey are in bad shape!) It's also the perfect social club. Where else, at your age, can you make new friends so easily? And it's doubly perfect because you don't have to get close and personal if you don't want to. Any oldtimers team accommodates two or three hermits, guys who come just to get their ya-yas out, shower, grunt enigmatically on their way out the door, and go back to their mysterious lives. A team accepts all kinds. And I'll ask again—where else can you yell uncontrollably, hug guys in joy, pout, brag, fart, and trade stock tips, all in two hours?

And it's inexpensive. Okay, I hear some of you whining already. Sure, you *can* buy $600 skates, and a $300 astronaut stick, and a glossy smoked shield, and a brand-new hockey bag with stewardess wheels, and play for three teams, and go to Santa Rosa and Vegas tournaments every year, and Hawaii sometimes too, and end up with no wife and a second mortgage on your house. That's up to you. But if you dust off your old tube skates and bring your own homebrew in your bag, you can enjoy an entire season of hockey for about five hundred bucks. Is that a deal, or what? Think of how much *you love the game*. For $500? I mean, how much do you spend on income tax every year? And you probably don't even *like* income tax.

And oldtimers is adapting "upwards." That is, as time has gone by and we have gotten older, new age categories have been blossoming just for us. Case in point, this year in Victoria there's a fairly large tournament, the Playmakers', that I can't play in because I'm still too young. *I'm fifty-two.*

So to us never-say-die types, you thirty-five-year-old rookies are indeed starting to look like kids—which I guess means we're starting to look old. And sure, maybe games in our age group might be starting to resemble hockey less than chess. But we're still having a good time . . .

Memory #11: The Green Flash

IT'S CHRISTMAS MORNING, 1973. I'm hungover, on a half-full jumbo jet with my UBC team, flying from Hong Kong to Tokyo. China had been a strange and heightened time, by far the most exotic journey I'd ever experienced—yet this Christmas morning felt profoundly empty.

Last night we'd spent Christmas Eve in Hong Kong, which wasn't China in those days. Hong Kong was bars, glitter, Western buildings taller and fancier than Vancouver's own, women with red lips and sparkling eyeshadow, and old guys in alleys selling cheap suits and bootleg cassettes. On the other hand, Beijing had the one hotel, a single brand of beer, pure cashmere sweaters selling for the equivalent of seventy-five cents (I bought three for my mother, two of which my brother stole to give to his girlfriend), and once from a bus window I saw what might have been the steamed-up windows of an actual restaurant. All the female comrades dressed in the same quilted black pyjamas as the comrade guys.

So, after a month in a severe China, we'd had a wild night of it in Hong Kong. My brother Bub and I had performed an especially festive brother act. Now, slouched side by side in midair, we moaned occasionally for each other in agreement that last night was fun and that this morning was not.

Last night had begun in various bars with the guys, all of whom confessed to dreadful homesickness brought on by being on the wrong side of the planet on Christmas Eve and all of whom, save Bub and me, wisely drifted back to a hotel bed. My brother and I had become enamoured of two "bar girls," those ever-present ornaments of Asian bars whose job it is to cozy up and hustle watered-down, overpriced drinks. (Rumour had it they might "go with you" if the price was right.) One of these bar girls thought my brother looked like, or might even be, Mick Jagger.

We bought them one drink for the thrill of it. They were gorgeous, feline damsels of the mysterious east, and we were goofs from North Van. Mine was named Joyce and Bub's was Lucy. We explained to them that we could afford only the one drink. They gulped it and wandered off, but wandered back later, bored, it being a slow night. Because they came back at all, Bub and I fancied ourselves witty and handsome.

To shorten a long story, suffice to say that although we were with Joyce and Lucy till dawn, nothing happened. It seemed they actually liked us, and we them. Once off the job they took us to weirdly dangerous bars and bought *us* drinks. At a well-lit intersection they soberly steered us away from a developing brawl that looked like a Bruce Lee film, one which they assured us would end in a death, it being the mob. In a '50s American diner with jukebox units in the booths, Joyce asked conversationally if I was homosexual when I put on the Bee Gees' "Massachusetts" out of nostalgia. We ate some truly strange food—snake, I think. We went back to "our place," and Lucy showed us how she could go into a monkey trance, that particular animal being, she explained, her last incarnation. Though Joyce wouldn't let me prove my true sexual orientation, she did speak shyly to me of marriage, and asked how big my house was in Canada.

They rode the taxi with us to the airport, where we cut in front of the team bus just as the guys began climbing off. Joyce and Lucy stepped out of the taxi and in plain view kissed us like the departing loves of their lives. The bus windows were full of eyes—Bub and I were heroes.

But we knew better. Their hints about marriage and Canada had grown pretty blatant in the last hour. They probably despised us and were only desperate to get out of Hong Kong and come to Gold Mountain, which is how they referred to America, of which Canada was a cold suburb. What should have been a great night inspired only loneliness. The night had been all tinsel, without any tree.

On the plane now I tried to deep-breathe myself into sleep before the growing headache made it impossible. I couldn't help but think of Christmas at home. I thought of my parents by themselves this morning. I remembered the Christmases of childhood, in Winnipeg, where Bub and I shared a room and woke up Christmas morning before dawn. My parents had a brilliant system worked out, whereby we were allowed to go help ourselves to our stockings and bring them back to bed. They always contained two comic books, a kids' hockey novel, puzzles, a rubber dart gun, oranges, and even some candy—stuff that would keep us going a couple of hours while they slept.

When we were allowed to dive under the tree for the real stuff, of course, we'd already seen it out the corner of our eyes during our run for the stocking: the Hespeler Green Flash, which vintage oldtimers will recall is a hockey stick. Every year we got a new one. In the days before slapshots and adolescent muscles, one new stick a year was all you needed. We did sort of know that the Green Flash wasn't the most expensive stick, but it was new, it smelled like freshly milled wood, and it looked full of goals. Maybe most important, it looked just like last year's, and it looked like next year's too. And, years later, on a plane, a remembered glimpse of the Green Flash brought with it the feel of my flannel pyjamas, the sound of a rubber dart sticking to glass, the smell of Dad's bacon and eggs.

"Hey," my brother nudged me out of a nod. Right, I was in a flying chrome monster roaring somewhere over the Sea of Japan. "Hey," said Bub, "I guess it's Christmas."

"I guess it is," I said, sounding as carefully neutral as he did.

"Where's the Green Flash?" he asked. His little smile was almost sly.

My God, he'd been having the same memories. Through my haze, I understood how close we were. Well, of course—we'd been shaped by the same stuff.

"Best stick in the world," I said.

"Damn right," said Bub.

We avoided eye contact because of the weight it would contain, which was all the sadness and all the good that had happened to us between the Green Flash days and now. But who could want anything more than to have someone else understand your life going by? Especially after a night you'd eaten snake and then tried to kill it with a bottle of Joyce's lychee-nut liqueur.

Memory #12: The Frozen Ponds of My Youth

THAT TITLE SOUNDS about as corny as it gets, eh? But this isn't a kid memory but an oldtimer memory, born of a car ride after a tournament in Saint John, New Brunswick. Me and Jim, a buddy on my Fredericton team, were driving out past the suburbs, a little tired after a late night, and he gave me a little elbow and tossed his head in the direction of the window and mumbled, "That's where I learned how to skate." I looked and saw this perfect, all-Canadian pond. Maybe twice the size of a real rink, it had hard, dark ice, smooth and wind-cleared of all snow. Perfect. It was a beautiful, cloudless day. The pond was empty of skaters. Jim stared at it until it was out of sight.

I don't know that I skated on more than one or two ponds, ever. A couple of rivers. One huge lake. I guess I'm just not all that old—I never did chase that frozen horse turd around the pond, Sears catalogues tied to my little shins. Those of you who did do that are probably reading this with a magnifying glass and grunting harshly at all the swearing.

But I *have* skated in some weird places, the rink at Toronto City Hall being among the weirdest. That infamous tiny rink in Burnaby where Cliff Ronning learned his hockey, the size of which probably kept *him* small, but forced him to learn how to dipsy-doodle on a dime like that. A second-storey mall rink in Los Angeles, where the skate-rental kiosk didn't have my brother's size so he had to rent figure skates and tripped on the picks every sixth step and as a result hated my parents for the rest of summer vacation. Hatchett Lake, Nova Scotia, during a blizzard. The Ottawa canal. The rink outside Mallow Road Kindergarten in Don Mills. A barn with a flooded floor near Brandon, Manitoba.

Maple Leaf Gardens. The old Vancouver Forum. The Ice Palace in Geneva, Switzerland. A fancy-assed outdoor rink in Megève, France, ringed by glass bars and bistros and rich après-skiers. Some weird old rink in Paris that smelled of cigars and squatted beside the Seine, a little below water level, I think. An outdoor rink high in the Italian Alps. The Seibu Arena in Tokyo. The flooded Queen's Square tennis courts in Fredericton. Also in Fredericton, my neighbour Steven's backyard rink. And, last but not least, the little outdoor rink in Niakwa Park, Winnipeg, where I spent hundreds of winter evenings growing up, chasing the bigger guys who kept the puck as long as they could, and once in a while getting to keep it for a few seconds myself.

There were others, but those are some memorable ones. Funny thing about rinks: you tend to remember them. The exact colour and brightness of the ice. The accumulations of snow, or the utter smoothness. The *smell* of the ice. And there are several different ice smells. Then, the wet-cigar and snow-melt smell of the room where you put on your skates — or, if there was no change room, the feel of planting your ass somewhere in the snow. And then, on outdoor ice, especially ice that's hard and brittle, there's the unforgettable *sound* of skating.

But this memory has mostly to do with that empty pond beside the highway on the outskirts of Saint John, New Brunswick. It was such a beautiful day. I wondered aloud where all the kids were. My buddy Jim, who had no kids of his own, shrugged. He said, "They play Nintendo now." Our hangovers got gently worse for a while.

Memory #13: The Earliest Frozen Pond of My Youth

I DON'T KNOW HOW OLD I WAS, but I remember watching my older brother first learning to skate, which probably puts me around four. He had the over-long stick tucked under an armpit, making the stick the third leg of a tripod, which is how everyone learned to skate. He ran on his skates, and he got going pretty good. I can picture this as clear as anything, even the big-eyed, hopeful look on his face. The rink was almost empty. It was outdoors, of course, and the sky was completely black. You couldn't see stars because the rink lights prevented it. It was cold. There was no adult near him. I don't remember him ever falling. My mom or dad, or both, were likely standing next to me.

Funny that I don't remember learning to skate myself (and some friends would argue that I never did), though I don't doubt it happened with a stick under the armpit, me running on my skates, left to my own devices. I do remember an early game of shinny, maybe the earliest. It was a rink with boards, somewhere on the outskirts of Winnipeg. But there were no lights strung over the rink. Instead, on a convenient little hill—more of a five- or six-foot rise is all—fathers had parked their cars and were sitting in them, engines idling, heaters on, headlights pointed onto the rink. It worked pretty well, except you were blinded if you skated one way, and you skated into your long shadow if you skated the other. I think my brother was out there, too, which means the kids were older than me. I don't remember touching the puck. I do remember not knowing which car my dad's was, except that one of them was definitely his, and he was there in that bank of lights shining in our faces, lights aiding the common cause, helping us play our game. I knew he had a Thermos of coffee, and I know now that he might have had something else in it. Since I have my own kids now, I know he watched me carefully, never bored, highly attuned to my progress as a skater and puck handler. And that he had lots to tell my mother later when we got home and I was in bed.

THIS SEASON SO FAR

April

I DON'T KNOW WHY I did it but I'm glad I did. The serious FeeFee thinks I'm an absolute idiot. So what else is new in that department? And isn't that why most of us play a bit of midnight hockey? To go a little idiotic, a little nuts, and escape the ongoing seriousness in our lives?

Anyway, I've finally understood that oldtimer health is as fickle as a teenage girlfriend. Sometimes it shuts you down, other times it's a go, but you never know why. That's just how it is. Miraculously, what happened is, my career-ending injury started getting a little better. Possibly it's the inversion table I bought, though I don't see what effect that would have on a leg. Maybe hanging upside down shocks the brain and makes it panic and send out all sorts of emergency super-healing ions, who knows? But I started noticing the healing process one evening when I bounded up the stairs to get the phone—my groin didn't grab and I didn't shriek. When I got to the top of the stairs, amazed, I ignored the phone altogether and tried gently stretching my brand-new leg. No pain. I stretched it a bit more. Just a dull twinge. So it seems that the snapped muscle, the ripped sinew, was healing up. Either that or the injured part had just sort of rotted away and lost all feeling.

Whatever the case, I figured I might be able to get in a last game or two.

And I did. I caught our last game of the season, a short road trip up near the airport at Panorama Rinks. I'm not sure why I did it. I had already regressed to shitty shape again after a month off. That glorious bit of jump was long gone. Guys would again blow by me, I would beat nobody one on one, and my passing would be tentative. What fun would I have? And wasn't I risking re-ripping a nearly healed muscle? What the hell was I doing? I didn't know, even as I stood in the dim storage room packing my gear, which I'd already hung on its off-season nails.

Why do we play? Why do we ever play? I suppose I've gone and written a book attempting to answer this very question. Negative capability. Second childhood. Reptilian brain. Ego gratification. Addiction to the zone. Delusions of lost grandeur. Boredom. Comradeship. Guilt-free beer. Fear of death. Brilliantly childish fun. We can pick any or all of those.

Packing my bag, I decided on brilliantly childish fun. Plus the cold beers after. Not even the most brilliant child gets to have a beer.

WHEN I GOT TO THE RINK and found the room, a few guys showed some surprise at this, my second return to action, but there was no uproarious celebration. Guys were used to my injuries. And most of them were of course hanging by a thread themselves. You could hear all the ibuprofen bottles rattling in the hockey bags as guys dug for tape or a pad.

There was a down feeling in the room. A general weariness, or maybe boredom. I noted that only half the guys were here. Besides Chris the goalie, we had only nine skaters, and three of them were spares. Well, it was a road trip, and a few were out with injuries, but still. We were playing the Primetimers (a decent name, combining their excellent eight-o'clock ice time with the tongue-in-cheek notion of being in the prime of life) and we were going to get pasted, because they'd stocked up with a few young guys, guys who *were* almost prime. But it wasn't just that we were going to lose, we were used to that. No, guys looked tired. Tired of each other. Maybe even tired of the game. On their faces I could see that a fifty-game schedule was definitely enough. Guys stared off into space, one skate tightened, the other not. Pregnant Mike looked dully wistful, wondering what, besides moose or dogs, he'd next have in his sights. Rich wasn't pacing and no jokes or coaching pointers coming out of him at all. I figured that, last game of the year, there'd be more guys, and some jollity.

I heard:

"We doin' anything later?"

"Dunno."

"It's the last game."

"So?"

"Shouldn't we go for pizza or something?"

"It's a Monday."

OUT ON THE ICE I warmed up, tested the leg, which felt, miraculously, completely fine. Out of shape, but no pain whatsoever. Weird, seeing as I actually thought I might need surgery to tie a snapped leg-cord back together.

Maybe I was meant to play this last game.

I took it slow. I had trusty Dave on right wing and I was content to try to get him the puck as much as I could, and then, if I could catch up, follow him in for some garbage, or maybe a drop pass. The game began, and it was sort of fun out there. Because of my injury, I told myself I had absolutely no defensive responsibility, and I didn't even pretend to *consider* backchecking. (Nobody seemed to notice much difference.) But it was okay: our line had time to make some passes out there, and back on the blue line Duane could see the ice really well and he fed us all night, and Dave popped a couple, one off a long saucer pass I was proud of, and we were down only one goal at the end of the second.

But the fatigue and sunken spirit evident in the room infected the bench as well. In my absence, the general whining and testiness had reached new thresholds. Big Bug was openly yelling at a couple of guys, supported by the secondary whiners, including Little Bug, who laughed. Big Bug, who had long been on our goalie Chris's case as well, over the course of the game wheeled and threw a couple of needless, and needlessly hard, passes, almost like shots, back to him. It was almost funny, but mostly not. I would've called his attitude "poisonous," except that it was more tired than that. Kind of a listless scorn. Once more, I made the decision not to play for this team again. Why pay money to feel not only physically shitty, but mentally shitty as well?

But, still, it was okay out there on the ice, actually playing. Our line was having some fun. The leg was fine. I hadn't lost all my timing. Rust hadn't claimed my body entirely. I could do the wily old veteran who sees the ice and makes nice passes. I could glide around like Jean Ratelle, try to stay open and maybe pop one if Dave could get it to me.

Then a wonderful thing happened. A truly wonderful thing.

I've already gone on about being an eternal defenceman, meaning I have cement hands around the enemy net. It's gotten somewhat better during my fifteen years of oldtimers and pretending to be a forward, but some things just don't change. Now, one thing that shows my defenceman nature is the way I shoot: I have an excellent snap shot. Even from the point—or better yet, crossing their blue line at speed—I can rip it pretty good, and if it hits a low corner it's probably in. Occasionally I'll put it right through a goalie. I'm bragging unashamedly only because I am about to debase myself by admitting that I don't know how to *aim*. That is, I *don't* aim. I take a quick look, maybe see a hole, but then I put my head down again to shoot the puck at the general area. A real forward doesn't do that. A real forward can see a hole and shoot the puck while looking at the hole, head up. Time and again I've had real forwards tell me politely, "Gee, Billy, you know you'd score lots more goals if you kept your head up." But I can't seem to. I'll watch Duane, who is also a converted D-man, come in and pick corner after corner, and the only difference in our shot is that his hands put the puck where his eyes are currently looking. Me, I'm looking down at the puck, and I don't know where the puck is going except generally. Which means—here's the real self-debasing part—which means that every single goal I've ever scored has been a fucking fluke.

All flukes. *I don't know how to aim.* The thing is, I don't really need to look down. It's like not being able to masturbate without looking down, rather than up at the magazine, where you should be looking. It's just needless habit. It's not as if I'm going to lose the puck if I don't look down. I can stickhandle and pass without looking down. So looking down is just psychological. Anyway, lately in warmup I've been trying to shoot without looking down. During the St. Louis drill especially. I'll come tearing in and see the hole over Chris's shoulder and I won't look down, won't look down, my wrists flick—and sometimes it's in the net. But during games I always freak out. I always look down.

You might already have guessed what happened, so I won't belabour it, though it was a thing of beauty. There's about five minutes left in the game. In their end, I pick up the puck in the corner and come out with it. I have time, and space.

Somewhere around the face-off dot I look up. There, on the short side over the goalie's left shoulder, is a hole about the size of an apple pie. I can feel my head wanting to dip down and check out the puck, but I don't let it. I keep my eyes on that hole. I snap my wrists. Puck flies to hole. Puck soundlessly dents twine. Arms in air, involuntary little yelp!

I've never scored a goal like that in my life. I'm a fifty-two-year-old dog with a brand-new trick. Here's the marvellous thing: oldtimers *can* get better. I'm not deluding myself. We can actually still get better.

And with that goal, we tie the game. Nobody really cares except me, I don't think, but I'm happy inside. I've never had a real sister, but this time it was quite tasty, kissing one.

BACK IN THE ROOM, nobody seems to want to do anything. Rich, who's normally so generous and jolly, wants to leave early tonight. The cooler is in his care and he wants to take it home and spray it out. Some guys aren't even in the shower yet when he says, "Last call." A guy from the next team using our room pokes his head in the door, asks how long we'll be. So it seems written in the stars: a last-game celebration just isn't going to happen.

Rich shouts "Last call" again like he means it and I almost knock heads with Duane as we rush to stoop at either side of the cooler. He grabs one, then two, then a couple more. He looks up, asks, "Parking lot?" and I answer by grabbing a bunch of beers myself. A few other guys stuff an extra beer or two in their bags.

The team disperses, one by one, out the door. A few guys call out a "see you next year," but most don't. Mostly it's a simple "later," if it's anything at all. True, there's the team meeting in a month or so, to discuss schedules and beer prices and who's retiring and what spare we should let come on full time. Then there's the team barbecue and bocce tournament. But I feel a sadness at these guys leaving. Maybe it's because I know deep down that I won't play again next year. Some of these guys I haven't chatted with tonight. One or two of them I might not have talked with all year, short as it was. Jimmy steps quietly out the door, and I wonder about his wife and their "religious problem." I still haven't asked anyone about Gene. Gene could be alive or dead, and I still haven't thought to ask. Aside from maybe Dave, after a third beer, I don't talk about real things with any of these guys. What's the point, then? Well, maybe that is the point.

The next team, a bunch of young guys, starts barging rudely in the door. We surrender our room without a struggle.

SIX OF US GATHER in the dark around Duane's dented old pick-up. We crack beers. Dave asks me what I'm up to this summer, and I tell him I want to take my two older kids kayak-camping. He's done that himself, he tells me, and he says it was great. We joke about how much beer you can cram into the beak of a kayak at the cost of how much food. And who *really* needs a tent? I ask him about his summer. He's rebuilt his old motorbike again, and now he's building a shed for it, with walls made out of a certain kind of river rock he's on the lookout for. He smiles and hesitates, asking me if I'm playing next year. I answer him with my own smiling question, "You?" It's an old joke, both of us tacitly agreeing that it's no fun without the other on the line, and we have a semi-serious pact to warn each other if we're quitting, to give the other guy time to find another team.

"I don't know," he says. "You?"

Duane hears us and gives us shit. Of course we're going to play, he tells us. How can we disagree with him? Duane, with his scars, his dozen truly serious injuries, his constant coming back from them, his bright eyes and enthusiasm out here in the parking lot. Here's a guy who played pro, and when he first began oldtimers he would go end to end ten times a game and score on five of them. Duane now operates at half speed—and yet he's keen talking about next year. Duane adds, in all seriousness, "I mean c'mon! Whattaya gonna do, go home and fucking *die?*"

Everyone there in the parking lot shrugs and bobs their head by way of agreeing that going home and fucking dying is the less attractive option.

Rich, who had been in such a hurry to leave, materializes at my right shoulder, a beer in hand. No explanation needed.

"You wouldn't believe how my granddaughter plays the violin, eh?" he says to me, out of the blue.

"Oh, yeah?"

"She played in front of three hundred people the other night. She's eight."

"Holy cow."

"She just decided one day she wanted to play the violin, and picked one up and it was incredible, she just *played* it, and now she runs to practice, whenever she can. Just loves it."

"Just picked it up and could play it?"

"That's right. It was incredible. I don't even like violin music, but it actually sounded good."

"And violins are so hard to play. No frets or anything."

"I know!"

"It's like she's a child prodigy or something."

"I know. She is. That's what her teacher says."

"Holy cow."

"I know. And I'm hopeless with music. Soon as my voice changed, I couldn't sing worth shit. But my wife really sings. Sings beautifully."

"Music is in the genes."

"It is. You should see her up there playing. Eight years old. You can't help but be proud."

"Well yeah!"

I pause for a moment, and think of something. It's something I've thought of before, but have never asked anyone about it.

"Do you get as proud of your grandkids as you do of your kids?"

Rich turns to me at this, and our eyes meet for the first time this conversation. His eyes have the warmest little smile in them.

"You do. It's different, but you really do."

In the meantime, Mel, a stubby spare who has aspirations of becoming a regular, has brought up a subject that's new to me: the team might be folding, or at least fundamentally changed. It seems that enough guys had been grumbling about getting blown out so often by younger teams that the idea was now simply to sign up twenty guys, divide in two, meet once a week, and play each other. Establish a core of guys for tournaments. One Victoria team that we often met in tournaments, the Blues, already had that arrangement.

"And the Pic-a-Pops do that," Mel said, nodding with raised eyebrows, as if to say we might be as good as the Saskatoon Pic-a-Pops if we did it too.

Out here in the parking lot it is definitely April. It's okay to be standing around with wet hair and our coats open. Now, I know that every Canadian who doesn't live on B.C.'s south coast is really sick of B.C. friends telling them how flipping warm it is, all the time, all winter long, exaggerating their pants off. But it's true that, come April, the pineapples are getting fairly heavy on the vine, and the banana tops are starting to poke up through the soil, and it's time to put the blades away and get out the sunblock and watch the lovely FeeFee shave her bikini line and—but seriously, that's a problem with Victoria, as far as hockey goes. By March and April it's no longer hockey weather and it's maybe too easy to say goodbye to it for another year.

I crush a beer can under my foot, easier to bag and recycle. Duane admonishes me, asking us all to just please toss the empty cans in the box of his pick-up, the side of which several of us are leaning on. Seems his ten-year-old enjoys cashing them in for the nickels they earn him. Me, I wonder about the wisdom of driving home at night with the aroma of a couple dozen fresh empties wafting off the ass of your truck—cop bait for sure, like blood scent to a shark. You've gotta hope the road-check officer plays some oldtimer himself, otherwise Duane'll be arguing with a more dangerous kind of ref, one who also won't change his call. I can picture Duane insisting that *he* didn't drink all of those beers, he probably drank only *half* of them. That's the kind of joke he'd tell a cop.

Anyway, who knows about next year. To play or not to play. Why do we keep playing? Out here in the dark parking lot it strikes me, more clearly than ever before. Though hockey is fun, and though it lets us drink a guiltless beer after, maybe the reason we play is really because we're still trying to fulfill an early dream. Maybe, on some level, aren't we *still* trying to become the man that the little boy pictured himself one day becoming? Becoming that man, scoring that goal, in front of all those people? It's something I wished I could run past Bub, who was at this moment, in all likelihood, standing in a similar parking lot somewhere, asking himself some similar questions.

Anyway, this team might not even be together next year, apparently. Even if it is, some of the better guys, and guys I'm most friends with, are gone. Can I stand the whining and general playground stupidity? And all this beer it makes me drink, can it be healthy? Can I afford another season where I pay for the whole schedule and get injured and play less than a third?

How much do I enjoy playing fat, at half speed? Do I really want to continue a hockey career when I'm one of the shitty guys? What about when I'm the shittiest guy! Because if I keep playing, that day will come. As will the day when the brain scan tells me that the news is bad. Will I just keep asking these same questions till then? When will I make my decision? Will I ever make it? Can I?

I arc another dead tin soldier high over Duane's pick-up box. My fabulous winger Dave leaps to grab it out of the air and stuffs it, an NBA alley-oop. No one says anything. Then I see Dave lift and rotate the foot he came down on, testing the ankle. He winces, he's hurt it. Dave catches me looking, we meet eyes, he shrugs at this new old injury, we burst out laughing.

No one has much more to say. Mention of the upcoming barbeque and bocce tournament causes a discussion about bocce strategy to break out, and the argument over tactics is as earnest and basically no different than any puck-talk on the bench. A few more cans land hollow in the back of Duane's truck. It's about time to shuffle off home.

But that goal I scored tonight? Like a real forward? Like a sniper? Picking the top corner while not watching the puck? That goal thrilled me. It could be the first of many just like it. If we're not deluding ourselves. We *are* getting better.

Acknowledgements

THANKS FIRST TO MY PARENTS, for making sure we always lived near a rink, or driving us when we didn't. And thanks to my brother Bob for occasionally passing me the biscuit, but also for reading an early version of this and telling me when it was too stupid, and when it wasn't stupid enough, and for correcting certain names and events. And to the formidable Dede Crane for understanding my passion to play and for encouraging me to sit down and write my "hockey fart-joke book." Thanks as well to Carolyn Swayze for arranging my trade to another team. And to Nick Massey-Garrison, for his expertise at helping me stop fooling around with it in my own end and bank it out cleanly off the glass. So, any time I've coughed it up here in these pages, it's my fault alone.

About the Author

BILL GASTON is the author of five novels and five collections of short fiction. He teaches at the University of Victoria and is the winner of numerous prizes, including the 2003 inaugural Timothy Findlay Award and the CBC/Canadian Literary Award. Of his story collections, *Mount Appetite* was shortlisted for the 2002 Giller Prize and *Gargoyles* for the 2006 Governor General's Award. He shoots left.